American Sports
in an Age
of Consumption

American Sports in an Age of Consumption

How Commercialization Is Changing the Game

CORY HILLMAN

McFarland & Company, Inc., Publishers
Jefferson, North Carolina

LIBRARY OF CONGRESS CATALOGUING DATA ARE AVAILABLE

Names: Hillman, Cory, 1978– author.
Title: American sports in an age of consumption : how commercialization is changing the game / Cory Hillman.
Description: Jefferson, North Carolina : McFarland & Compny, Inc., Publishers, 2016. | Includes bibliographical references and index.
Identifiers: LCCN 2016026779 | ISBN 9780786498888 (softcover : acid free paper) ∞
Subjects: LCSH: Commercialism in sports—United States. | Sports—United States—Marketing. | Sports—Economic aspects—United States. | Corporate sponsorship—United States.
Classification: LCC GV716 .H57 2016 | DDC 338.47796—dc23
LC record available at https://lccn.loc.gov/2016026779

BRITISH LIBRARY CATALOGUING DATA ARE AVAILABLE

**ISBN (print) 978-0-7864-9888-8
ISBN (ebook) 978-1-4766-2472-3**

© 2016 Cory Hillman. All rights reserved

No part of this book may be reproduced or transmitted in any form or by any means, electronic or mechanical, including photocopying or recording, or by any information storage and retrieval system, without permission in writing from the publisher.

Front cover images © 2016 iStock/Shutterstock

Printed in the United States of America

*McFarland & Company, Inc., Publishers
Box 611, Jefferson, North Carolina 28640
www.mcfarlandpub.com*

Acknowledgments

This book would not have been possible without the help and support of several people I wish to thank here. First, my thanks go to my wife, Abigail, and my stepchildren, Damion and Destiny, for their love and understanding throughout this arduous process. It could not have been easy given the time this book consumed in my daily life, but I will make up for it. I would also like to send a special thanks to my parents, Bob and Lee Ann Hillman, for their unconditional love and support throughout my life and for always being there when I need them. Thanks to my brothers, Chad and Chris Hillman, as well as to my sisters-in-law, Heather and Lori, my nephews, Landon and Brynn, and my uncle Chuck, my uncle Ken and my aunt Karen as well as to my cousins Olivia and Austin Hillman. I need to also thank my dissertation advisors Clayton Rosati, Josh Atkinson, and Dave Tobar, whose insights uniquely contributed to this book. And, of course, I would like to send a special thanks to Michael Butterworth, my dissertation advisor, whose wisdom was most responsible for this work and for whom I have the utmost respect as both an academic and a person. Thanks to my good friends Matt Lamb, Bryan Bohn, Ryan Anderson, John-Paul Staszel, Jacob Turner and Bruce Lillie for helping me survive graduate school and for sharing many of the good times we had. I would also like to thank Matt Maier and Brion White, my office mates while I was a doctoral student at Bowling Green State University, for the many laughs, insights, and conversations we shared as we occupied the bottom floor of West Hall together. And, finally, I want to thank all of the staff in the Communication and Dramatic Arts Department at Central Michigan University for believing in me enough to hire me and for believing in me enough to keep bringing me back.

Table of Contents

Acknowledgments v

Preface 1

Introduction: Sports, Democracy and Consumer Culture 5

ONE—Welcome to the Consumer Arena: Sports Stadiums and Consumerism 19

TWO—The Sports Gaming Culture 72

THREE—Does It Have to Be in the Game? Sports Video Games and Sponsorship 92

FOUR—"It's Not How You Play, but How You Look": Sports Merchandising and Consumer Spectacle 127

FIVE—Sports, Consumer Culture and the Prospects for Change 149

Chapter Notes 161

Bibliography 182

Index 191

Preface

This book began in the spring of 2009 when I was a doctoral student in the Media and Communication Department at Bowling Green State University. I was taking a class taught by Dr. Michael Butterworth titled Sports and Resistance in which we discussed how sports have served as a site of political struggle in the United States and abroad. After finishing the course, I decided to specialize my research in the emerging area of communication and sport, not only because it captured many of my interests and concerns but also because of what was happening in Detroit. In 2008, the city began dismantling historic Tiger Stadium, which, with few exceptions, had sat empty since the Tigers played their last game there in 1999. After watching YouTube videos of construction crews demolishing the all-too-familiar confines of my baseball-loving youth, I became sad because of what the stadium had meant to me personally. I was not alone.

I remember attending my first major league baseball game at Tiger Stadium when I was seven years old with my father, Bob, my two brothers, Chad and Chris, and my uncle Chuck on August 24, 1986. The fact that I even remember the exact date testifies to how important this was for me. Aside from that, I remember only a few disconnected fragments and moments from the game itself. We sat in the upper deck in left field where we watched an old timers' game before the Tigers were set to take on the Seattle Mariners. Hall of Fame pitcher Warren Spahn chatted with Tigers manager Sparky Anderson before the exhibition in his old, dusty, baggy Milwaukee Braves uniform. Tigers outfielder Larry Herndon slapped a broken bat chopper up the middle that struck Mariners pitcher Mark Langston in the throat. Unfortunately, I also recall that the Tigers lost, although I don't remember exactly what the score was. Years later, I would attend more games at Tiger Stadium

Preface

with my family, my Little League team, and even some of my teammates on the Saginaw Valley State University baseball team. As I watched the videos chronicling Tiger Stadium's destruction online, I felt I was losing an important connection to my past that the park had symbolized. In short, it felt much like a funeral. My experience was common among devoted Tigers fans who, in the various accounts that I read and watched on the Internet, discussed their personal memories of the famed ballpark as if they were mourning the passing of an old friend. Because of this, I wanted to understand why sports stadiums could evoke such emotional responses and why they were rapidly being replaced in the larger sporting landscape.

Thus, I decided to do research on what ballparks, stadiums, and arenas symbolized about our culture in both the past and the contemporary moment as historic venues were being torn down in favor of modern "corporatized" substitutes. Why was it that seemingly every team owner wanted a domed stadium during the 1970s and 1980s only to insist that these venues were obsolete by the 1990s? Did it, perhaps, have anything to do with the shifting social and economic values within the larger culture at the time that now considered any kind of history disposable if it served as a barrier to profit? But this work had already been done. So I focused my efforts on how the growing commercialization of sports both reflected and shaped a culture defined by consumerism. Furthermore, I was interested in how these trends were redefining both the meaning of sports and the ways that fans were expected to relate them. In short, it was becoming apparent that as sports were increasingly serving as a vehicle to sell the products of their commercial sponsors, their essential meaning was being lost.

Of course, this is not to say that a pre-commercial era of sports has ever existed, because this is simply not the case. Team owners and other institutional players have always conceived of them as a business designed to turn a profit. However, it is clear that sporting commercialization operates within fewer barriers and limits than it has historically. Commercial sponsors have taken center stage within ballparks, stadiums, and arenas as well as televised sport in a manner barely overshadowed by the action taking place on the field, court or ice. Thus, when one watches sports, whether in person or on television, they are pressured to engage the same market forces all too dominant in our culture as they are encouraged to increasingly embody the role of the

Preface

consumer. This book seeks to understand what kinds of messages fans encounter in their relationship with sports and the effects of those messages and to contextualize these communication processes within dynamics occurring in our social and political environment. This is not to suggest that commercialization has no role in sports, but rather too much of it tends to render them hallow and superficial as the entire fan experience of sports is being redirected toward serving corporate capitalism. Sports, thus, serve as a reminder of the degree to which the market is everywhere and how its logic determines contemporary social values and, ultimately, our political character itself.

While this book assumes a critical lens in understanding and explaining these issues, its often-cynical tone should not be mistaken as expressing a hatred toward sports. On the contrary, it is because I love sports that I decided to spend so much time researching them in order to further understand their importance to our culture. The growing commercialized character of sports, at both the professional and amateur level, is rapidly trivializing them as they are reduced to simply another branded cultural space all too familiar in our contemporary moment. While the market may indeed have a place in society, not everything meaningful to people should be reduced to simply serving it. Historically, people's lives included a space that existed apart from the market, but over the years these spaces are disappearing as more human activities are being reshaped and controlled by it. Again, there has never been a pre-commercialized era in professional sports. Yet one could be a sports fan without having to wholly engage or participate in the market side of sports. Today, however, almost the entire experience of sports fandom has been monetized to the point that one is *forced* to engage the market because there are few sporting spaces that exist untouched by it. Thus, being a sports fan involves constant reminders that one is a consumer first.

Finally, this book began as my dissertation, "The Sports Mall of America: Sports and the Rhetorical Construction of the Citizen-Consumer." I want to thank the anonymous reviewers who spent time reviewing the manuscript it became and offering helpful and practical suggestions for its further revision. Given its length, this required significant time on their part, and I am most appreciative of the support and detailed feedback I received from them. To be honest, I always thought about writing a book but always imagined it as something that

Preface

I would do someday, definitely not anytime soon. And when the project began, I was not sure if it would ever be finished, given my busy teaching and research schedule as a lecturer at Central Michigan University. There were times I struggled, but I am glad that I endured the stress and frustration. I am confident that the book has something interesting and worthwhile to say and I am happy that I had the opportunity to write it. It is now up to the reader to decide if it was, indeed, worth the effort.

Introduction
Sports, Democracy and Consumer Culture

It was a game that produced one of the most legendary and iconic home runs ever hit: Game 1 of the 1988 World Series between the Oakland Athletics and the Los Angeles Dodgers. The details have become the material of mythic accounts of the heroic struggle between the injured and horribly broken Kirk Gibson and the confident, ninth inning swagger of Athletics closer Dennis Eckersley, who had been called upon by manager Tony La Russa to preserve a 4–3 Athletics lead over the Dodgers. Gibson, who had been suffering from a stomach virus, a pulled left hamstring, and a swollen right knee, hobbled to the plate with two outs and a runner on first to face Eckersley, whose American League leading 45 saves cemented his reputation as the most dominating closer in major league baseball. Famed broadcaster Bob Costas would later recall the sound of Gibson's agonized grunts in the Dodgers' clubhouse while taking swings on a batting tee to prepare for a possible pinch-hitting appearance in the ninth.[1] This has merely supplemented the mythic scope of the game itself, as Gibson limped to the plate accompanied by the roar of cheers from hopeful Dodgers fans.

Gibson fouled Eckersley's first pitch, doubling over on the follow-through; it was a pathetic spectacle almost too painful to watch. Gibson would foul the next pitch away, nearly collapsing again as the count now stood at no balls and two strikes. Eckersley then tossed to first twice to hold the runner, Mike Davis, seemingly toying with the runner and the crowd. It seemed that it was over for both Gibson and the Dodgers in Game 1. Gibson chopped the next pitch to Mark McGwire, who barely fielded it just outside of fair territory, then took a pitch

Introduction

outside that nearly saw Davis picked off when Athletics catcher Ron Hassey snapped a throw behind the runner. After fouling another pitch and awaiting another throw to first, Gibson took the next two pitches outside to run the count full as Davis stole second base, representing the tying run, now in scoring position. Eckersley then gestured his catcher toward the mound as Dodger Stadium exploded in thunderous anticipation of an epic and historical finish. After Hassey returned behind the plate, Eckersley wound and delivered his old standby, a devastating slider. Undeterred, Gibson swung and drove the ball into the chaotic throng in the right-field seats, pumping his fists around the bases as the camera panned to Dodgers manager Tommy Lasorda leaping from the home dugout in childlike ecstasy. After Gibson was mobbed by his teammates at home plate, the fans continued to cheer. The Dodgers had struck a blow for the underdog.

It is in moments such as these that fans understand the allure of sports and their ability to provide both hope and heartache to millions. Yet today there is a pervasive feeling that sports are in trouble, robbed of their seeming purity by the unrestrained hands of commercialism that risk relegating sports to the larger commercial function they are often called upon to serve. While such sentiments risk overly romanticizing the past and glossing over the fact that professional (and, in many ways, college) sports have always been about business, there is no question that the commercialism of sports today asserts itself with unparalleled intensity. The purpose of this book is to examine how sports commercialism is connected to underlying changes occurring within our democratic culture. The intrusion of consumer culture into sports culture not only shapes and reflects a dominant political and cultural ideology but trivializes the character and essence of sports themselves.

Without question, consumerism today is awash with patriotic overtones, seen as uniquely defining what it means to be American while delivering the ultimate pursuit of happiness. This view has become so embedded in public consciousness that those who challenge the naturalness and pleasures of consumption are often dismissed as elitist, cynical, or perhaps clinically depressed. But the United States has not always been a consumer society, nor has it always viewed shopping as the embodiment of what it means to be an American living free in a democratic society. Historically, most people consumed goods to fulfill rather basic and mundane needs, and rarely was consumption seen as expressing one's individuality or demonstrating democracy par excellence.[2] Rather, it was the wealthy who were preoccupied with "conspicuous consumption," whose ownership of luxuries symbolized their class status, power, and sophistication.[3] This dynamic began to change with the coming of industrialization and mass production, which allowed goods to be manufactured cheaply, efficiently, and in greater quantities. By the end of World War II, "mass consumption was extensively reshaping the nation," as evidenced by the "American Dream" being defined by ownership of homes, cars, and appliances in carefully manicured suburban neighborhoods.[4] Thus, consumerism became endowed with national purpose during the Cold War as these mass-produced conveniences were celebrated as being tangible proof that capitalism was indeed superior to communism and that Americans were far better off than the Soviets.[5]

As manufacturing capacity increased by advancements in production that allowed more goods to flood the market, it led to the very real problem of too many commodities chasing too few consumers, which, left unresolved, could create a ripple effect leading to another recession or depression. One solution to what was known as the "crisis of overproduction" was to convince Americans to simply consume more in order to absorb the surpluses that businesses were generating.[6] This was the case after the conclusion of World War II, when American manufacturers, having been pulled completely into the war effort, had to redirect their efforts toward the consumer market in order remain profitable and, more important, prevent another economic cataclysm reminiscent of the Great Depression. Meanwhile, the American workforce, having experienced the rationing of goods during the war, was primed to fully enjoy the benefits of its labor by now being able to indulge freely in the re-emerging consumer marketplace. However, by linking consumerism to both national purpose and the American Dream, business leaders and political officials were channeling public notions of freedom and democracy toward a consumer ideal. While the "consumer republic" had been several decades in the making, interrupted of course by the Great Depression, it had now become the zeitgeist of American culture used to solidify its claims to exceptionalism.[7]

As the productive capacities of capitalism have continued to expand, intrusive marketing and advertising strategies have become

Introduction

the norm in order to not only sell the growing number of goods and services available but also create a competitive advantage. Furthermore, globalization and the disastrous "free trade" agreements that have accelerated it have been spurred by the need to find new markets in search of more consumers to absorb manufacturing surpluses produced in ever greater supply. In the United States, personal debt—once seen as undermining one's claim to self-sufficiency and independence—is now decidedly "normal," driven largely by the desire to keep up with a standard of living deemed necessary to be considered a decent and respectable member of society.[8] Thus, the association of consumerism and feelings of Americanness is the outcome of an unquestioned commitment to economic growth, which, consequently, expands the reach of the market in everyday life. Thus, regardless of the profits generated by large financial interests and their consolidation of market power, the game would always be driven by the imperative to acquire more. This would mean more invasive advertising and marketing strategies found in more places—including once sacred spaces such as public schools—all designed to further economic growth. And through the public's sheer exposure to these messages, consumerism would be further normalized as the primary purpose in American life.

As consumer culture became more entrenched in the public imagination, the relationship between fans and sports shifted to accommodate this new reality as the latter became more commercialized. While professional sports have always been a business designed for profit, this logic rarely extended beyond the sale of tickets, souvenirs, concessions, and a few well-placed commercial advertisements featuring, more often than not, local businesses connected to the community. However, as professional sports became increasingly popular, media networks started increasing their television coverage of sports to garner larger audiences and advertising revenues. Consequently, sports organizations became more "dependent upon media money for their very survival and their present organizational structure."[9] And as the model proved financially successful for both, sports coverage expanded into 24-hour sports networks, talk radio programs, and commercially supported Internet Web sites. Because of the growing visibility of professional sports within the media, corporations began attaching themselves to sports in greater numbers and, thus, further linked "the spheres of commerce and sports."[10] According to Sut Jhally, "given the prevalence of brand names in the athletic events themselves ... the blurring of the line between the two realms was so complete that, at times, it was difficult to tell exactly what one was watching."[11]

Indeed, sports and commercialism have merged so completely that it has become more difficult to separate the two. The Super Bowl has become a consumer spectacle without precedent in sports, with Super Bowl commercials often attracting more attention and admiration than the game itself. Meanwhile, the 1984 Summer Olympic Games that took place in Los Angeles, referred to by some critics as the "hamburger Olympics," started a precedent whereby the games would be more about elevating the sponsors than the athletic competitions themselves.[12] In all the major professional sports, the names of stadiums and arenas are routinely sold to corporate bidders, leading to often-clumsy monikers such as U.S. Cellular Field in Chicago or embarrassing pairings such as that of the New Orleans Pelicans with their home, the Smoothie King Center. In college sports, the level of commercialism has reached such a peak that the NCAA's insistent claim that its "student-athletes" are simply amateurs, not employees, seems preposterous. One example from media expert Matthew P. McAllister's study of the 2007 BCS Championship game revealed that 80 percent of the broadcast coverage contained some visible form of advertising.[13] Worse yet is fans' trying to keep track of the shifting sponsorships for bowl games such as the Holiday Bowl, which, since its inception in 1978, has had seven different corporate affiliations. So popular and lucrative are these partnerships for the NCAA that more postseason games are created simply to cater to more sponsors, including five new bowl games debuting in 2014 alone.[14]

Then there is the postseason men's basketball tournament, more commonly known as March Madness, which made $1.5 billion in advertising revenue in 2014, second only to the NFL play-offs for the most national advertising revenue generated for any postseason sports programming on television.[15] As a matter of fact, advertising revenues for the tournament have been increasing 8.2 percent each year largely due to inserting more sponsorship and product mentions within the broadcasts themselves. For the 2014 tournament, this even included brandishing the basketball net-cutting tradition with a corporate sponsor. As players from the University of Connecticut took turns clipping the ribbon from the net following their championship victory, viewers at

Introduction

home were reminded that Werner was "the official ladder of the NCAA."[16] With such massive revenues being generated by the NCAA from its advertising, sponsorship, and media deals, it is unsurprising that the debate is waging currently on whether college athletes should be paid. While NCAA president Mark Emmert has insisted that athletes "are not employees, they're students" in defense of his organization's amateur status, the players themselves are the only reason that fans watch at all and are the source of its—and its member schools— revenues.[17]

On the one hand, we hardly question these commercial practices and even have come to embrace them in many respects. However, this is not to suggest that the growing commercialism of sports has not gone without serious criticism, resentment, or backlash. The sale of stadium naming rights, for instance, has been critiqued as trivialization of the link between a stadium and its surrounding community that exemplifies crass commercial opportunism at its worst.[18] For example, many fans in San Francisco refused to acknowledge the new monikers of historically named Candlestick Park when it was renamed 3Com Park at Candlestick Point in 1996 and Monster Park in 2004, the name that remained until 2008.[19] Furthermore, many colleges have rejected stadium naming-rights deals for their football stadiums, including Notre Dame, Michigan, Ohio State, and Louisiana State University (LSU) in an attempt to resist the increasing commercialization of college athletics and to respect their institutional traditions.[20]

Moreover, fan criticism has gone beyond the sale of stadium naming rights to preserving the integrity of the playing field itself from the reach of aggressive marketing and advertising practices found elsewhere. In 2004, Major League Baseball announced their partnership with Sony Pictures to promote the upcoming release of *Spider-Man 2* by agreeing to place logos for the film on the bases in every ballpark the week before its release in theatres in June of 2004. The deal was rescinded shortly after its announcement due to an overwhelming wave of criticism from fans and purists who reminded the league that the playing field between the lines was no place for *Spider-Man* or any other form of advertising. In reaction, Commissioner Bud Selig stated that "the problem in sports marketing, particularly in baseball, is you're always walking a sensitive line. Nobody loves tradition and history as much as I do."[21] Since Selig approved the deal, we can easily dismiss his sentimental talk about "history" and "tradition" as public relations talk, a token nod to integrity above profit by a man who had witnessed and oversaw the unparalleled commercialization of major league baseball during his tenure as commissioner.

Moments such as these provide hope that limits, indeed, still exist regarding the extent to which fans will tolerate the kinds of advertising and marketing that are noticeably occurring through sport. However, these may be the dying cries of an aging generation; younger fans often consider the branding of cultural forms such as sports by commercial forces as natural, given, and inevitable.[22] To many of them, advertising and marketing are "cool, alternative, young, hip" and embody an understanding of their need for individuality and rebellion that consumerism promises to deliver.[23] One's identity, it seems, is almost shallow and invisible without consumer brands to give it expression and meaning. The corporatization of once-sacred spaces, such as public schools and universities, is probably rarely questioned by many students who have known nothing other than the branded culture they were born into. The naturalization of commercialism may open up possibilities for marketers and advertisers that are currently regarded as taboo for older sports fans when a younger generation of fans replaces them. For Millennials, brands are often "so inextricably connected with [their] lives that they don't even recognize them as brands."[24] Much of this has to do with the levels of engagement with consumer brands among Millennials at early ages, which conditions them to see logos and products as inseparable from life itself. Brand recognition is even trained via board games such as Logo Party, The Logo Board Game, and various alternative versions of Monopoly where, instead of fictional properties, there are recognizable companies. For those alarmed by the intensity of commercialization occurring in sports and its corresponding effect on their integrity, such celebratory acceptance of the branded culture does not bode well for those who claim that sponsorship of sports, while not wholly unnecessary, should not usurp the larger meanings and values that sports should reflect.

Perhaps another reason the union of sports and consumer culture is so problematic is because the former often operates as a potent metaphor for democracy.[25] At their best, sports symbolize larger cultural values such as merit, equality and fair play that purportedly represent the very essence of democracy itself. As I have alluded to before,

Introduction

the commercialization of sports is a consequence of not only the expansion of capitalism to secure greater profits to address the "crisis of overproduction" but also the attempt by large businesses to reshape the very definition of democracy to normalize consumption as the primary objective of life. It is no exaggeration to suggest that the contemporary political moment is confronted by significant challenges that pose a threat to the very definition and functioning of our democratic culture. The 2010 Supreme Court decision in *Citizens United vs. Federal Election Commission*, by claiming independent political expenditures as a form of speech protected by the First Amendment, removed many of the financial limits on the funding of political campaigns. While still prohibiting direct monetary contributions to candidates themselves, it would allow political action committees (PACs)—which often act as "shadow political parties"—to, in effect, "accept unlimited donations from billionaires, corporations, and unions to buy advertising, most of it negative."[26] This was followed by legitimate concerns that wealthy donors could purchase greater influence among politicians more beholden to returning the favor once elected to political office. Without question, this would be a significant further step toward reshaping democracy for the benefit of capitalism and the wealthy instead of the welfare of more ordinary citizens without the monetary influence to "speak" as equally as financial elites.

Current economic policy is predicated on the belief that any limitations that act as barriers toward capital accumulation should be eliminated in the name of economic growth.[27] When President Ronald Reagan addressed the New York Stock Exchange in 1985 with the promise that he and his administration were going to "turn the bull loose," he was expressing a commitment to let the economy run wild by eliminating "burdensome" regulation and government spending standing in the way of profits.[28] However, the strategies of "Reaganomics" were largely a reinvention of policies partly responsible for the Great Depression, which began in 1929, leading to the plea by economists such as John Maynard Keynes that capitalism needed to be properly regulated to avoid further economic disasters in the future.[29] Reagan's policies followed the "trickle down economics" doctrine that assumed that the results of providing advantages to the wealthy would "trickle down" to everyone else in the form of more jobs, higher wages, and an increased standard of living. A study conducted by the International

Monetary Fund (IMF) in 2015 found that such policies, long known to be based on fallacy, have contributed to increased income inequality while also hampering economic growth.[30] The effect has also been held partially responsible for the gradual disappearance of the middle class and, consequently, the tougher financial realities for American workers as a whole commonly struggling with higher debt, stagnating wages, and job insecurity.

However, these policies were already being pursued and implemented before Reagan was elected to political office, even if he was the first American president to endorse them so proudly and vigilantly. Known as neoliberalism—which should not be mistaken for what it means to be politically "liberal"—this economic philosophy assumes that the primary responsibility of government should be to serve the interests of business. As David Harvey writes, "it proposes that human well-being can best be advanced by liberating individual entrepreneurial freedoms and skills within an institutional framework characterized by strong property rights, free markets, and free trade."[31]

Furthermore, the concept of the "market" would be tied to the idea of "freedom" while government policies designed to regulate the former would be seen as a betrayal of the right of individuals to fully enjoy the benefits of the latter. Neoliberalism as a policy objective was a response by elites to preserve their class power due to financial and global instabilities that threatened it during the 1970s: the removal of the gold standard, the rising unemployment and inflation, and a dwindling tax base ineffective to meet rising social expenditures. Neoliberalism would further loosen the obligations the wealthy had to the public by cutting their taxes, slashing funding for public institutions such as schools, and dismantling labor unions where they existed.[32] Meanwhile, more government money would be directed toward the wealthy in the form of subsidies paid for by cutting social programs designed to assist middle- and working-class Americans, such as public investments in education.[33] According to the Center on Budget and Policy Priorities, "when this funding is cut, colleges and universities [in particular] look to make up the difference with higher tuition levels, cuts to educational or other services, or both."[34]

In order to understand the effect of these policies on sports and the consumer culture that increasingly defines them, it is important to note how the policies have fundamentally altered social relations

Introduction

between people. As the market and its requisite commitment to profit increasingly influence government policy, it comes to define more aspects of everyday life. One effect is that competition becomes the primary relationship between people, because without job security and government safety nets and with scarcer possibilities for upward mobility citizens must "fight" one another for the opportunities that are available. This has many consequences, but two of them are of interest here: (1) citizens become preoccupied with attaining social status and wealth because of greater social intolerance toward "losers,"[35] and (2) greater degrees of distrust result between people because of the assumption that everyone else is only motivated by self-interest and personal gain. The latter is not wholly unreasonable, because it operates within the context of an economic system and philosophy that, in fact, privileges individuality at the expense of more communal values such as sacrifice, cooperation, and a selfless concern for others. Meanwhile, consumerism would be seen as a means of "keeping score" in terms of our relative individual value in our competition with others. The attainment of personal wealth, regardless of its impact on relationships, families, and communities, was the only true purpose through which all of our efforts should be directed. The penetration of the market and its worldview in once-exempt social and personal activities is not seen as intrusive or manipulative but rather evidence of its willingness to serve the public anywhere and at any time. Meanwhile, entrepreneurs such as Mark Cuban, Jay-Z, and Steve Jobs, among others, would become cultural "heroes" worthy of admiration and unadulterated praise.

Of course, there are many who disagree with this value system, either entirely or partly, but it has become without question a dominant ethos in the United States. So intensely has it influenced public thinking that is not uncommon for people to think of themselves as brands.[36] And when individuals begin to view themselves as consumer products dedicated to building the right image that demonstrates they are "winners," this becomes evidence of how strongly people identify with the imperatives of consumer culture in the first place. Unquestionably, this value system is strongly embedded within social media, where "friends" become "followers" and the self becomes more malleable in service to appearances, especially by younger people whose lives are often defined by their presence in these mediums.

Sports, Democracy and Consumer Culture

Thus, the transformation of fan culture into consumer culture in sports is partially supported by an apparatus that normalizes the centrality of consumption and the market in daily life. Of course, this is not the entire story and the commercialization of sports is also the consequence of less abstract processes that are perhaps more clearly evident. In professional sports, escalating player salaries introduce a cost to team owners, which sports sponsorship and the leveraging of new revenue streams are designed to compensate. However, it is also fair to say that these additional revenues these sources provide are not simply an effect of rising salaries but also a significant cause of them. Currently, the NBA pays its players the highest salaries in all professional sports, with the league average approximating $4.5 million per player.[37] Without the monies created by sports sponsorships, television rights, new stadiums, and licensed merchandising, salaries would not be able to increase to such levels. And while many fans may criticize the players themselves for the levels of commercialism the fans do not like, not to mention the higher costs of attending live sports events, it is often the greed of ownership and other institutional players largely responsible for it.

Today's sports owners often view their team as a platform to market other business assets operating under their control, such as Walt Disney's former ownership of the Anaheim Angels and the Anaheim Mighty Ducks, so named after a Disney movie.[38] Then there is hip-hop star Jay-Z, recruited by Brooklyn Nets owner Bruce Ratner as a team investor for his promotional savvy, who used his stake in the franchise not only to design the team uniforms but also to market other holdings bearing his name.[39] Even NBA commissioner Adam Silver celebrated Jay-Z as a "true virtuoso in terms of his crossover abilities in both entertainment and sports business."[40] So shameless was Jay-Z in his willingness to market his endorsements, the rapper began mentioning them in his song lyrics, including his association with Hublot, a producer of luxury watches. His song "Otis," for example, includes the line "new watch alert—Hublots," and which caused demand for the company's product to "skyrocket".[41] Thus, Ratner saw Jay-Z as the ideal pitch man to secure profitable sponsorships for the Nets, not to mention the value of the Jay-Z "brand" to the team and the NBA themselves. It is unquestionable that the growing popularity of sports, along with their all-too-visible presence in the media, attracts a specific kind

Introduction

of ownership class who see operating a team as an easy way to make money. They are the quintessential neoliberal faithful who view sports, and fans for that matter, as simply a collection of "revenue streams." And this belief system is not limited to professional sports but is also well represented in supposedly "amateur" organizations such as the NCAA, where profit often trumps integrity without apology.

Of course, none of this is intended to imply that team owners from previous eras were entirely motivated by a higher purpose, either. Plenty lacked anything that resembled a soul, especially when it came to their treatment of their players, the public, or fans. Pitcher Steve McCatty, after being asked to comment on Oakland Athletics owner Charlie Finley's heart surgery, remarked that "it took eight hours. Seven and a half to find the heart."[42] Of course, there was also the infamous owner of the New York Yankees George Steinbrenner, who once paid a spy to follow outfielder Dave Winfield, issued haircut memos to players whose hair was deemed too shaggy, and bullied the city of New York so often with relocation threats that they finally capitulated and agreed to build the Yankees a new ballpark.[43] Yet despite these more egregious examples, these "old school" owners were often emotionally invested in the teams they operated and rarely did they view the team as simply another property or business holding charged with "[maxing] out every last cent."[44] Today, most owners approach teams as corporations designed to do what any business should: exhaust all possibilities that could lead to profits. The consequence is that fans are consistently hailed as consumers, whether at stadiums and arenas with the multitude of "fan-friendly" amenities available or at home with sports broadcasts becoming more indistinguishable from television commercials.

This book is a criticism of what sports have become, how their relationship with fans has changed, and how their pairing with consumer culture risks emptying the deeper social meanings and values of sports that make them enjoyable to watch in the first place. In the pages that follow, there will be many negative observations made about sports, but be assured that they originate from my deep admiration for sports. It should also be noted that the unholy union between sports and consumer culture both reflects and shapes the quality of democracy too commonly reduced to be simply about shopping, materialism, and self-interest. When seemingly everything important in society is being redirected and redefined in the image of neoliberal capitalism, we may come to expect something less from sports than what they are capable of giving. We may simply see the commercialization of sports as "common sense" and as a mere by-product of just the way things are. But in doing so, we are conspiring against ourselves. For the value of sports lies in the emotional attachments they are capable of fostering, the alternative visions they provide of what a more just society may look like, and the hope and optimism they often inspire. But when all of this becomes secondary to the larger commercial function they are often called upon to serve, we risk losing an important connection to a human institution that, at its best, reminds us we are more than simply machines, workers, and consumers. Sports, of course, are not perfect and perhaps there are better things that we could do with our time. But they are far from meaningless and what they have become requires no less than a discussion of what we have become in the process.

One

Welcome to the Consumer Arena
Sports Stadiums and Consumerism

In April of 2012, Marlins Park opened in Miami as the new home of the Miami Marlins, replacing the cavernous multipurpose facility shared with the Miami Dolphins since 1993, when the Marlins entered the National League as an expansion franchise. For a team plagued by low attendance and waning fan interest, the new stadium signified a new beginning for a once-prominent franchise that had won two World Series championships in 1997 and 2003 but had recently become a mediocre has-been. As an added incentive to encourage fans to pay to see the Marlins in their new stadium, the organization hired Ozzie Guillen as manager and acquired Jose Reyes, Heath Bell, Mark Buehrle, Carlos Zambrano, and Carlos Lee in what promised to be a new beginning for Marlins baseball. Unlike the designs of the newer "retro" baseball stadiums that had become the norm in Major League Baseball since the early 1990s, the design of Marlins Park was intended to illustrate the contemporary, forward-thinking character of Miami. Marlins owner Jeffrey Loria pondered, "Was I looking for a retro stadium? Did we have that in mind? I said, 'No retro, art deco, no looking back.' Miami is a spectacular city looking ahead. We need to be looking forward."[1] What he had in mind was not a ballpark that exploited baseball nostalgia. Rather, the stadium resembled a large aquarium and a rave all rolled into one.

As part of its architectural aesthetic, the Fort Lauderdale–based company Living Color Enterprises designed two saltwater fish tanks that would serve as the backdrop behind home plate. Speaking to the essential novelty of this feature, MSNBC noted that "in addition to the spectacular new stadium that features a retractable roof, pool, sculptures, and other amenities, the 37,000 LEED Silver certified stadium also includes something no other ballpark can claim—two custom saltwater aquariums that flank either side of home plate."[2] Of course, this was somewhat of an understatement, as one of its other prominent spectacles included a 75-foot marlin and flamingo carousel beyond left center field that would animate each time a Marlins player connected for a home run. Reflecting a tacky aesthetic without precedence in major league baseball, to baseball purists and traditionalists the rainbow-colored eyesore was an offensive display of hubris. Furthermore, the Clevelander, a nightclub located near the pool in the new stadium beyond left field, would be branded as a trendy yuppie hot spot, including half-naked female dancers and waitresses, body painting, and live DJs for those seeking a reprieve from watching baseball.[3]

Meanwhile, several states to the west in Texas, the Dallas Cowboys take the field in their new, corporately named facility known as AT&T Stadium, which opened in 2009. The $1.2 billion stadium, commonly referred to as "Jerry World" after Cowboys owner Jerry Jones, features the typical array of upscale leisure options and amenities that typify new stadiums but also includes a Ford dealership displaying the auto company's prized new models.[4] Prior to the game, fans can enjoy live music and entertainment on both the AT&T Plaza and Miller Life Plaza located at opposite ends of the facility.[5] And, as part of the Cowboys' naming rights agreement with AT&T, the stadium is outfitted with Wi-Fi capabilities, providing fans with on-the-spot Internet connectivity that can be used to advertise team sponsors.[6] The revenue from the deal has been celebrated as a win-win that will allow the city of Arlington the opportunity to pay off the debt for the facility in 15 years, as opposed to the originally projected 30.[7]

Arguably, its more noticeable features, however, are the twin, high-definition television monitors extending between the 21-yard lines that simulates the living room experience most fans have become accustomed to in their engagement with sport. The $40 million price tag for the large Mitsubishi HDTVs exceeded the entire cost of the Cowboys' previous home, Texas Stadium, which opened in 1971 and closed

One. Welcome to the Consumer Arena

following the 2008 season.[8] The NFL asked the team to raise the large, in-house television known as "Jerry Vision" over worries that it could interfere with game play.[9] As a matter of fact, these concerns became reality during a 2009 preseason game between the Cowboys and Jacksonville Jaguars when Jacksonville kicker A. J. Trapasso hit the television with a punt.[10] When the commissioner asked Jones again to raise the television, he declined by indicating that it would interfere with the stadium's visual appeal.[11] While the television was touted as a fan-friendly amenity that would bring fans closer to the action, its primary purpose for Jones was to sell advertising space for a corporate elite willing to pay big money for the opportunity to pitch their wares before a captive audience. According to Jones, "[fans] can't turn away, so you can hammer them with your message."[12] Meanwhile, he compared the stadium to a "modern day Colosseum [sic] of Rome" while Jack Hill, Director of Stadium Construction, bragged that "we think it will be a lot of years until a new stadium will top us."[13]

NFL commentator Al Michaels reinforced Jones' metaphor during the Cowboys' inaugural game at the new facility on ESPN's *Sunday Night Football*, gloating that "what the Roman Coliseum was to the First Century is what Cowboys Stadium is to the 21st Century."[14] The commentary was supplemented by a video montage that included images of the Great Pyramids in Egypt, the Parthenon, the Great Wall of China, the Taj Mahal, and, of course, the Roman Coliseum. In between the celebratory and sycophantic fanfare from the national sports media, a few critical voices emerged that were not so impressed with such publicly funded excess. One was *National Post* columnist Bruce Arthur, who remarked: "[Michael's] timelines don't quite work out, but just as the Roman Coliseum became the centre of an empire in decline, so, too, will the new Cowboys Stadium be the symbol of the American empire's end."[15]

Clearly, much in the sporting landscape has changed in recent decades, as evidenced by the consumer-oriented spectacle of new sports stadiums. While the stadium "experience" may, perhaps, justify in the minds of fans the higher cost of attendance, it is revealing of a darker truth that is worth exploring: specifically, how middle- and working-class fans are increasingly priced out of attending sporting events altogether even while their tax dollars are diverted toward funding the construction costs of these new sporting palaces in the first place. Given the abundant leisure and entertainment options for fans, it is clear that team owners use these amenities to draw upper-income fans to the stadium who have the disposable income to spend on consuming that "experience." Those with more limited incomes, while not excluded from the option of purchasing a ticket, are simply not as profitable a "revenue stream."

*****

New sports stadiums have been championed by civic officials as a way to create jobs, stimulate consumer spending, and generate economic development in otherwise decaying and deteriorating urban centers.[16] Between 1990 and 2010, there were 104 new sports facilities built for Major League Baseball (MLB), the National Football League (NFL), the National Basketball Association (NBA), the National Hockey Association (NHL), and Major League Soccer (MLS) franchises in both the United States and Canada, compared to 128 facilities the previous 90 years.[17] The reasons, according to new stadium supporters, are clear. A professional sports team gives cities national and international visibility compared to cities without major league sports, which provides them an advantage in attracting jobs and other forms of investments. Companies, as is often claimed, are attracted to cities with professional sports franchises because they can be used as part of the companies' sales pitch to recruit "talent." And with more cities wanting professional sports teams than the available supply, team owners wanting a new stadium can often threaten to relocate to pressure municipalities to comply.[18] Yet economic analyses have consistently shown that new stadiums do not stimulate the economic renewal promised, nor do they do much in the way of creating more jobs and increasing tax revenues to justify their expense.[19]

Meanwhile, when citizens and civic officials do, in fact, reject a proposal for a new stadiums they are often accused of not caring enough about their teams to pony up the funds for a new stadium, ballpark, or arena. And for cities with a losing team an existing stadium is often used as an excuse as to why a team is not competitive. This is one of the reasons why, when teams receive a new stadium, the hype for the facility is often fueled by marquee free-agent signings and acquisitions as "evidence" that team owners, blessed with a new stadium, can now field a "winner." Thus, team owners who received a new

One. Welcome to the Consumer Arena

stadium did by often leveraging three variables: (1) the emotional connection between fans and teams that can be exploited by threatening to move a team if a new stadium is not built, (2) the supply-demand issue of professional sports franchises that ensures team owners have relocation options if they do not receive the facility they want, and (3) the fear of cities potentially losing their "major league" status.[20] Opponents to a new stadium are often characterized as either sports haters or, in some cases, "job killers."[21] Meanwhile, once the facility is built the profits generated are almost entirely retained by the owners, while the public remains responsible for paying for it, often for decades. Some stadiums are funded through the sale of federally tax-exempt bonds to wealthy shareholders, which, after interest is paid, means that the city will pay much more for a facility beyond its initial asking price. Team owners may "contribute" to funding part of a stadium's cost, often by selling the naming rights and personal seat licenses, instead of directly from their own pockets.[22] In other cases, such as Nationals Park in Washington, D.C., the public covered the entire construction cost for their coveted new facility without any financial input from ownership.[23]

An oft-cited example of how all of this works can be found in Cleveland, which, since the early 1990s, has constructed three new stadiums for its professionals sports teams: Jacobs (now Progressive) Field for the Indians, the Gund (now Quicken Loans) Arena basketball complex for the Cavaliers, and Cleveland Browns (now FirstEnergy) Stadium. These, along with the Rock and Roll Hall of Fame, were to be the centerpieces that would transform Cleveland's reputation from a Rust Belt tragedy to America's "Renaissance City."[24] The story of how all of this came to be is a cautionary tale of greed reflecting how an economically vulnerable city was taken advantage of by selfish and rapacious ownership groups.

When Cleveland Indians owner Steve O' Neill passed away in 1983, rumors circulated that the team might be purchased by an ownership group that wanted to relocate the franchise to Florida. Without plans for a new ballpark to replace Cleveland Municipal Stadium—the home of the Indians and Browns at that time—a new proposed tax initiative was seen as the only possibility for keeping the Indians in Cleveland. Often mocked as the "Mistake by the Lake," Cleveland Municipal Stadium was built by the Federal Works Project Administration in 1931 with the hope of securing the city's bid for the 1932 Olympics. Funded in part by $2.5 million in local taxes, a rarity at a time when most stadiums were privately funded by team ownership, Municipal Stadium exemplified Cleveland's vibrant economy and its national reputation as the American capital of steel manufacturing.[25] Celebrated for its awe-inspiring size and aesthetic appeal, the Indians set attendance records as fans clamored to see one of the most formidable franchises in the major leagues during the 1940s and 1950s. By the 1970s, however, Cleveland's once-prosperous economy was devastated from the effects of deindustrialization that led to the exporting of both industry and jobs. The Indians, meanwhile, had become the all-too-predictable perennial cellar-dwelling team in the American League, the seeming ideal microcosm of Cleveland itself. It seemed appropriate perhaps that Municipal Stadium became a joke in major league baseball. According to Neil deMause and Joana Cagan, "teams dreaded the trip to frigid Cleveland Municipal Stadium, with its bitter winds of Lake Erie and its tiny crowds, cramped locker rooms, and out-of-date scoreboard."[26] In short, the stadium became a nightmarish reminder of the city's once-unshakeable optimism and the embarrassing reputation of its once-beloved team.

Thus, a new stadium was seen as necessary to solidify any chance of keeping the Indians in Cleveland in the wake of O'Neill's passing. However, city voters rejected a proposal in 1984 that called for a new domed stadium for the Indians as part of a larger redevelopment effort of the city's Central Market in downtown Cleveland. In 1986, Richard and David Jacobs purchased the Indians and, because they were real estate developers who made their fortune in the city, it appeared that the team's future would remain in Cleveland. Yet the owners argued that the Indians would not be able to compete as long as they remained shackled to Municipal Stadium. In 1990, the Central Market Gateway Project was formed in an effort to secure a home for the Cleveland Indians alongside a new arena for the Cleveland Cavaliers as part of another ballot initiative in 1990. Major league baseball Commissioner Fay Vincent stated that a failed vote would spell the end of the Indians in Cleveland. However, such possibilities never materialized, as the vote passed with narrow support. To fund the project, the initiative called for a "sin tax" on alcohol and tobacco-based products sold in the city, a burden that critics argued fell disproportionately on lower-income groups.[27]

One. Welcome to the Consumer Arena

Jacobs Field opened in 1994 and was regarded as symbolizing the rebirth of the Indians as they cruised to their first postseason appearance in 41 years the next season, followed by five more between 1996 and 2001. Unsurprisingly perhaps, the Indians set a major league record for most consecutive sold-out games at 455, a streak that did not end until 2001.[28] Next door, fans at Gund Arena witnessed the Cavaliers continue its streak of five straight play-off appearances. Despite the successes of Cleveland's teams in these two sports, the promised economic benefits did not accrue to citizens as a whole. Both facilities benefited from property tax subsidies costing Cleveland city schools $3.5 million, leading to further budget cuts in educational spending.[29]

Of course, the fact that both the Indians and Cavaliers were playing in new facilities angered Cleveland Browns owner Art Modell, who was allegedly left with promises from the city that Municipal Stadium would be renovated. After rumors were reported in the sporting press that he might relocate the Browns, Modell reassured fans that he had no intention of leaving Cleveland. After all, the Browns had one of the more passionate working-class fan bases in the NFL and games at the Municipal Stadium, despite its aging edifice, were regularly sold out. Yet, behind the scenes, Modell was negotiating a deal with the city of Baltimore, which was promising a new stadium if Modell was willing to move the team. Baltimore had been the site of one of the most infamous franchise relocation heists in sports history when the Colts, after a failed stadium deal, moved in March of 1984 to Indianapolis, where a new domed stadium, built with the hope of enticing an existing NFL franchise, awaited them. Having learned the difficult emotional lesson of refusing to succumb to the demands of team ownership, Baltimore was more than willing to replace the void left by the departed Colts by promising Modell what he ultimately wanted. As news of the secret deal circulated in the press, the city of Cleveland urgently approved the extension of the funds generated by the "sin tax" on alcohol and cigarette sales originally created for new stadiums for the Indians and Cavaliers to include renovations to historic Cleveland Municipal Stadium. However, three days after this proposal was announced, Modell explained that the Browns were moving to Baltimore anyway.[30] Betrayed, Cleveland football fans regarded Modell as the quintessential villain signifying all that was wrong and impure with professional sports by callously taking away their beloved team for no other reason than Baltimore's promise of a new stadium.

Modell tirelessly defended the decision, stating the unfairness of playing in the dumpy, obsolete, and uncharming Municipal Stadium while the Indians and Cavaliers played in new, state-of-the-art venues merely blocks away. Furthermore, he claimed that the Browns were $50 million in debt, which he blamed on "local politicians' indifference to the team's plight and on escalating player salaries."[31] However, an investigative story in *Sports Illustrated* stated that the debt was a consequence of Modell's miscalculated business decisions. After the city of Cleveland claimed that it was losing money by having to finance the operating expenses of Municipal Stadium, Modell signed a 25-year lease with the city in 1973 whereby he would assume control of these expenses. In exchange, he would be able to collect rent from the Browns and Indians for the use of the facility and retain all stadium revenues, including parking, concessions, and advertising signage. Shortly after the deal was finalized, Modell realized that the stadium was in need of extensive renovation and had to take out loans to offset the maintenance costs. Meanwhile, stadium revenues collected by the Indians were embarrassingly low because few were willing to pay to see such a lousy team play. Over the years, Modell attempted to swing various business deals, including selling his own stadium company, purchasing land for a new stadium, and attempting to sell it back to his stadium company well above its appraised value, but was not able to recoup his investment.[32]

While such circumstances appeared to justify Modell's anger over not being offered a new stadium for the Browns and the team's subsequent move to Baltimore, recent evidence has surfaced in the wake of Modell's passing that the city, indeed, offered to build him a new facility.[33] However, Modell refused, perhaps believing that his existing lease on Municipal Stadium, despite its mounting losses, was a better deal than a renegotiated lease with the city if a new stadium was ultimately built. After the Browns' departure, then Cleveland mayor Michael White met with the NFL in 1996 about the prospects of football returning to the city and was told such a possibility hinged on building a new stadium. After further negotiations with the NFL, the city agreed to tear down vacant Municipal Stadium to build a new $220 million facility funded largely by tax dollars. Ironically, news reports suggested that the Indianapolis Colts and the Cincinnati Bengals might relocate to Cleveland to play in its new stadium, perhaps as a gambit to pressure their home cities to build new stadiums for their respective teams, an outcome that ultimately happened for both.[34] However, since the city had already committed to a new stadium as part of its deal with the NFL, Cleveland was ultimately awarded an expansion franchise that would retain the name of the Browns.

Yet, despite optimistic claims that such massive investments in professional sports in Cleveland would stimulate economic renewal within one of the nation's poorest cities, the reality is that the situation in the so-called "Renaissance City" has actually worsened within the last decade. According to the most recent census data, the number of Cleveland residents living in poverty is 36.9 percent, an increase from 31.1 percent a decade earlier. Meanwhile, the number of children living in poverty within the city exceeds an astonishing 50 percent.[35] The example of Cleveland could easily be dismissed if it were merely an anomaly; however, evidence shows that such outcomes, based on the premise that building new stadiums will generate economic renewal, are unfortunately the norm. According to sports journalist Dave Zirin:

> The landscape is made worse by the fact that during the economic boom of the 1990s, the longest period of economic expansion in U.S. history, publicly funded stadiums became the substitute for anything resembling an urban policy in this country. These stadiums, ballparks, arenas, and domes were presented as a microwave-instant solution to the problem of crumbling schools, urban decay, and suburban flight.[36]

In order to understand why new stadiums are seen as the solution to urban blight and economic stagnation, we need to revisit the history of stadium construction in the United States. Of course, such has to be examined within the context of the changing political dynamics of urban governance within the last few decades. As will be seen, there are clear "winners" and "losers" when cities finance new sports facilities and, sadly, it is often the "losers" who civic officials and team owners promise will benefit the most from a new stadium or arena in order to rally public favor for its tax dollars being used to build the facility.

*****

American Sports in an Age of Consumption

During the late nineteenth and early twentieth century, the population within America's urban centers swelled as an expanding manufacturing-based economy promised jobs and economic opportunity.[37] It was around this period that the Cincinnati Red Stockings baseball team became the first professional sports franchise in 1869, subsequently going undefeated in their first season.[38] Early ballparks during this time period were not urban landmarks, nor were they considered visible symbols of civic pride and identity, often including little beyond an outfield fence to prevent fans from rushing the field and disrupting play. Since these early facilities were often temporary, hastily constructed ballparks, it was common for a team to have several "homes" within their host cities in a given season.[39] It was not until owners became convinced that professional baseball could be profitable that they funded the construction of more permanent ballparks, usually built of wood and other durable materials. Yet when fire destroyed the Baker Bowl in 1894 and the Polo Grounds in 1911 due allegedly to fans' careless tobacco use, newer facilities were constructed from a combination of concrete and steel.

Around this time, sports became a common target by Protestant moral reformers because they provided working-class fans a recreational space to drink, smoke, and gamble, pastimes that the reformers considered objectionable, impure, and ungodly.[40] For many fans, sports gave them a needed escape from the often-mechanized discipline and mind-numbing monotony of factory labor. However, since many of these social reformists were wealthy, many team owners sensed financial opportunity in placating them. After Albert Spalding renovated Lake Front Park in Chicago in 1883, he hired a security staff to police fans in the bleachers where the majority of the smoking, gambling, and drinking took place.[41] Meanwhile, when the National League was formed in 1876, league policy prohibited Sunday baseball and the sale of alcohol at games and demanded that players abstain from drinking both on and off the field.[42] Such "purification policies" represented a vivid attempt by early ownership groups in professional baseball to alienate the working class through a façade of moral righteousness that catered to the biases and prejudices of upper-income fans. As I will argue later, these policies have made a resurgence in new stadiums and arenas across the United States.

As the architecture of ballparks and stadiums became more grand

and spectacular, they began to be regarded as a tangible symbol of a city's industrial might and cultural sophistication. For example, Forbes Field in Pittsburgh was built to reform the city's blue-collar image and demonstrate to the nation that it was committed to "cultivating an emerging upscale citizenry."[43] In New York, the opening in 1922 of Yankee Stadium, whose opening game attendance reportedly was in excess of 70,000 fans, was partially intended to solidify New York's status as a world-class city. While team owners labored to maintain the allegiance of upper-income fans by offering exclusive seating options and higher ticket prices, the bleachers became synonymous with the working-class fan.

With the outbreak of World War I, a vast majority of the workforce was pulled into military duty, creating labor shortages in manufacturing plants in northern cities. Consequently, a growing number of African Americans migrated north in search of jobs and economic opportunity that became available because of these shortages.[44] This led to a noticeable demographic shift of the urban population in several major cities such as Detroit, Cleveland, and Pittsburgh. Between 1910 and 1966, the number of African Americans living in the industrialized North increased from 800,000 to 9.7 million.[45] Yet like other facets of public life, seating in major league ballparks was racially segregated, with African American fans routinely confined to the outfield bleachers.[46] As further evidence of the segregationist divide in professional sports, the Negro Leagues, established by Rube Foster in 1920, became "perhaps the largest and certainly most geographically diverse black-owned business in the United States."[47] Not only did it provide a space for African American ballplayers to compete on a professional level, but the league also generated employment opportunities rarely available elsewhere for black accountants, bookkeepers, and trainers.[48] Some of major league baseball's most archetypal and iconic players, such as Satchel Paige, Willie Mays, Hank Aaron, and Jackie Robinson, played some or most of their professional career in the Negro Leagues.

While boxing had long been desegregated, along with professional football in 1946, Robinson's crossing of the official yet unofficial color barrier when he debuted with the Brooklyn Dodgers in 1947 was a major symbolic and political victory for African Americans, owing to the cultural significance of baseball in American society.[49] Of course, while the Dodgers have been memorialized in sporting mythology for their progressive strides in racial and ethnic inclusion, there is evidence that the signing of Robinson was also economically motivated.[50] John Paul Hill writes that "the dramatic population shifts triggered by the war helped the integration campaign.... Noting the changing demographics, critics of the color line appealed to baseball's pocketbook by maintaining that integration would swell black patronage."[51] With more African Americans living in cities that hosted major league teams, owners contended that signing black baseball players would be the ideal marketing pitch to increase overall attendance. Former Negro League star Buck O'Neill stated that

> Branch Rickey [the Brooklyn Dodgers owner who signed Jackie Robinson] saw how ... [Negro League teams] put 30,000 fans in his ballpark. He saw how we drew 40,000 in Yankee Stadium, 30,000 in Griffith Stadium in Washington and 50,000 in Chicago. This is the reason he signed Jackie Robinson—not because he was thinking about blacks. He was thinking about money.[52]

To be sure, some teams resisted integration years after Robinson made his debut with the Brooklyn Dodgers in 1947. For example, the Boston Red Sox waited until 1959 before promoting infielder Pumpsie Green to the major league club after passing on the opportunity to sign future Hall of Famers Willie Mays and Robinson himself. In April of 1945, the Red Sox held an integrated tryout at Fenway Park during an off day for Negro League players Marvin Williams, Sam Jethroe, and Jackie Robinson. According to *Boston Globe* reporter Clif Keane, who was present at the tryout that day, Red Sox owner Tom Yawkey allegedly shouted from the stands to "get those niggers off the field." Unsurprisingly, the Red Sox did not contact any of the players following the tryouts and went on to earn the dubious distinction of being the last major league team to integrate.[53] Of course, resistance toward integration was not confined to baseball. In 1962, Washington Redskins owner George Marshall publicly touted his refusal to sign African American players until President John F. Kennedy and his administration gave Marshall an ultimatum that he do so or be locked out of his new stadium in Washington, D.C.[54]

These events transpired in the context of growing racial tension in American cities as many whites feared the possibility of the desegregation of residential neighborhoods and public schools. The presence of blacks in professional sports, alongside the Supreme Court's decision in the landmark *Brown v. The Board of Education* added fuel to these

One. Welcome to the Consumer Arena

anxieties. What followed was a massive population migration, otherwise known as "white flight," from the inner cities to the surrounding suburbs aided by increases in government subsidies for mortgages and the funding of a complex highway system. In 1956, congressional approval of the Interstate Highway Act under President Dwight D. Eisenhower ensured that the growing suburban population could travel to and from work with greater ease and convenience.[55] By 1957, 70 percent of the homes sold that year were located in suburban neighborhoods that, coupled with discriminatory housing and lending practices, ensured that these spaces would remain predominately white.

These shifting geographical dynamics signified a threat to the bottom line for professional sports franchises, as many stadiums, ballparks, and arenas were located in the same inner cities that whites were fleeing from. Businesses deserted the urban landscape and moved to the suburbs, further eroding economic opportunities for African Americans confined largely to the city. In areas like Cleveland, the negative impact of these trends was intensified by the relocation of manufacturing jobs to the Sun Belt in the South, exacerbating long-boiling racial tensions that led to race riots in the 1960s.[56] Meanwhile, arguably the most well-known race riot occurred in Detroit in 1967, politically energized by the abuses of law enforcement, scarce and low-paying jobs, deteriorating schools, and the massive blight and disinvestment caused by the fallout of white suburbanization.[57] Few jobs meant few workers paying taxes, and city treasuries became overburdened by the need to cover social and infrastructural needs to the point that cities such as Detroit became littered with abandoned buildings, poor roads, and transient homeless residents. These realities were interpreted by many in the white suburban community as "evidence" for the negative attitudes and stereotypes they already held toward the black community, who were consequently blamed for ruining once-thriving urban centers.

Thus, many team owners began pursuing new stadiums in the suburbs because their existing facilities within the inner city were not favorably situated to attract a more affluent, predominately white suburban fan base. Where this was not possible, city officials and team ownership built new stadiums located strategically along highways so that suburban fans could attend a game without actually visiting the city. During the late 1960s, the "first wave of public stadium building" was in a full and invigorated swing, as multipurpose stadiums (which could be shared by professional baseball and football teams) were built in St. Louis (Busch Stadium), Pittsburgh (Three Rivers Stadium), San Diego (Jack Murphy Stadium), Cincinnati (Riverfront Stadium), and Philadelphia (Veterans Stadium), all inspired by the bowl-shaped design of Shea Stadium in New York.[58] However, when the Cleveland Cavaliers relocated from the city to the nearby Richfield suburbs in the 1970s it was viewed as part of a nationwide trend whereby "many teams sought to follow their wealthier fans to the suburbs to avoid the conflicts and tensions that were dominating so many of America's urban centers."[59] The Detroit Lions moved from the city to the suburbs of neighboring Pontiac while the Pistons relocated to nearby Auburn Hills. In Chicago, journalists reported that White Sox owners Jerry Reinsdorf and Eddie Einhorn neglected to provide routine maintenance for old Comiskey Park located in a predominately black neighborhood on the city's South Side. By letting the stadium fall apart, they aimed to justify to civic officials that a new stadium was desperately needed, preferably in the western suburbs of Chicago.[60] While they did not ultimately receive the suburban ballpark that they had envisioned, a new stadium was built for the White Sox in 1991.[61]

Returning to the issue of multipurpose stadiums, these futuristic, modern facilities symbolized an early attempt at urban renewal. A new stadium represented faith, hope, and promise for a brighter future and would be used to lure suburban and out-of-town visitors to neglected, urban locations to shop, be entertained, and play. When Riverfront Stadium opened in Cincinnati in 1970, it was praised as a "world class" facility that served as a tangible indication of civic achievement at a time when many inner cities were in a rapid decline.[62] In the same year, the opening of Three Rivers Stadium in Pittsburgh was commemorated by front-page treatment in the *Pittsburgh-Post Gazette*, which noted how "it obviously made a big hit with first nighters. Clearly they fell in love with it. They used adjectives such as terrific, great, and fantastic. But the most commonly heard word was: beautiful."[63] These sentiments are worth noting because many of these stadiums would later be criticized as ugly architectural embarrassments devoid of personal charm and character, especially in the case of baseball after Camden Yards in Baltimore inspired the "retro" ballpark fad which, like the multipurpose Shea Stadium before it, spawned many copycats.

There is no question that the great stadium construction wave of the 1960s and 1970s was partially galvanized by racial factors. While many of these multipurpose facilities were the ideal "two for one" solution to accommodate the needs of professional baseball and football teams, their geographical locations catered to the preferences and anxieties of predominately white, suburban fans. Whether these stadiums were situated near highways that provided easy accessibility in and out of the city or within the "safe" confines of suburbia altogether, the shifting racial demographics of the American landscape certainly influenced these developments. The city had become defined within the cultural imagination as a crumbling relic of uncontrollable poverty, crime, and racial tension that contrasted with the predictable safety and security of the suburb.[64] Yet, as Robert Fishman notes, "every true suburb is the outcome of two opposing forces, an attraction toward the opportunities of the great city and a simultaneous repulsion against urban life."[65] Unlike the dull, bland sterility of the suburbs, the city offered a seemingly endless array of thrill, novelty, and excitement. However, the fact that many cities were seen as being "dangerous" scared suburbanites and out-of-town visitors away from traveling downtown. Many of the inner-city stadiums built during the 1960s and 1970s did not bring about the economic renewal that had originally been envisioned, nor did they do enough to repair the image of the urban landscape. Beginning in the late 1980s and early 1990s, civic officials and business leaders sensed political and economic opportunity in pursuing more aggressive forms of urban renewal that would involve larger-scale investment in sports, tourism, and entertainment. In essence, the goal was to create a Disneyfied urban playground for the benefit of suburbanites, corporate socialites, yuppies, and out-of-town visitors.[66] The success of these attempts would hinge on the degree to which civic planners could make these visitors feel "safe" by shielding them from visible instances of poverty and its unfortunate consequences.[67]

This is not to suggest that those who visit the city are not entitled to some degree of personal safety and security, nor is it intended to downplay the issue of crime in impoverished urban environments. However, much crime is an inevitable outcome of concentrated levels of poverty created by underfunded schools, the lack of decent-paying and stable jobs, and neglected, deteriorating neighborhoods. Elijah Anderson's sociological research in a Philadelphia ghetto demonstrated a "code of the street" whereby violence and a display of overall toughness was a necessary survival strategy within the neighborhood he studied. Furthermore, such anger is born out of frustration from feeling alienated from mainstream society, a nagging and persistent hopelessness, and the often-persistent patterns of racial discrimination from law enforcement, some of whom harbor negative stereotypes toward black America. These factors are uniquely responsible for the cyclical nature of the poverty and violence that characterize poor inner-city neighborhoods.[68] However, the mainstream narrative is that crime and poverty are the by-products of individual failure, lack of responsibility, and personal laziness.[69] In short, the urban poor, like those in the rest of the United States, are blamed for their lot while the structural causes of poverty and crime are often unacknowledged and unexamined.

Thus, new sports stadiums are seen as a quick fix to the material problems of the inner city. Gentrification—more commonly referred to here as urban renewal—involves rebuilding the city to attract and benefit the wealthy, often leading to the displacement of poorer residents through increased rents and property values along with the demolishing of public housing to make way for more luxurious condominiums and apartments.[70] The goal is not simply to lure more affluent residents but also to transform the city landscape into a consumer-oriented playground for the benefit of visitors, most notably suburbanites who live outside the city. Thus, new sports stadiums, which are often located within planned "entertainment" districts that include nightclubs, bars, convention centers, casinos, and upscale restaurants, communicate the notion that the space is "safe."

While pinpointing an exact origin of the new age of urban renewal may be controversial and difficult, the opening of Baltimore's Oriole Park at Camden Yards in 1992 is often cited as the beginning of the latest wave of new stadium construction in professional sports. Situated on a former rail yard for the Baltimore and Ohio Railroad's Camden Station adjacent to the B&O Warehouse (which currently stands visibly beyond the right-field wall), the stadium would serve as the prominent showpiece of a rejuvenated and rehabilitated Inner Harbor in Baltimore. As baseball's first "retro" ballpark, Camden Yards' architecture paid homage to a "Golden Era" in America with exposed brick and steel similar to that of pre–World War II ballparks and a vast, hypnotic view of the Baltimore skyline beyond centerfield. The stadium was nationally celebrated for its ability to transplant fans into a mythic and romanticized past of American innocence and its conscious rejection of the bland uniformity of modern, cookie-cutter ballparks, stadiums, and arenas.[71]

Thus, the success of Camden Yards lay in its ability to cater to a widespread nostalgic yearning for yesteryear not only within the culture at large but within the game of baseball itself. It seemed to offer a momentary reprieve from the many problems and issues that fans complained were ruining the game, such as escalating salaries, lack of loyalty to one's team as a consequence of free agency, and arrogant and often-unapproachable athletes. Furthermore, it provided Disneyfied access to a past in a manner that could be bought and consumed while honoring a time when baseball itself was regarded as "just a game." For example, Boog's Bar-B-Q featured nightly appearances from former Orioles slugger Boog Powell that "[harkened] back to an era when professional ballplayers and other celebrities actually lived in the same neighborhoods as the fans who admired them."[72] These, and other attractions, provided fans a safe and selected engagement with the past without the burden of having to confront its more uncomfortable realities. Ironically, while Camden Yards offered a convenient and family-friendly re-creation of the past, much of the district's history in terms of its community and architecture was destroyed and replaced by a shallow, gentrified simulation of its past that would be more palatable and comforting to visitors.[73] Without question, Camden Yards established a new standard in professional sports that can be seen in every arena, stadium, and ballpark that has been built since. Namely, that owners must offer a consumable "experience" with a seemingly endless buffet of novelty and distraction apart from the games themselves. To the degree to which this can be accomplished, the results can be quite profitable.

Because of the astounding success and celebratory fanfare of Camden Yards in Baltimore, Major League Baseball owners leveraged new "retro" ballparks of their own in places such as Cleveland, Detroit, Denver, Houston, Philadelphia, Pittsburgh, San Francisco, San Diego, St. Louis, and Washington, D.C., each accompanied with the optimism of signaling an urban renaissance and needed economic growth. Meanwhile, many NFL, NBA, and NHL teams would receive new stadiums and arenas of their own, as civic officials wanted to avoid the charge of favoritism if a ballpark was built for a baseball team and not for teams in other sports.[74] In many cases, team owners threatened to move their team out of town to pressure their home cities in ponying up the money to fund a large percentage of their construction.[75] Stadium fever had reached such a pitch that, in some instances, team owners dispensed with all logic and reason in arguing for a new facility to replace a stadium and/or arena barely years old.

In 1993, the Alamodome opened in San Antonio, Texas, in an attempt to lure an NFL team to the city at a cost of $186 million, largely funded by a controversial and unpopular city sales tax increase.[76] When the city did not get the NFL team they wanted, the massive arena became the new home of the San Antonio Spurs at the beginning of the 1993–1994 season. By 1996, Spurs ownership was already demanding a new arena, claiming that they were losing money playing in a facility built for football, not basketball. To be fair, there may have been some merit in their complaints, because despite sectioning off the Alamodome with a curtain to reduce its size, the stadium had poor sight lines that distanced fans from the action. Ownership began hinting to the San Antonio press that without a new arena more suited for basketball the team might move to nearby Austin. Spurs owner Peter Holt proposed the construction of a new, $157 million, 18,500-seat arena that would be funded by a $20 million contribution by the Spurs, while the remaining amount would come from diverting some of the tax revenue away from the East School District. Unsurprisingly, the school district voted against the funding mechanisms that Holt proposed.[77]

However, the county would later approve a new arena in San Antonio in 1999 and the fate of the Alamodome was finally sealed less than ten years after it first opened its doors.[78] Today, the arena hosts college bowl games and conference basketball championships, spring-training baseball exhibitions, circuses, and motor sporting events.[79] Civic officials yet remain convinced that the city may get the NFL team that justified building the Alamodome in the first place.[80] News reports have suggested that the Oakland Raiders—who have been long leveraging a move to Los Angeles to get a new stadium at home—are now considering relocating to San Antonio. Given the short shelf life of modern stadiums, it is unlikely that this would occur without plans for a new facility. Meanwhile, Spurs ownership proposed they would fight a move

One. Welcome to the Consumer Arena

unless they are allowed to purchase a controlling interest in the franchise, contending that competition with an NFL team would compromise Spurs sponsorships and suite and ticket sales.[81] Since Spurs ownership presumably value the merit of the "free" market, which celebrates competition as invaluable and democratic, such anger is loaded with an all-too-visible irony.

Perhaps a more egregious example can be found in the case of Miami Arena, which was built specifically for the NBA expansion Miami Heat, who began their first season in 1988–1989. As early as 1993, the ownership of the Heat concluded that their newly completed arena was economically obsolete and inadequate, arguing that it did not have enough luxury boxes, seating capacity, or advertising space.[82] While Heat ownership threatened to move the franchise without a new facility, the Heat's current lease with Miami prohibited the city from building any "large-scale indoor facility that would compete with Miami Arena."[83] By 1996, Heat ownership agreed to cover the entire $165 million cost for a new arena in response to public opposition to tax dollars being used to finance a new facility while still paying for the old one. Even though the deal seemed to be a fair bargain on the surface, Dade County would still fleece taxpayers to the tune of $6.5 million a year to cover the operating expenses at the Heat's new home. Not impressed, opponents of the new project circulated petitions and collected 48,000 signatures, forcing a public vote on the manner. Aside from being angered by tax dollars going to benefit a billionaire owner, citizens also argued that the waterfront location, where the proposed new arena would be built, should be converted into a public park instead.[84]

Of course, there is a more twisted element to the story that made the integrity of the Heat's argument that a new arena was desperately needed a little more questionable. The proposed waterfront facility would be packaged as a larger redevelopment project of the 70 acres around the Port of Miami and would include shops and restaurants, as well as an expansion of the port itself for the benefit of Carnival Cruise Lines.[85] As the new arena project was being discussed with civic officials, Mickey Arison bought out the other owners of the Heat, which had previously been co-owned by Mickey's father, Tom Arison; Lewis Schaffel; and Billy Cunningham. It was no coincidence that Mickey was also the owner of Carnival Cruise Lines and would stand to benefit from a new waterfront arena situated next to a renovated port to drive tourist business to both the Heat and the cruise line itself. So determined was Arison to get his new arena that he pulled out all of the public relations stops he could muster to sway the public to vote in favor of the project. These included free balloons, miniature basketballs, and sending Heat players through Miami neighborhoods to sign autographs, take photos, and make emotional speeches regarding how much they loved the city and needed the voters to keep them there. Even head coach Pat Riley made appearances in which he made clear that, without a new facility, the city would lose its basketball team. In Liberty City, for example, he spoke to a large, enthusiastic crowd comprised mostly of schoolchildren, reminding them that "the Miami Heat belong here in Dade County" while encouraging the kids to "make sure to encourage your parents to vote."[86]

The reality is that Miami had already lost one franchise, which new arena supporters often pointed to in order to remind voters of what happens when owners do not get what they want. The Florida Panthers, who shared Miami Arena with the Heat since entering the NHL as an expansion franchise in 1993, claimed that they also needed a new home to be profitable. Broward County to the north agreed to build a new $212 million arena to be shared by both teams, providing a date by which the Heat and the Panthers had to accept or reject the offer.[87] On the day of the deadline, the Panthers agreed to move to Sunrise, Florida, in Broward County when the arena was finished in 1998. Meanwhile, the city approved a $210 million sports complex on the Miami waterfront to keep the Heat in Dade County, which would later be amended to include a privately funded arena in exchange for the country covering its operating expenses. That is when the public voiced its opposition, signed petitions, and forced a public vote, after which Coach Riley and his players showed up in communities with balloons, basketballs, and motivational speeches. Few could blame the public on the matter, however. Miami Arena cost $53 million to build, with $46 million of it being funded by taxpayers, and was barely a *half* decade old by the time Heat ownership began lobbying for a new facility while threatening to walk if the city balked at their demands. By the time the public vote took place, the county was still on the hook for the remaining $38 million in bonds sold to finance Miami Arena, which would not be fully repaid until 2018.[88]

One. Welcome to the Consumer Arena

The Arison PR gravy train would ultimately work, as the public voted in favor of the new arena as well as the larger redevelopment project on the Miami waterfront.[89] Meanwhile, Miami Arena would later be sold in 2004 for $28 million to a wealthy Boca Raton investor who hoped it could be used as a "niche venue" for concerts and other seasonal events.[90] However, due to the glut of concert, athletic, and entertainment venues in Miami, coupled with the arena's inconvenient geographical location relative to its competitors, Miami Arena was ultimately demolished in 2008. For the Heat, the $215 million American Airlines Arena opened in 1999 and was celebrated for being "everything the Heat's old home wasn't—big, plush and state-of-the art" and included an outdoor balcony showcasing the "breathtaking vista ... [of] the downtown skyline, Biscayne Bay and Miami Beach."[91] In many ways, however, the venue is a gigantic corporate advertising pitch for American Airlines, which purchased the naming rights. A gigantic replica airplane welcomes visitors from the arena roof outside while the "Flagship Lounges" inside, named after the airline's series of premium lounges in American airports, serve as luxury box heaven for wealthier patrons.

While Heat ownership did pay for the entire construction costs of its new home, the facility sits on a piece of prime waterfront real estate valued at $38 million provided free by the city while its annual operating costs are subsidized by county taxpayers.[92] Furthermore, this "sweetheart" deal included a revenue-sharing agreement with the city of Miami. After taking its share of profit, the Heat would write a check to the city for whatever money remained after recouping construction costs, deducting past losses, and covering facility upgrades, as well as 60 percent of the leftovers. Furthermore, the agreement would only "kick in" if the Heat made $14 million in profit from the arena that year.[93] Before 2013, the team had paid nothing to the city, prompting former Miami-Dade commissioner Katy Sorenson to remark that "the Heat, as usual in these deals with the county, got way more than they should have and the county got not nearly enough."[94] In 2013, after the Heat made tens of millions in profit in that year alone, the city finally received its first long-overdue check for a "whopping" $257,000. Then, adding insult to injury, the Heat asked the city to increase its annual operating subsidy for American Airlines Arena from $6.5 million to $17 million. If an average person fleeced an entire county for millions, he would be labeled a criminal, thrown in prison, and publicly scorned for ripping off taxpayers. But when you are a wealthy businessperson this kind of hustle is often celebrated as being savvy and smart.

*****

To be sure, new stadiums, ballparks, and arenas could avoid much of this controversy if significant amounts of public money were not consistently funneled toward the cost of building them. Historically, publicly funded facilities in professional sports were uncommon, with the Rose Bowl in Pasadena, California, Solider Field in Chicago, and Municipal Stadium in Cleveland serving as rare exceptions to the norm whereby team owners paid for new stadiums and arenas on their own.[95] This changed when the hapless and hopelessly mediocre Boston Braves moved in 1953 to Milwaukee, where the new, publicly funded County Stadium awaited them. Few could blame the Braves for wanting out of Boston, where they were often considered a second-rate attraction consistently overshadowed by the more successful and nationally recognizable Red Sox. In their final season in Boston in 1952, for example, the Braves drew an embarrassing 281,000 fans, who, if anything, probably enjoyed the extra leg room more than watching their team cruise to a 64–89 record. By way of contrast, the new Milwaukee Braves attracted over 67,000 fans in their first two games at County Stadium alone and, by the end of the season, had eclipsed the 2 million mark in attendance, a mesmerizing 750 percent increase from the year prior. Because of the success of the Braves in their new home in Milwaukee, "teams began to see the value of a new publicly funded stadium."[96] Consequently, they began pushing their home cities to fund new stadiums and a great wave of stadium construction occurred in New York, St. Louis, Houston, Oakland, Anaheim, Cincinnati, Pittsburgh, Philadelphia, and Kansas City. Ironically, the Braves would last just a little over a decade in Milwaukee, migrating in 1965 to Atlanta, where a more architecturally modern, publicly subsidized facility awaited them in a larger television market in the south.

Of course, the political climate has shifted significantly in recent decades to a time when team owners financed their own stadiums and arenas. Today, civic officials are often beholden to powerful business interests to attract or maintain jobs and, in the case of professional

One. Welcome to the Consumer Arena

sports, to save a city's beloved team(s) by using tax dollars to pay for new stadiums and arenas. With the offshoring of production and manufacturing to areas outside of the United States where businesses take advantage of cheaper, non-unionized labor, these jobs have largely been replaced by low-paying jobs in the service sector. Thus, businesses no longer need to invest in sizeable and relatively permanent manufacturing plants, which, because of the cost of building them, ensured in many cases that businesses stayed in one place. Instead, many headquarter their operations in rented retail and office spaces, allowing companies to be much more mobile than they used to be. Under conditions of neoliberal capitalism, this means that cities have to compete much more aggressively with one another to either lure businesses to their region or appease the companies that already reside there. Often, this occurs through favorable tax breaks, government subsidies, infrastructural investments, and other enticing incentives.

Of course, having professional sports teams is often promoted as providing a city a significant advantage in having "major league" status that grants them national and international visibility.[97] Some believe that public investments in new sports stadiums and large entertainment districts will attract white-collar companies to their cities. Location in areas with an abundance of leisure options can be used to recruit high in-demand working professionals who consider an area's quality of life vital and important. However, the issue tends to overlook the fact that, for the residents already living in a city, their tax dollars are being used for the benefit of projects that, in many cases, they will be priced out of enjoying. Furthermore, no evidence exists that companies are relocating to cities just because they have a major league sports franchise. As Neil deMause and Joana Cagan note, "welfare as we know it may be dead, but corporate welfare is alive and kicking."[98] For residents, attracting white-collar businesses does not benefit them if they do not have a college education. Meanwhile, upscale leisure options such as trendy clubs and outdoor cafés may not benefit them unless they can afford to look the part. Nor do these benefit them if they are unable to afford a drink or a decent meal in many places that purposely price them out to remain exclusive. In the case of sports stadiums, they do not benefit when they cannot afford a ticket for a stadium they helped pay for. Thus, their anger and opposition are justified when primarily affluent visitors and suburban residents, who can afford the higher ticket prices and $8 beers, enjoy the benefits largely at the resident's expense.

Thus, the question remains as to why the public votes in favor of publicly funded stadiums to begin with. In most cases, they do not, as most stadium referendums are routinely voted down by the public.[99] Part of the reason is that, in many cases, such a vote only occurs after opponents circulate a petition and garner enough signatures to put a proposed taxpayer-funded sports stadium on the ballot.[100] The fact that the issue is being voted on in the first place is already indicative of significant public opposition. Unless enough people ask for a publicly subsidized stadium proposal to be put on the ballot by signing a petition, many civic officials and team owners are able to strike a deal without public input or approval. However, if a referendum is offered and the public rejects a new stadium deal there are options for officials to maneuver around the vote and fund a stadium anyway. In Seattle, voters rejected the sale of $336 million in bonds for a new stadium for the Mariners to replace the Kingdome only to have the decision later overturned by the Washington Supreme Court.[101] Years earlier in Cleveland, 56 percent of city residents voted against a taxpayer subsidy for a new baseball stadium for the Indians. In response, civic officials extended the vote to the surrounding suburbs, where the subsidy garnered the necessary support.[102] This kind of voter gerrymandering had also been successfully used after Denver city residents disapproved funding for Coors Field, the current home of the Rockies. In some cases, such democratic process are sometimes mocked altogether, as in the case of the mayor of Chandler, Arizona, when a proposed spring training facility appeared on the ballot. When asked what he thought the outcome might be, he stated that "if voters pass this, we will move forward. If the voters don't pass this, we'll still move forward."[103]

It is not uncommon for civic leaders to make exaggerated claims about the economic benefits of new publicly funded sports stadiums, the numerous jobs that will be created, and the fan spending that will be stimulated in and around the ballpark, stadium, and arena.[104] Academic analyses of the economic impact from these projects have repeatedly indicated that they contribute little to no economic growth and, in some cases, cities are worse off with a new stadium then they were before. For example, sports-related employment makes up approximately 1 percent of all private-sector jobs and many of them are seasonal, low paying, and, in the case of stadium construction, temporary.[105] As Cleveland union activist John Ryan indicates, "none of these are jobs that the mayor hugs his kids and says, 'I hope that you can get one of those jobs someday.'"[106] Moreover, the entertainment budget of most fans remains unchanged regardless if a new stadium is built; thus, whatever "new" spending that is generated by a new facility is merely transferred from someplace else that might have received it before, such as movie theatres, shopping malls, hotels, and restaurants located farther away.[107] Yet a new stadium provides a comforting set of illusions that appears to offer convincing proof of economic activity and growth, such as the high demand for tickets in a new stadium, the "buzz" taking place in nearby restaurants and bars before and after a game, and a previously neglected and deteriorating piece of downtown real estate having been given a significant face-lift. The persistent fact remains, however, that whatever economic activity is taking place is simply diverting money from other recreational activities that fans would have spent their money on if these sports-related options simply did not exist.

Furthermore, a new stadium or arena receives most of its usage when its home team is in season and, in the case of football, it is more difficult to justify a multi-million-dollar investment for a new facility for a team that might use it a dozen times in a given year. Consequently, when a city invests in several new sports facilities for its teams, these stadiums and arenas are located within close proximity of one another in order to ensure economic activity virtually year round. To be fair, some indirect benefits may be created by their construction. A new facility tends to attract media coverage when it opens and, for a moment at least, a city becomes the center of national attention. In other cases, a state-of-the-art "world-class" facility could serve as an important source of civic pride.[108] However, the tangible value of these alleged benefits is difficult to quantify and measure.[109]

*****

One primary yet often-overlooked reason why team owners want a new stadium is because many of the existing stadiums and arenas were built during a time when ownership believed that the primary product they were selling was sports. When their teams were winning, this clearly was a much easier sell. Today, however, the paradigm has shifted, as team owners aim to provide fans a consciously crafted "experience" apart from the spectacle of sports themselves. After the opening of Oriole Park at Camden Yards in Baltimore in 1992, it became clear that designing a stadium as a consumer-driven theme park could be not only profitable but also a hit with fans. While "real" sports fans would continue to be drawn mostly to the action on the field, the stadium experience would work to drive more casual "fans" into the stadium who might be less interested, perhaps, in watching a game than in having many things to do. When this paradigm shifted after Camden Yards opened, owners in older facilities began pressuring their home cities to fund a new facility, often by threatening to move elsewhere if they a city refused. Meanwhile, owners in relatively new facilities, such as the Miami Heat ownership, felt cheated because they were shackled playing in a new arena that operated under an obsolete philosophy that privileged sports over an experience.

Numerous examples abound that exemplify this new ideology. As the Cleveland Indians Baseball Company remarked about new Jacobs (now Progressive) Field, fans "are offered a customer focused experience in an attractive, comfortable environment featuring a variety of amenities, concessions, and merchandise options."[110] Meanwhile, Texas Rangers president Nolan Ryan stated—after 39-year-old Shannon Stone died from falling over a railing to catch a ball thrown into the stands by outfielder Josh Hamilton—"we're about making memories.... You can see how many people come into our ballpark with gloves, just hoping to have that opportunity [of catching a ball]. That's just part of the experience of being here."[111] Perhaps more transparent is the comment made by a representative involved in the planning of the Atlanta Braves' home Turner Field, who said that "if we are going to hook people on baseball, we don't do it by making them sit through nine innings. If we can make the experience more pleasurable, we should."[112]

In many cases, team owners whose teams played in older venues claimed that these facilities were lacking the amenities that made it impossible to deliver a "fan-friendly experience." One option would be to simply renovate a stadium or arena, but many owners concluded that this was too costly and, in the case of older venues, structurally impossible due to the limitations imposed by their original design. However, there are a few examples where ownership pursued this route, as in the case of Kauffman Stadium in Kansas City. In 2009, much of the stadium's renovations involved converting the open lawn areas beyond the outfield fences into "party areas," including the Pepsi Party Porch, the Budweiser Patio, and the Rivals Restaurant and Sports Bar, all funded through a sales tax increase.[113] Such examples are the exception, as most owners aggressively pursue new stadiums and arenas in which these consumer-driven amenities can be implemented from scratch. Often, they justify the construction of a new facility or the upgrading of an existing facility on the basis that their home stadium and arena has become economically obsolete. Simply put, this means that these facilities are missing revenue streams that are commonplace in more "state-of-the-art" and "fan-friendly" new stadiums and arenas. Team owners often hide these motivations behind the oft-repeated claim that such amenities are intended to benefit the fans themselves by ensuring that they are comfortable and sufficiently entertained. If such claims are left unexamined, the owners appear to be selfless in caring so much about the fans. However, owners' appeal to "fan friendliness" is little more than a rhetorical cover that often conceals a more selfish motivation: to create additional ways for fans to spend money and, consequently for owners, to make money.

However, it is one thing for owners to create these additional revenue streams, but it is another for owners to make sure that that they are maximizing them. The common refrain that professional sports are pricing out working-class fans is not facetious, nor is it an exaggeration. Lower- and working-class fans' more limited incomes render them undesirable for team owners compared to more affluent fan groups who have more money and a willingness to spend it. Treated simply as "revenue streams" themselves, certainly not all fans are created equal. The inclusion in a new stadium of more luxury boxes, party decks, swimming pools, trendy nightclubs and bars, and concession stands offering exotic fare such as sushi and martinis is designed to appeal to the consumerist inclinations of upper-income fans. Meanwhile, the overwhelming message to fans, whether wealthy or not, is that they are expected to assume the role of a consumer, much less a fan. The extent to which teams are successful in attracting upper-income fans is anchored by the following variables: (1) the novelty of the stadium experience that makes it "the place to be," (2) the constant surveillance of fan conduct to ensure fan safety, (3) higher ticket prices that effectively but not completely price out lower-income fans to ensure the exclusivity of that experience, and (4) a winning and competitive team that, through increased demand for tickets, increases the price beyond the affordability of the average fan—thus, more exclusivity.

Older stadiums and arenas have often been viewed as being more democratic than the newer facilities that have replaced them, especially in the case of the large, multipurpose stadiums that rarely experienced sellouts for sports such as baseball. According to Daniel Rosensweig, "tickets were cheap and readily available, meaning that, for perhaps the only time in baseball's history, live professional games did in fact seem to be 'for everyone.'"[114] The stadiums themselves had a decidedly working-class feel and the experience of attending a game was more spontaneous, lively, and unpredictable than in newer sports stadiums that often have a more corporatized, Disneyfied, and regulated feel. Many owners claim this makes their venues more family friendly and that the visible presence of security guards and stricter regulations policing what fans are allowed to do are designed to ensure safety while providing clean, "family-friendly" entertainment for everyone.[115] While this may be true to a degree, it is also the case that this is done to attract upper-income fans, many of whom associate "rowdy" fan behavior with the working and lower classes. Most MLB and NHL teams have team-specific "fan code of conduct" policies that stipulate, with some ambiguity, what fan behaviors are prohibited, while the NFL and NBA have similar league-wide policies that all teams and fans must adhere to.[116] These policies bear a striking resemblance to the "purification policies" that early professional baseball teams once used to discourage working-class attendance in order to attract more affluent patrons.[117]

For example, the Sun Life Stadium (the home of the Miami Dolphins) fan code of conduct prohibits, among other things, "obscene or indecent messages or clothing," "intoxication or other signs of impairment related to alcohol consumption," and "interfering with others' enjoyment of the game." Fans are encouraged to report violations to ushers and law-enforcement and stadium personnel via text message, with violators being subjected to "ejection, Season Ticket revocation, and possible arrest."[118] For years, all of these were considered part of the experience of attending a game and owners made few attempts to curb behaviors that, if anything, were regarded more as a nuisance than

One. Welcome to the Consumer Arena

a threat. In older venues, many fans reported the greater degrees of freedom related to how they were allowed to behave and express themselves. Thus, sports offered for fans a momentary reprieve from many of the rigid constraints and social norms that characterized everyday life.[119] This is not to suggest that fans were allowed to do what they pleased. Rather, it demonstrates to a large degree how new sports stadiums and venues today are catering to a different kind of fan, one that demands and feels entitled to a more disciplined and controlled experience. In the "old" days, team owners were merely trying to sell tickets and were less concerned with who was buying them. Today, owners are concerned with not only getting people into the stadium but also attracting the "right" kind of fans who are affluent enough to be able to spend more money while they are at the game. When attending a sporting event is no longer the "mundane" experience of watching a game and buying a few hot dogs but now the spectacular experience of stadiums with restaurants, bars, and gaming experiences, team owners make more profit by attracting the kind of people who have more money to spend on these activities. Families, thus, represent an ideal "revenue stream" because parents with children often spend more money at a game to feed and entertain them then they would have spent if they attended alone. And as the costs of attending live sports have increased in recent years, more families are priced out due to this reason. Thus, the families being targeted, unlike in years past, are a *specific* kind of family of a particular socioeconomic status. So while fan code of conducts are may be manufactured to ensure family friendliness on the one hand, they also operate on a deeper symbolic level as a form of classism and exclusion on the other hand.

In the NFL, these codes have been extended beyond the stadium and now regulate which behavior is allowed during tailgate parties and other kinds of pregame festivities. In Buffalo, Ken Johnson's antics made him such a celebrated local icon that he became part of the spectacle of attending a Bills game. While his customary tradition of cooking raw meat on the hood of a 1980 Pinto was considered benign, the Bills determined that his pregame ritual of drinking Polish cherry liqueur out of a bowling ball was not family friendly. Prior to the Bills' home opener in 2010, Johnson was told to move from a nearby stadium lot because his conduct was offensive to parents. In an interview, Johnson stated that "I do push the limits, so I can't scream too loudly. But you wonder how many people go to games because of characters like me. I think I add to the experience."[120] However, Johnson's experience was attractive to the wrong kinds of fans. According to Jeffrey Miller, the NFL Director of Strategic Security Programs, the NFL was targeting these kinds of behaviors in order to remain profitable during the economic recession. Thus, he reasoned that they had to be sensitive to the preferences of upper-class fans, who typically were less impacted by the recession and could still afford to attend games and might interpret Johnson's behavior as working-class, fraternity-inspired nonsense. "Irregardless [sic] of the fact that he may have been doing this over the course of a number of years, it doesn't make it right. People taking shots out of a bowling ball has the effect of repelling families."[121]

It is telling how the Bills attempted to drive upper-class attendance to home games by creating a "family-friendly" environment, something that, at first glance, does not appear to have any particular social class dimension. After all, one could argue, as many team owners do, that policing the kinds of behaviors that have made Ken Johnson legend are designed to benefit everyone, regardless if they are wealthy, working-class, or poor. However, this overlooks the fact that ownership attempts to be "family friendly" have only arisen within the most recent wave of new stadium construction in the last few decades. In older stadiums and arenas, families still attended games without the firm expectation that they would be shielded from sometimes rowdy and carnivalesque fan behavior, even if some of it might have made parents uncomfortable. Today, however, new stadiums and the larger urban development projects that they are a part of are largely designed to lure suburban residents into the city in order to spend money and rejuvenate urban economies.[122] Thus, team owners have resorted to being "family friendly" in order to alleviate generalized fears and anxieties that suburbanites harbor toward the inner city with its lower-class "Other" where many of these new stadiums and arenas are located.

Suburban fans expect that when they attend games they are to be provided the same sheltered and controlled experience that they have grown accustomed to living in the suburbs (and, in some cases, gated communities). Thus, to stem the anxieties of the suburban class who are asked to travel downtown to see a game, stadiums and their surrounding environment must show that surveillance is everywhere, that security is alert and vigilant, and that elements not deemed "family

One. Welcome to the Consumer Arena

friendly" are policed and contained.[123] These practices should not be regarded as all that surprising, as researchers have consistently found that Americans today have higher levels of generalized fear and anxiety than in previous decades.[124] As Ronald Lee and Shawn T. Wahl note:

> It does not seem so many years ago, as we reminisce through an admittedly sentimental lens, that kids went running out the front door in the morning, ran all over the neighborhood with friends, congregated in a vacant lot to play ball, and then came home again for supper. Now, we have indoor playgrounds, supervised sports leagues, nannycams, and surveillance cameras mounted in school doorways.[125]

Despite the fact that crime rates (violent, property, theft, murder, etc.) have consistently decreased, with few exceptions, since the early 1990s, the perception that "the world is a dangerous place" continues to escalate. This phenomenon has largely been attributed to the mass media, who, despite the decrease in crime in recent decades, have increased crime-based programming.[126] This is not only the case with the local news, where the saying "if it bleeds, it leads" has become a cliché, but also with the creation of cable networks such as Investigation Discovery, whose brand involves recycling past sensationalized crime stories in a documentary drama format. While such content drives ratings due to the fascination and fear Americans have toward crime, its effect is a paralyzed and fearful public. Consequently, Americans are increasingly convinced that crime is a more pressing and troubling problem than it actually is. Meanwhile, appearing to be tough on crime has become an almost standard strategy for politicians hoping to be elected to political office.[127] More prisons are built, more mandatory sentencing is instituted, and greater surveillance efforts are called for in order to reassure the public with a sense of safety and security. Ironically, when these occur, it reinforces the narrative that crime is out of control because these greater measures are assumed to be a response to a growing problem. And it is in this context that relatively benign fan activities in sports stadiums, such as intoxication, the wearing of "offensive" T-shirts, and the use of "obscene" language, become viewed as potential threats in the minds of many fans already primed to be on high alert.

However, this high alertness extends beyond the chronic anxiety that one may be a victim of a criminal act to a more diffuse and generalized fear of moral contamination, especially in the case of upper-income Americans. The German philosopher Friedrich Nietzsche in his text *On the Genealogy of Morals* argued that morality had an upper-class, elite origin. The behavior of the wealthy and powerful became the barometer of moral superiority in contrast to the masses who were assumed to be deviant, dirty, and immoral thieves. In short, one's class standing was believed to be indicative of one's moral character.[128] Nietzsche's genealogy of morals seemed to offer one account as to why the upper classes often attempt to insulate and distance themselves from those regarded to be both their economic and moral "inferiors."

The suburbs historically, with all their exclusionary practices, were assumed to be "safe" precisely because of the efforts undertaken to ensure that minorities and lower and working classes were kept out. Discriminatory lending practices and higher rent and property values would be used to keep out the "undesirables." Yet as suburbs gradually became more socially and racially diverse, gated communities became more common, appealing to wealthier citizens seeking more exclusive and homogenized communities.[129] In sports, fan codes of conduct aim to target and prohibit behaviors believed to be associated with working- and lower-class fans to similarly filter them out. Family friendliness may, on the one hand, benefit parents who want to shelter their children from rowdy fan behavior and its alleged contaminating effects. On the other hand, such "family-friendly" practices have emerged as team owners catered to a more financially affluent class. Perhaps it is fair to say, at risk of overgeneralization, that when more working-class fans attended sporting events, many of them were probably less concerned about how rowdy fan behavior might impact their kids. In contrast, upper-income fans are more intolerant and snobbishly dismissive, especially toward behaviors they associate with being typical of their social and economic "inferiors." And when working-class fans attend games the fan codes of conduct are designed to remind them to behave with "class."

I will caution the reader that I am not suggesting that all upper-income fans are moral prudes or that working-class fans are less responsible parents than anyone else. However, I would suggest that team owners operate by these very assumptions and they are reflected almost everywhere within the built environment and experience of new sports stadiums. Given that many of these fans prefer their experiences to be exclusive, fan codes of conduct, higher ticket prices, and more expensive consumer options provide symbolic reassurance that certain classes of people are kept out, either coincidentally or by design. The gradual disappearance of the working-class fan from live sporting events is viewed as necessary to satisfy those upper-income fans who do not wish to "rub elbows" with them. As a matter of fact, the skyrocketing cost of game tickets, in many ways, is the draw itself. As famed Frankfort School cultural theorist Theodor Adorno noted when talking about the bourgeois fascination with high cultural arts forms like opera, "the consumer is really worshipping the money that he himself has paid for the ticket ... he has not 'made' it by liking the concert, but rather by buying the ticket."[130] While there are many legitimate upper-income sports fans who would pay to see their team play regardless if they played in a new stadium or not, the more casual upper-income fan is likely more enchanted by the experience for sale and its high cost than the action taking place on the field, ice, or court. New sports stadiums have become a new kind of gated community that aims to keep certain people out for the benefit of the fans inside.

The pricing out of the working class is both well noted and documented, not only by sports writers but also by the fans themselves. As Dave Zirin comments, "it's no exaggeration, and even a cliché, to point out that the working class people have been priced out of attending sports events; it's no longer possible for kids to trade in some milk bottles for tickets to the game."[131] When the $1.3 billion new Yankee Stadium opened in the Bronx in 2009, Yankees Chief Operating Officer Leon Trost explained that "we've tried to reflect a five-star hotel ... [with] a ballfield in the middle."[132] Meanwhile, one Yankee fan lamented the closing of the old Yankee Stadium, stating that "if you build a new stadium for more luxury boxes, what that means is that you leave ordinary fans out. It will be a stadium for corporations, not a stadium for you and me."[133] As a matter of fact, the exorbitant price tag of new stadiums is largely due to providing amenities. New Yankee Stadium, for example, features 51 luxury suites, two expansive outdoor suites, eight party suites, several martini bars, a video conference room for business rental, and an exclusive members-only club.[134] None of these amenities are designed or intended for working-class fans; rather, they exist simply to make the ballpark more inviting for corporate elites and upper-income patrons by reflecting their expensive tastes.

*****

American Sports in an Age of Consumption

As I have argued, the appeal to family friendliness is wrought with classist dimensions and is not as innocent or inclusive as it may appear on the surface. Furthermore, this new paradigm has created a noticeable and significant tension regarding the pervasive sponsorship of professional sports by beer and alcohol companies. More specifically, teams have had to navigate the contradiction between profiting from the sales of alcoholic beverages at ballparks and arenas while, at the same time, maintaining their commitment to family friendliness. The effort to do both simultaneously raises questions regarding exactly where the line between the two is drawn. As part of Captain Morgan's sponsorship agreement with Major League Baseball in 2010, the company sent its bearded pirate mascot to throw out the first pitch at ballparks across the country. Simultaneously, MLB.com urged fans to "make plans to hang with the Captain on one of his stops this year" while posting a video archive of past appearances by the company's icon.[135] Meanwhile, Captain Morgan's sponsorship agreement with the NFL included a promise to make a charitable contribution each time a player was spotted on camera doing the Captain Morgan pose during a televised game, a deal that the NFL later judged was in violation of league rules.[136]

Returning to baseball, the mascot of the Milwaukee Brewers, known to fans as Bernie the Brewer, was a fan favorite at County Stadium prominently known for sliding into a large beer keg to celebrate Brewer home runs. Such antics personified Milwaukee's beard-wearing working-class culture and solidified County Stadium's reputation as "baseball's blue collar bastion."[137] In 2001, the team began play in the new, publicly financed Miller Park, named after the famed Miller Brewing Company, which negotiated a 20-year $41.1 million dollar naming-rights deal with the club.[138] Unfortunately for the Brewers faithful, Bernie's beer keg was noticeably absent in the new ballpark in an effort to make it family friendly, replaced by the empty spectacle of Bernie the Brewer sliding unceremoniously down a yellow slide onto a flat scaffold to celebrate Brewer home runs instead. The sanitization of Bernie the Brewer symbolized a departure from the Brewers' blue-collar image and tradition toward a more suburbanized and Disneyfied direction. Never mind the obvious irony of a stadium named after a beer company, or that the team itself is called the Brewers, or that the park is nicknamed The Keg by fans "for the alcoholic beverages sold

One. Welcome to the Consumer Arena

there and after which the park is named."[139] Bernie's keg, however, celebrated the working-class culture that defined County Stadium. Its inclusion would have interfered with the team's attempt to cater to a more affluent fan base, many of whom would have found Bernie's keg objectionable.

The case of Miller Park and Bernie the Brewer is representative of the tension between selling alcohol at games because of its profitability while simultaneously offering an appealing product to the family-friendly crowd. To be sure, there is a strong connection in the cultural imagination between beer and sports. As Lawrence Wenner notes, "wetting one's whistle while watching sports has become a naturalized artifact of fanship. Beer, in particular, has a longstanding cultural association to those enmeshed in sports."[140] However, when one pauses to reflect on this relationship one realizes that the consumption of alcohol contradicts what we imagine sporting and athletic excellence to be. For example, sporting success depends on the honing and development of fine motor skills, while drinking alcohol impairs and inhibits them. Sports are presumably good for your health if you participate in them, while beer, however, is not.

Wenner describes the relationship between beer and sports as an example of "sports dirt" where the cultural logic of sport is being borrowed to make the consumption of alcohol seem more attractive.[141] Through their sponsorship with sports, beer and alcohol companies are hoping that the positive emotions people have toward sports will be transferred to the product they are selling. Thus, sports become yet another cultural vehicle to sell and market a product, and evidence shows this to be an effective and profitable strategy. For example, Chicago Cubs fans consume approximately 29,000 cups of beer per game at historic Wrigley Field, while beer and wine sales increase an average of 34 percent during the week of the Super Bowl.[142] While such statistics may appear self-evident and unsurprising, the relationship between alcohol and sports was not always welcomed by team owners because the former attracted working-class fans to ballparks. As a matter of fact, the history of alcohol and sports is no less a discussion on inclusion, as purification policies limiting or banning the consumption of alcohol at sporting events historically were designed to appease upper-income fans who aspired to clean living. These policies were designed to repel working-class fans in order to satisfy the desire of the affluent to not have to mix with the "underclass." This happened in the National League, which in its early years prohibited the sale and consumption of alcohol at games while banning Sunday baseball to conform to upper-class values. It was not until the American Association was established years later that fans were allowed to purchase alcoholic beverages at professional baseball games, giving it its nickname as the "Beer and Whiskey League."[143]

Of course, it would take several years before fans, sports, and beer were seen as a natural partnership. Thus, it was unsurprising that when beer companies were trying to market light beer to male consumers who dismissed it as feminine they used sports to assure them that one could drink light beer and still be a man. In 1973, McCann-Erickson developed the first Miller Lite ads, featuring sufficiently masculine NFL stars Matt Snell and Ernie Stautner, that incorporated the soon-to-be well-known slogan of "Tastes Great, Less Filling." This was later followed by the "Miller Lite All Stars" that included sporting icons such as Mickey Mantle, Dick Butkus, John Madden, and Deacon Jones, all marketed as "real men" who enjoyed the taste and masculine bravado provided by light beer. Within five years, sales for light beer increased from 7 to 31 million barrels a year.[144]

Today, the relationship between alcohol and sports is seen as less innocent and many professional sports franchises are regulating its consumption within their stadiums and arenas more. While this appears to be the case with fan codes of conduct, these efforts potentially cut into a very lucrative and profitable revenue stream. Yet owners have found that they can get the benefits of both by advertising fan codes of conduct via team Web sites and stadium announcements to cater to families while building lavish "party areas" to contain and separate the party crowd from the former. Rhetorically, the name "party area" (or "party deck" in some instances) implies a space where the rules governing fan behavior are much looser and more flexible while offering a greater degree of relative freedom. Thus, the more rigid norms in modern sports stadiums are suspended because of the shared understanding of those who occupy these spaces that they are all there to have a good time. For families, the clear designation of these spaces makes these easily avoidable by them and ensures that the "party" crowd will be kept separate from the "family-friendly" crowd to each's mutual and maximum benefit.

One. Welcome to the Consumer Arena

In other instances, alcohol sales are sometimes restricted to upper-class patrons presumed to be more responsible when it comes to their alcohol consumption habits. In 2014, the University of Arkansas announced a partnership with concessionaire company Sodexo to sell beer and wine within indoor club areas at Donald W. Reynolds Razorback Stadium, where the school's football team plays its home games. Citing the need to be in compliance with the policies of the Southeastern Conference (SEC), the university restricted the sale and consumption of alcohol elsewhere in the venue and required that one actually had purchased a ticket for the indoor club areas to be eligible to purchase alcohol. Given the fact that the costs of these tickets are several hundred dollars apiece, this privilege is virtually inaccessible to all but the most affluent fans, who can afford the costs. According to University of Arkansas Athletic Director Jeff Long, "we are pleased that Sodexo will be able to utilize its expertise developed through implementing and coordinating similar programs around the country."[145] While a motivation behind this new policy may be to make these indoor club area tickets more appealing while still curbing underage drinking in general-seating areas, it does reveal an assumption that the wealthy consume alcohol more responsibly than others. The announcement of the policy, for example, did not come with warnings regarding possible consequences for being intoxicated or wasted.[146] This owes to either a degree of privilege and entitlement that individuals of high social status become accustomed to or a belief that such problems will not be an issue.

In the case of the latter, a fundamental ideological principle in our culture is the widespread assumption that the wealthy are morally superior to those beneath them. The United States has long regarded itself as *the* ideal meritocracy, premised on the belief that one's social standing in society depends on one's moral virtue, talent, intelligence, work ethic, and productive usefulness. The wealthy, it is often assumed, excel in these areas and deservedly occupy the upper rungs of society, whereas the poor are presumed to be deficient in some or all of them. Meritocracy assumes personal responsibility for one's station in life because of the belief that it results from one's own efforts, strengths, weaknesses, and fortitude. While this belief does not completely dismiss the fact that some are born ahead of others by virtue of the advantages inherited from their parents, economic opportunity is assumed to be available to anyone with the character to seize it.[147] Its appeal as a cultural axiom owes to its simple and uncomplicated explanation of how success is achieved in a society while offering a reassuring worldview that the wealthy should not feel ashamed of their material abundance while others have to survive with decidedly less. After all, as the meritocratic philosophy goes, everyone gets what they deserve; it is an intellectual and material form of justice.

As philosopher Alain de Botton explains, "faith in an increasingly reliable connection between merit and worldly success in turn endowed money with a new moral quality. The rich were not only wealthier, it seemed that they might also be plain *better*."[148] In essence, meritocracy is nothing more than a recycled ideological principle with a long historical precedent that assumed that kings, queens, and wealthy aristocrats were divinely chosen by a higher power to rule and to be admired.[149] The only difference between this notion and meritocracy is that the latter conforms to a more democratic and secularized vision of society. However, since meritocracy carries with it vestiges of this old philosophy, it perpetuates the "godlike" status that both wealthy individuals and celebrities enjoy in our culture. With the normalization of neoliberalism and its corresponding worldview as common sense, one's value and worth to society are wholly determined by the market. As competition is parlayed as the only natural relationship between human beings, values not serviceable to the market, such as integrity, solidarity, and an empathetic concern for others, are largely devalued in our culture and mocked as hopelessly naïve and idealistic. As market philosophy and its emphasis on competition as a self-justifiable good penetrate deeper into social life, social status has become a more prominent preoccupation with more people.[150] It provides validation that we are succeeding in the alleged meritocratic game of life.

Social status is defined as "value and importance in the eyes of the world," which in the Western world "has been awarded in relation to financial achievement."[151] Without question in the United States, consumer goods are rarely consumed for their usefulness and utility but rather to the degree that they can be used to symbolically communicate our "value." As ticket prices have escalated in recent years, resulting in large segments of fans being effectively priced out, attending live professional sports can have status-enhancing effects. Major League

One. Welcome to the Consumer Arena

Baseball's Fan Cost Index, which tabulates the average cost of attending a game for a family of four, estimates that the typical cost of attendance is approximately $213.[152] This includes the cost of four average-price tickets, two small draft beers, four small soft drinks, four regular-sized hot dogs, parking for one car, two game programs, and two "least expensive, adult-size adjustable caps."[153] For the NBA the average cost of attendance using the same criteria is $333.58, while for the NFL it is a whopping $479.11.[154] This is not surprising considering that NBA and NFL teams play fewer games than their MLB counterparts, who have 81 regular-season home games to sell tickets for. Regardless, it is clear that the cost of attending games of the three major professional sports in the United States effectively prices out many fans who are financially unable to bear the burden of skyrocketing ticket prices, outrageous parking fees, and expensive concession and souvenir items. Because professional sports have become more exclusive, the stadiums themselves have a certain degree of "status currency" similar to other social and cultural events virtually off-limits to all but the most affluent customers. Thus, attending sporting events in expensive venues is a way of generating social status for those able to afford the cost of admission. As a matter of fact, this is precisely why some kinds of fans are drawn to these venues in the first place.

*****

After the 2014 season, the Chicago Cubs and the city of Chicago finally reached an agreement to renovate historic Wrigley Field, the legendary ballpark that in recent decades has acted as a veritable time capsule of the pre–consumer wasteland of modern capitalism with its lack of authenticity. The $500 million project would include sensible upgrades such as additional traffic lights around the ballpark and a new parking plan that would offer shuttle service to and from Wrigley Field from distant lots.[155] One notable exception was the newly constructed Captain Morgan Club connected to the ballpark, which includes enough high-end novelty to appeal to the upwardly mobile and networking-hungry professionals who are its target demographic. While the club is technically open to anyone, the expensive drink prices courtesy of "its many premium options" and "rotating selection of specialty cocktails on tap"[156] are enough to ward off poorer fans without the money to indulge in these options. The fact that the bar is labeled a "club" contributes to its sense of exclusivity that will appeal to the self-important "anybody who is anybody" crowd.

Meanwhile, the expansion of the bleachers—excuse me, the Budweiser Bleachers—would yield additional advertising signage to complement the advertising barrage courtesy of the new LED scoreboard in right field. New and expanded luxury suites were regarded as essential to create a world-class facility. While these suites were touted as a necessary renovation to an aging ballpark, it is clear that the primary motivation is revenue streams by first creating the suites and then targeting a more affluent fan base in order to maximize them. Of course, Cubs chairman Tom Ricketts claimed that the renovation was merely an issue of fairness, stating that "what I didn't understand was that we're the only team in baseball that ... [had] these restrictions."[157] As Wrigley Field is a historical landmark, the Cubs could not make these renovations without approval from the city. According to Ricketts, the Cubs were preventing from making revenue on par with other major league clubs. Yet *Forbes* has consistently reported that the Cubs are one of Major League Baseball's most profitable franchises, valued at $1.8 billion as of 2015, with over $300 million in revenue in 2014 alone.[158] Yet the national and local sporting media in Chicago repeated Ricketts' comments without question that the Cubs were a "loser" in modern sports, playing in a historic facility without the necessary revenue streams to be competitive with other clubs. Worse yet, Cubs players echoed his sentiments, emotionally appealing to diehard Cub fans whose team had not won a World Series since 1908 to support these renovations by suggesting that Wrigley Field partly was to blame. In 2013, Cubs pitcher Kerry Wood lamented that Wrigley Field had become a burden, claiming that "I don't think you're gonna get free agent players coming over to spend time here when facilities are what they are compared to everyone else's in both leagues."[159] Ironically, Wood himself had signed as a free agent with the Cubs the previous off-season.

While Ricketts was finally given permission from the city of Chicago to make his proposed renovations to the ballpark, it was not without criticism or controversy. Owners of neighboring buildings beyond right and left field, whose rooftop views made them a hot selling ticket in their own right, filed lawsuits against the Cubs. They alleged that the new Jumbotrons in left and right field, the increase in outfield

One. Welcome to the Consumer Arena

signage, and the extension of the outfield bleachers—all of which obstruct the view from these buildings—were Ricketts' attempts to punish rooftop owners for refusing to sell their buildings to the team.[160] Meanwhile, the proposed renovations were not finished by Opening Night in 2015 and the Cubs were forced to open the season with Wrigley Field's famed outfield bleachers, which resembled a steel and concrete disaster area, off-limits. Worse still, there were only four functioning bathrooms for 35,000 fans on Opening Night, prompting many fans to urinate in empty beer cups and against concourse walls.[161] Levy Restaurants, located in Wrigley Field, would later be hit with several health code violations due to the storing of food at improper temperatures, leaking beer lines, and ice-cream buildup in its coolers.[162]

While the renovations of Wrigley Field were not without hiccups, they signified an extension of the "yuppization" that had long been under way on Chicago's North Side. In 2011, the Cubs renegotiated a brewing-rights deal with Old Style Brewing Company, which had built its reputation as a visible badge of working-class culture.[163] Many speculated that the agreement with Old Style "was an anachronism to the frequent criticism from crosstown White Sox fans that Wrigley is filled with yuppies less interested in the game than taking photos of one another."[164] For anyone who has ever lived in Chicago, the decision to root for the White Sox or Cubs is, for some fans, rooted along social class dimensions. The South Side of the city the White Sox call home is known for being the dirty ghetto of Chicago's neglected underclass, while the North Side where the Cubs play is known as the playground of the city's "mover and shakers," hipsters, and trendy enthusiasts. While getting White Sox tickets was relatively easy and affordable even when the team was doing well, obtaining tickets to see the Cubs at Wrigley Field was difficult and expensive. While there are *true* Cubs fans sprinkled in the seats at the legendary ballpark, they are surrounded by many whose joy in Cubs baseball is less a question of devotion and loyalty and more about the self-importance they feel because they can afford the tickets. In other words, they are less interested in baseball than the social status to be gleaned from being seen at Wrigley Field, which has developed the same unfortunate reputation as any exclusive nightclub or hangout in the city.

As should be clear at this point, professional sports teams are catering to a more affluent crowd who have the money to spend on the many indulgences that have become standard fare at stadiums across the country. While this has been addressed by many academic treatments on the subject, what has been ignored is *how* team owners are able to attract a more upscale fan base. It is precisely the exclusivity of the experience of attending professional sporting events that serves as both the bait and the magnet. For some, exclusivity promises safety and security when traveling downtown to see games because the "lower-class riff raff" cannot, for the most part, afford to get in. For others, exclusivity validates one's social class status and standing in society; the ability to partake in an activity financially off-limits for others raises the status capital associated with the event. The more exclusive the sporting event, or any cultural activity for that matter, the more one's status is elevated. Country clubs across the United States, for example, operate under the same philosophy and ethos.

For this reason, most contemporary sports stadiums, both new and old, have become what I refer to as *statuscapes*, which are landscapes or physical spaces that are sought after by the financial elite because of their exclusivity and their ability to keep members of the "lower" classes out. The greater the degree to which this can be accomplished, the more social status is bestowed upon the individual who can "get in" by affording the cost of admission. In New York, a Manhattan residential address is regarded as essential in order to earn and claim membership in the city's elite class, similar to Beverly Hills in California, where the upper class buys not only a home but also the 90210 zip code to validate their self-importance and class standing. Operating under similar principles, professional sports stadiums through high-priced tickets, exotic concessions, and pricey leisure options can reasonably be considered statuscapes to the degree that they can price out less affluent fans. Of course, this is premised on both demand and esteem; teams that have difficulty drawing fans because they either play in an "old" venue and/or field a losing team diminish their status capital. Exclusivity not only demands that people are kept out but also depends on *how many* are kept out. In other words, the greater the demand for access, coupled with the scarcity and high cost of that access, the greater the status capital associated with a landscape, cultural event, and leisure activity.

When the 2014 Super Bowl, for example, was held at MetLife

One. Welcome to the Consumer Arena

Stadium in New Jersey, only 35 percent of the tickets for the game were made available to the general public while the remainder were held for wealthy corporate executives and official league sponsors.[165] Many of them were probably more interested in what their Super Bowl ticket symbolically demonstrated regarding their own class standing rather than seeing the game live and in person. Unsurprisingly, these mega sporting events are particularly popular for celebrities, many of whom are more interested in being spotted by the news media at the biggest and most exclusive sporting event in the United States than in watching football. At the 2014 Super Bowl, journalists snapped pictures of actors and media personalities such as Hugh Jackman, Kevin Costner, Jennifer Garner, Denis Leary, Harry Connick, Jr., and Spike Lee as they graced the "red carpet" outside the stadium prior to the game.[166] Examples such as these lend credence to the fact that the Super Bowl is more of an exclusive social event for the wealthy and powerful whose membership and status are often predicated upon being seen at big-ticket events such as the Super Bowl. Because social status is often elusive and fragile, owing to the endless competition and effort that goes into attaining it, it must consistently be demonstrated in material ways. As Thorstein Veblen noted, "in order to gain and to hold the esteem of men it is not sufficient to possess wealth or power. The wealth or power must be put into evidence, for esteem is only awarded on evidence."[167]

New sports stadiums and arenas constitute such "evidence" for team owners who consider a new facility a symbolic homage to their legacy as well as a physical expression of their own economic power. Furthermore, such facilities are particularly appealing to wealthy business executives in the cities in which they are located because they provide a charming and sophisticated backdrop for negotiating business deals and schmoozing potential clients. According to Mark Yost:

> Frequent guests in [Washington Redskins] owner [Dan] Snyder's box include former Federal Reserve Chairman Alan Greenspan and his wife, NBC news correspondent Andrea Mitchell, [former and late] congressman and NFL quarterback Jack Kemp, and other Washington power players. In Charlotte, bankers rather than politicians hobnob on the club level of Bank of America Stadium before Carolina Panthers games. At Denver's Invesco Field at Mile High Stadium, oil, gas, and real estate executives gather before Broncos games in the club level sponsored by American Airlines.[168]

American Sports in an Age of Consumption

The selling of naming rights and other forms of sponsorship on the one hand provide additional sources of revenue but on the other hand rhetorically convey to company executives that a venue is "business friendly." Luxury suites take on the additional character of being treated as offices away from the office, while the luxurious and spectacular confines of a new stadium or arena become something that executives "show off" to their clients as if they were their own.[169] Worse yet, league officials have made various threats to cities in order to get them to pony up the necessary funds to build these lavish sporting palaces largely at great cost.

In 2000, then Major League Baseball Commissioner Bud Selig announced his plan to eliminate two teams in order to restore competitive parity between small- and large-market clubs. Although a "blue-ribbon" panel recommended that contraction could be avoided through increased revenue sharing, luxury taxes imposed on high-spending franchises, and an international draft, Selig ignored these suggestions. Instead, he proposed that the Minnesota Twins and Montreal Expos should be eliminated, the teams of two cities struggling to garner necessary public support for new stadiums.

To be fair, the contraction of the Montreal Expos seemed to be a sensible choice due to waning fan support and embarrassingly dismal attendance numbers in the cavernous and uninviting Olympic Stadium. The facility had been built for the 1976 Olympics and was subsequently renovated for the Expos, who had been playing at nearby Jarry Park since entering the National League as an expansion franchise in 1969. However, Selig's contraction gambit was actually the second time in recent decades that Montreal fans were told that they might lose their team. Previously, Major League Baseball threatened to revoke the franchise in the early 1970s after the team and the city failed to secure a new stadium.[170] However, when the International Olympic Committee awarded the 1976 Summer Olympics to Montreal on the condition that newly constructed facilities be put to long-term use the Expos were saved, as Olympic Stadium—built specifically for the Olympic Games—would be converted to a baseball stadium. Unfortunately, the ballpark would later prove to be a financial disaster, largely due to numerous structural failures such as the "retractable" roof that never worked properly. In total, Olympic Stadium would cost the city of Montreal a near-record-breaking $1.4 billion (topped only at the time by "new"

One. Welcome to the Consumer Arena

Wembley Stadium in London, built at a cost of $1.5 billion), a debt that would not be repaid until 2006, two years after the Expos played their final game in Montreal.[171]

Meanwhile, the Minnesota Twins were a championship-caliber club with a loyal fan base yet were unable to garner enough public support for financing a replacement for the Metrodome, built in 1982 at the end of major league baseball's "dome fever" era. In response to Selig's contraction threat, the Metropolitan Sports Facilities Commission successfully sued the Twins to honor its performance clause to play in the Metrodome in 2002. While the plans for contraction were never realized, the city of Minneapolis took the threat seriously enough that a new stadium initiative eventually passed in 2005. In the meantime, Major League Baseball purchased the Montreal Expos for $120 million in 2002 with ambitions of relocating the team in a more financially lucrative market willing to entice the league with a new stadium offer it could not refuse. Shortly thereafter, Washington, D.C., offered an unprecedented deal in which the city promised not only a new ballpark but a facility financed entirely by the public.[172] Selig agreed to the deal and the Expos departed Montreal after the 2004 season for the nation's capital, where they were renamed the Washington Nationals. As sports economist Andrew Zimbalist notes:

> A plausible explanation for the contraction gambit is that owners were seeking leverage in the stadium and player markets. Threaten to eliminate the Twins and maybe Minneapolis or St. Paul would finally put up the public funds to build the team a new facility. Threaten to eliminate the Expos and maybe the Washington D.C. market would produce a solid ownership group and support stadium funding.[173]

In recent years, several organizations such as the Montreal Baseball Project—started by former Montreal Expos outfielder Warren Cromartie—have been lobbying Major League Baseball to bring baseball back to the city, stating on its Web site that "in recent months, a new attitude toward baseball has developed in Montreal" while promising "to turn desire into action by taking the necessary steps to see the game return."[174] Next to these words is a sketch diagram of a proposed new ballpark, obviously a necessary step if the city of Montreal were to be awarded a major league franchise.

Here we see the tired and replayed dynamic of what occurs when a city loses its team after the public refused to finance a new stadium for them. In 1997, Claude Brochu, the managing general partner of the Expos, announced his proposal for a $250 million 35,000-seat retro-style ballpark similar to Camden Yards, claiming that he would he would move the team without it. While some Quebec officials were supportive, Premier Lucien Bouchard did not authorize the required public funding, claiming it would be unethical to divert public money toward a ballpark when the city was already cutting funding for its hospitals. Furthermore, Bouchard reiterated that the debt associated with Olympic Stadium was not yet paid off.[175] Years after the Expos departed for Washington, D.C., organizations such as the Montreal Baseball Project began lobbying Major League Baseball to bring baseball back to the area due to the city's more favorable attitude toward a new publicly financed stadium.

As we have seen, a similar pattern can be found in Cleveland after Browns owner Art Modell moved his team to Baltimore because he wanted a new stadium. Baltimore, meanwhile, was more than willing to build him one after its dearly beloved Colts moved to Indianapolis a decade prior after the city balked at the idea of a new facility for the team. Cleveland then "learned" its lesson, committed itself to a new publicly financed stadium, and was rewarded for doing so by the NFL, who gave them an expansion franchise. A further example can be found in the NFL with the Houston Oilers, who relocated to Nashville to become the Tennessee Titans after team owner Bud Adams' unsuccessful lobbying for a new stadium to replace the Astrodome. After Houston "learned" its lesson, it quickly financed new stadiums for the Astros and an NFL expansion team, the Texans. Team owner Bob McNair stated "[After the Oilers' departure] there was a concern we could lose the Astros. It was a wake up call."[176] Meanwhile, Oliver Luck, former Oilers quarterback and then member of the Houston County–Houston Sports Authority, remarked "that's the irony. [Bud Adams'] ... leaving was the catalyst for a massive public funding of stadiums [in Houston]."[177]

Returning to the example of the Montreal Expos and Premier Bouchard, it is exceedingly rare for governmental officials to weigh the public interest so heavily when it comes to issues of tax dollars being funneled toward private investment opportunities. In the United States, when issues of public welfare and private business interest clash it is often the latter that is given unquestionable priority.[178] Under conditions of neoliberalism, the role of government is defined as providing a favorable business climate, even if the interests of the public are harmed in the process. When a new stadium was being proposed for the New York Yankees, Bronx borough president Adolfo Carrion fired any commission members who disapproved the appropriation of public funds for the ballpark.[179] After the funding was ultimately approved and construction under way, the Yankees went on their then typical high-spending shopping spree, signing free agent All-Stars C.C. Sabathia, A.J. Burnett, and Mark Texiera for a combined $423.5 million.[180] As the ink was drying on the contracts, the Yankees demanded an additional $380 million in funds from the city treasury for "cost overruns" including $150 million for a high-definition scoreboard in center field, $138 million in food and beverage costs, and $50 million for delays created from pending lawsuits regarding the facility.[181] The city not only obliged, but Mayor Michael Bloomberg pledged $324 million in budget cuts for New York City public schools on top of an unannounced midyear cut of $100 million.[182] As the Yankees and Mets—who were also opening a publicly financed facility at the same time—were "ushering a new level of luxury in baseball," taxpayers largely footed the bill for two stadiums that many would never be able to afford to see the inside of.[183]

In Detroit, the city announced in July of 2013 its plans to file for municipal bankruptcy due to an $18 billion debt and a $400 million operating deficit.[184] Six days later, the Michigan Economic Development Corporation gave its preliminary approval to for a new $650 million arena for the Detroit Red Wings with 60 percent of the cost to be covered by taxpayers.[185] Predictably, many Detroit residents wondered how a bankrupt city was able to find the money to commit to a facility to replace Joe Louis Arena, which, despite lacking many of the modern amenities of new sports stadiums, was structurally sound. In a press conference, Governor Rick Snyder defended the decision, stating emphatically:

> [The new Red Wings arena] is a catalyst project. This is going to be where the Red Wings are. Who doesn't get fired up in Detroit for the Red Wings? Come on now, the people that are criticizing us are people from outside of Michigan. This is something that is important to all of us.[186]

Aside from the "us" versus "them" rhetorical gesture, Snyder was exploiting the rabid fan excitement over the Detroit Red Wings' record consecutive play-off appearances to sell an economically questionable funding project as a matter of fan loyalty and Michigan pride. While it is true that the new arena would be paired with a $200 million redevelopment project near the site to create an "entertainment and commercial district" of restaurants, bars, office space, and apartments, the notion that the new Red Wings home is to be a "catalyst" is far from a sure thing. One only has to revisit recent history to see the same promises associated with the public funding of new sports stadiums in Detroit.

When ground broke for Comerica Park—the new home of the Detroit Tigers—in 1997, then Michigan governor John Engler said that the new stadium would serve as a symbol of Detroit's economic renaissance.[187] Denise Illitch, daughter of Mike Ilitch, who owns the Tigers, Red Wings, and Little Caesars pizza chain, boasted that "over the years, there has been a lot of talk, a lot of rhetoric of saving downtown [Detroit]. But ... [the opening of Comerica Park] is more than talk. It's proof that things are finally changing."[188] In 2002, wide-eyed optimists viewed the opening of Ford Field as the new home of the Detroit Lions with the same kind of religious fervor and unabashed enthusiasm. Lions chairman William Clay Ford, Jr., purported that the new facility would "showcase the city's turnaround."[189] When the NFL announced that Detroit would host the 2006 Super Bowl—a common gesture in professional sports to award cities with new stadiums with championship and All-Star events—it was supposed to generate $372 million in revenue.[190] Furthermore, the Super Bowl would be an opportunity to rehabilitate on an international stage the city's image as a crumbling and neglected urban wasteland.

But none of the economic renaissance of job creation and opportunity associated with these new stadiums or Detroit's newly built casinos ever came to fruition. In 2005, Census Bureau data revealed that the city's unemployment stood at a dismal 14 percent, with nearly a third of the city's residents officially living below the poverty line.[191] Years later in 2010, Detroit mayor David Bing announced that he was going to "shrink" the city by plowing blighted neighborhoods and relocating residents, serving for some as a "modern day Trail of Tears for Detroiters."[192] Then, in 2013, came the announcement that the city was filing for bankruptcy, with Kevyn Orr, the city's emergency financial manager appointed by Governor Synder, announcing that "significant

One. Welcome to the Consumer Arena

cuts" in pensions for retired city workers were necessary. Michael Wells, a retired Detroit Public Library employee, stated "[pensions] are deferred income. Had I not had a pension, perhaps I would have gotten several more dollars an hour and that would be OK. I would have taken that money and invested it in some kind of mutual fund or stock."[193] In other words, the pension money was already earned by city workers who were paid less money than their counterparts elsewhere with the difference being deposited into their pensions while they were employed.

In November of 2014, a federal judge approved the city's bankruptcy while also permitting the cutting of pensions and retiree health care.[194] Noted economist Robert Reich stated that bankruptcy could have been avoided had Detroit drawn its city boundary to include the surrounding suburbs. He writes:

> In drawing the relevant boundary to include just the poor inner city, and requiring those within that boundary to take care of their compounded problems themselves, the whiter and more affluent suburbs are off the hook. "Their" city isn't in trouble. It's that other one—called "Detroit." It's roughly analogous to a Wall Street bank drawing a boundary around its bad assets, selling them off at a fire-sale price, and writing off the loss. Only here we're dealing with human beings rather than financial capital. And the upcoming fire sale will likely result in even worse municipal services, lousier schools, and more crime for those left behind in the city of Detroit. In an era of widening inequality, this is how wealthier Americans are quietly writing off the poor.[195]

Of course, many would complain that inner-city Detroit's fiscal problems were not the problem of the suburbs, who should not be financially responsible in the first place. However, Detroit, like many other northern industrialized cities, witnessed a mass exodus of white residents to surrounding suburban neighborhoods such as Auburn Hills, Rochester, and Gross Pointe Woods. This was caused by demographic changes that occurred as many African Americans moved to northern cities seeking employment in automobile-manufacturing plants in Detroit, stoking racial tension between white and black residents competing for jobs.[196] With the flight of many white middle-class residents to the surrounding suburbs in the 1960s and 1970s, jobs and other investments followed them. That, coupled with discriminatory housing and lending practices, ensured that blacks would largely be kept out. Meanwhile, Detroit's auto industry was threatened by imports flooding the American consumer market that were often better built and more fuel efficient, leading to further economic woes.[197] What followed was a devastating trend of unemployment, as few jobs remained, lower tax revenues were generated by the city because of that unemployment, and, consequently, the government was unable to finance essential city services and other monetary commitments. As Detroit fell apart, the prominent narrative in Michigan was that all of this was occurring because of the African Americans "ruining" a once-thriving urban center. Meanwhile, the Detroit suburbs are within the top five nationally for high-technology, engineering and architectural employment. The city, however, has dismally low property values, underfunded schools, high crime, abandoned buildings, and streets where 40 percent of the streetlights do not work.[198] Yet the complexity of Detroit's economic situation is jettisoned in favor of a more simplified explanation in which blacks are blamed for the sorry state of affairs within the city itself.

While Detroit unquestionably is in need of some degree of investment to revitalize itself, evidence has repeatedly shown that financing new sports stadiums and other entertainment amenities merely benefits tourists and out-of-town visitors at the expense of a city's more vulnerable population who are often pushed out.[199] Furthermore, urban governance has shifted toward increasing political power for various financial interests as cities compete with one another to demonstrate their business friendliness. It is clear that Detroit's bankruptcy was partly motivated to remove itself from its financial commitments to free up capital to shoulder tax subsidies for financial investments that would have been nearly impossible with its significant debt. Given Detroit's dire situation, Tigers and Red Wings owner Mike Ilitch is viewed as the city's savior, whose entrepreneurial muscle and business acumen will lead the city toward its long-delayed renaissance. After serving on Detroit's Renaissance Board, Illitch secured many of the rights for his Olympia Development Company to rehabilitate large areas of the city, including the historic Fox Theatre, which he purchased.[200] Given his willingness to undertake such a massive project at a time at which investments in Detroit were nonexistent, Ilitch gained significant political leverage to map the transformation of the city. Emmett Motin, Director of Economic Development for former city mayor Coleman Young, boldly claimed that "if not for Mike Ilitch, there may not be a Detroit."[201] Commissioner Bud Selig echoed these sentiments, suggesting that "what Mike Ilitch has done for the city, sociologically, is stunning. Here is an owner that understood the social responsibilities as well as anyone could. Not everything may have been in his best interest, but it was in the best interest of Detroit and Michigan."[202] The deification of Ilitch is typical under neoliberal capitalism, in which wealthy entrepreneurs are regarded as unsung heroes and the courageous vanguard of the public's welfare.

Ilitch began pushing for a new home for the Red Wings as early as 2006 and his success at getting a publicly funded arena was inevitable given his political power in the city of Detroit.[203] The new state-of-the-art facility would stand as a physical symbol of Ilitch's status and ambition, a tangible demonstration of his wealthy and economic legacy. During the 2005 MLB All-Star Game festivities at Comerica Park, *The New York Times* reported that Major League Baseball contemplated holding an All-Star event at the Tigers' previous home, Tiger Stadium, but were told by Ilitch that the facility was structurally unsafe.[204] As it turned out, the city had provided the Tigers owner with $2.5 million since the stadium closed after the 1999 season to provide maintenance and security at the Tiger Stadium site, yet Ilitch spent only a portion of that money to do so. Some speculated that he was concerned that if the park was maintained it would overshadow Comerica Park, which Ilitch wanted to showcase instead. Meanwhile, various preservation groups, such as the Michigan & Trumbull group, submitted bids to civic officials to be allowed to provide basic upkeep and maintenance of Tiger Stadium, only to be denied by the city. Gary Glaser, producer of the documentary *Stranded at the Corner* that chronicled the struggle to save the historical ballpark, claimed that "the city is not going to do anything Ilitch doesn't sign off on."[205] In 2009, the structure of Tiger Stadium was torn down, and in 2015 the Detroit Police Athletic League and the Old Tiger Stadium Conservancy received approval to develop a sports complex on the site. This would include replacing the original playing field with artificial turf for baseball, football, lacrosse, and cheerleading events.[206]

Like old Tiger Stadium, Joe Louis Arena is considered an architectural relic that lacks the amenities and spectacle to adequately represent Ilitch's financial empire. Built in 1979, the arena was Detroit's attempt to prevent former Red Wings owner Bruce Norris from moving the team to the suburbs following the Detroit Lions and Detroit Pistons exodus to the nearby Pontiac Silverdome. At the time, the lease signed between the Red Wings and the city of Detroit was regarded as one of the most "owner friendly" in professional sports. Given the neoliberal transformation of urban governance since, the lease is no longer regarded as being as advantageous as it once was. Today, team owners have used relocation threats to get not only a publicly funded stadium but also low-rent or rent-free agreements that allow owners to retain revenues (such as parking) that historically would have gone to the city.[207]

Within the original Joe Louis lease agreement that Ilitch had with the city, he had to pay an annual $2.6 million "use tax," $25,000 monthly in rent, a 10 percent ticket tax for all arena events, a 10 percent surcharge on concession sales, and 7 percent of the revenue generated from suite rentals.[208] Furthermore, Olympia Entertainment, the network owned by Mike Ilitch that controls the rights for Detroit Red Wings television broadcasts, had to pay the city of Detroit 25 percent of its cable revenue. When the lease expired in 2010, Ilitch and the Red Wings continued to play in Joe Louis Arena despite ownership not having renewed or renegotiated a new lease. As they did so, the Red Wings failed to make the promised payments stipulated in the old lease under the convenient assumption that they no longer applied.[209] Worse still, reports surfaced that Ilitch never made the promised cable revenue payments owed by his company Olympia in 30 years, an amount projected to be as high as $70 million. Surprisingly, a new lease was not formally completed and signed until 2014 and evidence surfaced that there was a "$3 million dollar gap in the agreed-upon-lease compared with the previous one."[210] Moreover, the new lease included language that specified that any outstanding disputes (likely referring to the unpaid revenues owed to the city by Ilitch) between the city and Red Wings had been resolved. While the agreement included a deal by Olympia to pay $5.175 million to Detroit, which some have speculated refers to past debt related to cable revenues never paid, the amount is significantly less than what was originally owed. The new lease also agreement included a "non-compete clause," which means that "the city can't use the Joe Louis Arena for anything once … [Ilitch] vacates it," virtually sealing its fate for demolition once the Red Wings relocate to their new home in 2016.[211] John Lauve, a resident of Detroit who attended the council meetings regarding the lease, stated "[it] is just inconceivable, and it should not be signed." Another attendee, Victoria Glenn, argued that "this is an ongoing effort to destroy the heritage of Detroit."[212]

One. Welcome to the Consumer Arena

While many will argue that the development plans will provide a needed economic stimulus for a decaying and deteriorating urban center, it is also the case that the ambitious redevelopment plan has enticed speculators to buy their share of property on the hope that the gamble will pay off. Cleveland Cavaliers owner Dan Gilbert, who was born in Detroit, "has gone on a downtown building buying spree, rehabbing dormant buildings and moving his Quicken Loans employees and other companies into them."[213] Because the proposed site is blighted with abandoned buildings and other visible signs of poverty, land is being sold cheaply, but once the Red Wings arena and other proposed developments are completed that will raise property values significantly. Of course, all of this will depend on the cleansing of Detroit of its poorer citizens in the area in order to entice an affluent, upwardly mobile consumer class whose high-spending ways and discretionary capital will be required for this new consumer playground to fully realize its value. The branding of the new Detroit as a space of fashionable consumption for the social-climbing faithful has already begun. In 2015, the Michigan Civil Service Commission advertised a networking and job fair in the city with flyers and laminated brochures emblazoned with the message:

> Detroit is the home of the nation's best high tech startups, cutting edge medical researchers, fashion trendsetters, unrivaled restaurants, world-renowned museums and affordable places to lives. Ever wonder where all the up and comers are going? We can show you! Join us to get the inside scoop on what's going on in Detroit from people who live, work, and play in the city. Dinner is included![214]

In the new model of democracy being fashioned by neoliberalism, one's right to citizenship is determined by one's capacity and willingness to consume. For those on the lower rungs of the economic ladder, government no longer feels any degree of accountability or responsibility as the increasing hegemony of market-based thinking casts them off as disposable and irrelevant. As we have seen, the funding of new sports stadiums and the environment they provide to cater to upper-income fans is a microcosm of these transformations occurring with the political culture at large. Consumer culture has gone political and is increasingly regarded as the very essence of democracy itself. However, this conceptualization is highly misguided—in a pure democracy all citizens should be treated equal. Yet in the consumer democracy that now prevails, some people are more equal than others.

Two

The Sports Gaming Culture

The United States is a culture dominated by entertainment, as evidenced by a media marketplace that has become saturated with options that entice us to "tune out"—from cable and satellite television packages offering hundreds of channels to on-demand music and video streaming, video games, and social media. Unsurprisingly, sports programming can be found 24 hours a day, 7 days a week, courtesy of such entities as ESPN, Fox Sports 1, CBS Sports Network, and a barrage of regional sports networks, not to mention all the sports talk radio personalities dominating the radio dial. In this mediasphere, sports "experts" can be found everywhere, offering exhaustive and sometimes-trivial commentary on player performances, locker-room gossip, managerial decisions, statistical analysis, and a redundant fascination with player salaries. It is for all of these reasons, as some analysts claim, that sports are in serious trouble. In a frenzied and cluttered entertainment market where this is simply too much to choose from, the long-assured hegemony of professional sports seems to grow increasingly precarious and uncertain. Audiences have simply become too fragmented along a constantly expanding media and entertainment chain that shows no sign of alleviating or stopping. As Irving Rein, Philip Kotler, and Ben Shields note, "in a marketplace so crowded, the search for fans has become essential to the very survival of sports."[1] Yet this search is yielding diminishing returns, as many of today's youth find sports too time-consuming an ordeal of delayed gratification compared to the allure of the Internet, which caters and contributes to their ever-shrinking attention spans.

In the United States, the NFL has witnessed a 10.6 percent decline

Two. The Sports Gaming Culture

in viewership among audiences between 18 and 49 between 2010 and 2014 on its football networks, including CBS, Fox, NBC, ESPN, and, of course, the NFL Network.[2] According to sports and entertainment marketing expert Kirk Wakefield, "this segment is not passionate about the NFL like older age groups," and he adds that "the social status of NFL teams and players may be deteriorating compared to other pastimes and interests that are more personally engaging."[3] Meanwhile, according to a recent ESPN Sports Poll, the number of 12- to 17-year-olds who identify as "avid fans" has decreased from 40 percent to 30 percent between 1995 and 2013 for the NBA while for MLB it has declined from 25 percent to 18 percent over the same time period. For men's college football and basketball, popularity in terms of their avid fan bases has remained relatively steady, while the only sport to show any significant growth is Major League Soccer which is now as popular as major league baseball among the demographic measured.[4] However, television viewership for MLS games is noticeably low, averaging a paltry 220,000 for games televised on ESPN's networks. This prompted Rich Luker, who developed the methodology and conducted the research for the ESPN poll, to admit that "avid MLS fans between the ages of 12 and 17 are not watching much MLS on TV."[5] Michael Printup, president of the Watkins Glen International, one of the largest racing tracks in the United States, suggests that these issues stem from the monopoly digital devices have on youth culture, stating:

> We don't see the youth coming in. The millennial, the younger adults 18 to 35, is our target. We spend millions of dollars a year to target that group. But it's hard.... Every sport from the NFL to the NHL is struggling ... [attracting] the 18 to 35 demographic. They call them weird. They call them difficult. They only want to look at their computers.[6]

Perhaps worse still is that many younger fans prefer playing the video game versions of professional baseball, football, basketball, hockey, and soccer to watching games on television. One adolescent gamer stated that "when you watch [sports] on TV it's just boring. I like the [video] games better because you ... can make the [basketball] player pass or shoot it. But when you see it on TV, you're just watching."[7] While still serving as NBA commissioner, David Stern expressed concern that sports video games were becoming a substitute for watching games on television and, thus, could jeopardize its media revenue in the future. At the same time, Stern iterated that "the competition for eyeballs is so intense now that if our consumers are not consuming us on television, we would rather have them consuming us on a video game than doing something else."[8] Not only are sports video games becoming graphically sophisticated and, thus, more "real"; they also deliver a degree of interactivity that youth culture demands in its engagement with popular culture. Passively watching sports on television is commonly regarded as *boring* and not in keeping with a new cultural ethos that emphasizes engagement and involvement beyond "just watching."

One fan activity that bridges the gap between passive spectatorship and interactivity is fantasy sports, involving more than 41 million participants in the United States and Canada alone.[9] This is more than triple the amount of fantasy sports players a decade ago in 2004, when 13.5 million participated. Most fantasy sports enthusiasts are male (80 percent), are Caucasian (89.8 percent), and have a bachelor's degree or greater (78.1 percent), and about half (46.8 percent) pay to play in leagues that require membership fees for possible cash payouts. The Fantasy Sports Trade Association, meanwhile, represents the interests of fantasy sports companies who sense great financial profitability in an industry estimated to be worth several billion dollars.[10] Not only have fantasy sports attracted the attention of optimistic and ambitious entrepreneurs who see them as part of a lucrative growth industry to hawk their brands; fantasy sports also have significantly transformed how fans follow, discuss, and ultimately consume sports.

While there is a great deal of strategy involved in managing a fantasy sports team, the rules and objectives are relatively comprehensible and straightforward. Individuals form leagues, engage in a draft where they take turns selecting players, and compete head-to-head earning points based on the real-life statistical performances of their selected athletes in order to outscore their opponents. In most cases, owners can trade their players with one another, set a reserve roster where players can be placed when they are not in the starting lineup, release players who are injured or are performing poorly, and pick up "unowned" players who the owners speculate will produce points for their team. For some fantasy sports stimulate interest in a sport they may otherwise pay little attention to, while for others they create an opportunity for "serious" fans to demonstrate their superior sports knowledge.[11] In between, people play to foster camaraderie and connection between

Two. The Sports Gaming Culture

themselves and their friends and/or co-workers,[12] while many see fantasy sports as a form of legalized sports gambling in the case of leagues such as Draft Kings, which offer cash payouts.

There are many conflicting accounts regarding exactly how and where fantasy sports began and who should ultimately be credited with inventing them. Some argue that the origins can be located in Strat-O-Matic, a simulated baseball game that included a set of cards featuring actual major league baseball players and a pair of dice whose value after being rolled was determined by the possible outcomes listed on individual player cards.[13] Others cite the development of Rotisserie Baseball by journalist Dan Okrent and his colleagues, who created a game very similar to modern fantasy sports where participants would pick players and compete based on the real-world performances of the players they chose.[14] Since this occurred before the advent of the Internet, playing was hard work and labor intensive, requiring participants to scour box scores and calculate their fantasy points by hand. Because of this, fantasy sports had limited appeal. Both Strat-O-Matic and Rotisserie Baseball were regarded, at worst, as relatively antisocial activities for "geeks" seeking their statistical fix in a largely isolating and time-consuming activity that few understood.

As the years passed, the Internet would change the status of fantasy sports due to the many conveniences it offered: access to real-time stats that, often, were calculated automatically for one's selected players, the ability to compete with other participants on a global scale, and the ease of online communication, by which one could coordinate drafts much more simply.[15] As a consequence, fantasy sports leagues online exploded in popularity, many of them free of charge, through league Web sites and affiliated companies such as ESPN. Today, fantasy sports have become an annual ritual for the "serious" fan. For professional sports leagues and their respective television networks, fantasy sports mean big audiences and, consequently, big money. Research has demonstrated that people who play fantasy sports watch more sports on television, including games they would have no other vested reason to watch.[16] According to the Fantasy Sports Trade Association, the average fantasy sports participant spends almost 18 hours "consuming sports per week."[17]

Because of this, professional sports leagues and their teams understand that fantasy sports are necessary for being able to negotiate higher television rights deals with national and regional sporting networks. These, meanwhile, are willing to pay the higher asking price because larger audiences means that these networks can increase the amount they can charge for advertising. At the same time, the decreasing popularity of many professional sports among younger audiences poses a threat to media revenues. Thus, fantasy sports are viewed as the mechanism to "save" sports by making sports spectatorship interactive in a way these audience demographics demand. Of course, for fantasy sports to accomplish the purpose they are designed to fulfill participants have to think of managing a team as a full-time commitment. Almost three-quarters of fantasy sports players visit four to six fantasy sports Web sites to obtain "insider" fantasy information while mobile applications are being developed daily to provide convenient access to cheat sheets, real-time fantasy news and stats, check scores, "talk smack" (which, if effective, motivates more effectively the desire to win), and make trades and other transactions.[18] Ironically, one can keep up-to-date regarding how his team is doing without actually watching any games on television. It is also becoming more common for fans to watch sports only to see how their players are doing, courtesy of "season-ticket" television and streaming packages that gives fans access to all of the televised games occurring across a given league.

*****

Of course, one way to encourage participants to take fantasy sports more seriously and create a more voracious market for stats, expert analysis, and real-time updates that networks and leagues are providing is to up the ante by allowing players to compete for money. Fantasy sports leagues that offer cash payouts are not new, but the confusion over whether these Web sites were legal halted their growth. This changed in 2006 when the federal government passed the Unlawful Internet Gambling Enforcement Act, which prohibited, among other things, gambling on "games of chance" online. However, they carved out a special exception for fantasy sports, which was regarded as a "game of skill." Thus success was not determined by chance but rather the relative sports knowledge of participants. The law stated that one could legally place wagers on fantasy sports provided that: (1) the outcome is not determined by any one real-life sporting event or individual athletic performance and (2) the outcome is based on player knowledge of the "accumulated statistical results of sporting events, including any non-participant's [i.e., the athletes'] individual performances in such sports events."[19] As a consequence of this loophole, speculators invested millions in pay-to-play-to-win fantasy Web sites such as FanDuel, which began in 2009, and DraftKings, which started in 2012.[20] Today, DraftKings advertises that it has over one million active users and is reportedly worth $900 million in an industry that, it is predicted, "will continue to flourish, racking up hundreds of millions of dollars in revenue."[21]

Professional sports leagues have been so impressed by the ability of these sites to generate interest, increase audience shares, and make money that many of them are lining up to buy in. In 2015, Major League Baseball announced that it was extending its "under-the-radar partnership" with DraftKings, which would give the league an ownership stake in the popular fantasy sports web site.[22] This deal was touted as "smart" by industry insiders because it would provide the MLB with "new revenue … and more importantly, boost engagement with fans, particularly those in the coveted 18-to-35 male demographic."[23] This followed a partnership between DraftKings and the NHL, FanDuel and the NBA, and interestingly team-specific deals between FanDuel and the Dallas Mavericks, Washington Redskins, Orlando Magic, Brooklyn Nets, New York Knicks, and Chicago Bulls, among others.[24] Perhaps more chilling is that Fan Duel even has a partnership deal with sportswriter Jay Glazer, who writes for Fox Sports.com and is an insider for *NFL on Fox*. No longer taboo, advertisements for play-for-pay sites such as FanDuel and DraftKings are prominent in local and national sports broadcasts.

In actuality, the line between fantasy sports as a "game of skill" and a "game of chance" is a very thin and murky one indeed. This is especially the case given that both FanDuel and DraftKings offer one-day "no commitment" fantasy leagues. While yearlong fantasy leagues mitigate the influence of chance given the large sample of outcomes involved, "one-day" fantasy leagues are more beholden to chance. Regardless of one's skill and knowledge, there is no foolproof means to determine whether a star player will have an off day, succumb to injury, or perhaps be left out of the starting lineup. Then there is the possibility in baseball that a game could be rained out or postponed.

American Sports in an Age of Consumption

As of this writing, there are several pending lawsuits against FanDuel and DraftKings that could either challenge or reinforce the legality of "one-day" fantasy leagues, which did not exist at the time the Unlawful Internet Gambling Enforcement Act was passed in 2006.[25] While these cases confront a multitude of legal issues, of relevance here is the issue of whether outcomes are largely determined by chance or skill. Because of the significant levels of unpredictability due to the influence of good/bad luck, one-day fantasy leagues are more subject to a "single act of randomness."[26] Lawyers representing these Web sites will obviously boast that there are many participants with a history of success in one-day fantasy leagues that could not be explained by chance alone. As a matter of fact, these Web sites pay their more "successful" players for their use in marketing materials to promote a rags-to-riches narrative of "regular Joes" garnering huge winnings by playing fantasy sports. Chris Prince is one such player whose winnings of over $650,000 are posted on FanDuel's Web site with the quote "playing in one day and getting paid the same day is awesome."[27]

Other fantasy sport gurus have quit their jobs in order to pursue their hobby full-time, such as Peter Jennings, who left Charles Schwab in 2011 and, afterward, went on to win the $1 million DraftKings tournament later that year.[28] As Jennings states, "it's much like trading on the stock market, except you are buying individual players ... you're always crunching numbers and it's very hard to be a good player."[29] The issues not only involve the ethical quandaries regarding major professional leagues aligning with fantasy sport sites that offer a service akin to gambling, but the trivialization of sport itself for personal gain. As Jennings' quotes suggests, athletes are simply "stock" to which he has no personal attachment or commitment, a disposable commodity bought and sold in the fantasy sports marketplace. If this is the mechanism through which major professional leagues hope to engage the coveted 18-to-35 demographic, the relationship between fans and sports will be less significantly altered. This new model of "fandom" being proposed likely means that fan will be less concerned with team win/loss records, pennant chases, and championships and more concerned with the isolated productiveness and performance of individual athletes. Sporting contests will be increasingly scrutinized with the cold rationality of statistical analysis and trends, rather than the beauty of a well-timed pass, pinch-hitting heroics, or an unbelievable diving catch to save or win the game. It is no stretch of the imagination to see that this is fandom without feeling and commitment. Supporters of sites such as FanDuel and Draft Kings may contend that these criticisms could be extended to fantasy sports in general. However, in more casual fantasy leagues where the stakes merely involve bragging rights, participants often make more playful choices, such as selecting players from their favorite teams or a sleeper perhaps woefully undervalued or maybe following a gut intuition that a selected athlete will have a breakout year. On sites where money is on the line, such charming sentimentalities have no place—fantasy sports have become more serious. As stock market mogul Gordon Gecko reminds his protégé Bud Fox in the movie *Wall Street,* "Don't get emotional about stock, kid!"

An equally curious effect of fantasy sports is the way they encourage sports fans to more identify with the general managers and the owners of teams themselves rather than the athletes who long garnered their admiration. Dave Zirin writes that "fans used to dream of being John Riggins, the Washington Redskins Hall of Fame running back. Now they want to be Dan Snyder, who owns the Redskins."[30] Meanwhile Thomas Oates argues similarly that fantasy football provides participants an opportunity to engage in "vicarious management," which "invites audiences to identify with the institutional regimes of the NFL (and the authorities who conduct them) rather than with the athletes."[31] In today's culture, athletes are no longer regarded as "heroes" in the same ways they used to be. Rather, it is savvy entrepreneurs like Steve Jobs who are more often elevated to the status of secular deities. In the cultural imagination, Jobs was an unapologetic risk taker, selflessly leading the masses toward a technological utopia of consumer convenience, free choice, and personal expression and liberation. His Apple products have become our technological organs and cultural life support system in an age that too often places blind admiration in these gadgets to alleviate our problems and most pressing anxieties. Likewise, Theo Epstein (general manager of the Chicago Cubs) and Mark Cuban (owner of the Dallas Mavericks) have become sporting icons themselves, praised for the managerial genius in reviving faltering franchises and leading them toward a championship renaissance. In today's discourse, it is not really the athletes who win Super Bowls or World Series; it is the movers and shakers in the front office who put a winning team on the field, court, or ice. The fact that Epstein is young in a culture that worships youthfulness and Cuban a memorable personality in a society that values attitude adds credibility to their status as entrepreneurial "heroes."

For this reason, many participants see fantasy sports—whether money is on the line or not—as an opportunity not only to see if they are cut from the same managerial cloth as the Epsteins and Cubans of the world but also to test their "entrepreneurial selves." The entrepreneurial self has now become dominant as neoliberal, free-market governmentality has become the model by which institutions should operate and the way citizens should think about themselves.[32] With the decline of the "welfare state" in which governments and elected politicians are supposed to make decisions on behalf of the public's welfare, neoliberalism aims to restore moral responsibility by casting individuals to think of themselves as more or less on their own.[33] Public institutions are commonly regarded today in political and social discourse as enabling the "laziness" of the poor and offering a place for "overpaid" and "unaccountable" people to live high on the taxpayer's dime with often-disappointing results. The undercutting of public institutions and services is believed to eliminate these safety nets, provide discipline, and embolden people to "pull themselves up by their bootstraps."

Meanwhile, the entrepreneurial self generates a new mode of citizenship whereby individuals are expected to think of themselves as their own businesspeople and brands, led by self-interest in order to further themselves materially and economically in society.[34] Morals and ethics are deemed irrelevant because these involve collective considerations, despite the insistence that this new model will yield a more morally just society. Furthermore, individuals are taught that the public has no responsibility to them nor should they rely on institutions to provide them the support they need to succeed. Rather, individuals have to make various investments on their own to ensure their livelihood without assistance from others. For example, education under conditions of neoliberalism is increasingly regarded as an individual, not a public, good. The decline of state investments in higher education is propagated by the argument that because students alone will financially benefit from a college education, they alone should pay for it. This is far removed from the belief long held to be true in society that education was a public investment that benefited the culture as a whole.[35] Instead, citizens are taught to think of themselves as "free agents" who are responsible for their own personal bubble and only afterwards the welfare of the communities they live in. As former prime minister of the United Kingdom Margaret Thatcher, who zealously pursued these kinds of neoliberal reforms during her tenure, stated:

> There's no such thing as society. There are individual men and women and their families. And no government can do anything except through its people, and people must look after themselves first. It is our duty to look after ourselves first and, then, also to look after our neighbors.[36]

According to political economist David Harvey, this "always look out for number one" ideology is regarded as common sense in a culture that commonly dispenses with the notion of public commitments once regarded as an indispensable aspect of citizenship.[37] The persuasiveness of this idea stems from American's increasing economic uncertainty, creating anger and cynicism then directed by civic leaders toward public institutions—and consequently the "parasitic public"—in order to justify their dismantling. Human relationships, meanwhile, are recast from camaraderie and cooperation to competition and self-interest where other people are regarded as an obstacle to one's material and economic advancement. In many cases, as evidenced by popular discourse on the subject, other people are an enemy, cannot be trusted, and are as equally self-absorbed.

Within the context of fantasy sports, sports fandom itself becomes a competition to not only demonstrate one's knowledge of sports but, more broadly, seek a kind of self-esteem and worth we are told can only emerge from competition. As citizens are increasingly taught to view themselves as economic subjects (i.e., their own personal business entity or brand), fantasy sports offer participants a simulation in which to test their entrepreneurial selves. By assuming the role of an owner, fans are provided an opportunity to indulge the fantasy of being a part of the managerial culture of professional sports where entrepreneurial logic is dominant. In doing so, fantasy sports encourage participants to identify with the ownership and management class of professional sports while further alienating them form the athletes themselves.[38] By virtue of the Internet, many fans have access to "insider" information such as up-to-date statistics, scouting reports, and draft analyses that decades earlier would have been only available to the management class of sports and, to a lesser extent, sports journalists. This deepens

American Sports in an Age of Consumption

the level of identification fans have with the institutional powers of sports while diminishing the status of the athlete to their bare-bones productivity, ultimately disposable if they are "not doing their job." While sports fans have always held a degree of contempt for under-performing players, never before have fans felt more certain about the decisions management should take in replacing them. With the abundance of insider information and sports content available to be consumed, "real" fans talk about sports like an "expert" and, in many cases, from the rationalized perspective of management itself. This ultimately represents a new way of relating to one's favorite sports and teams, less based on sentimental loyalty and commitment and more that of a critical observer speaking like a general manager.

Because of this transformation, some critics contend that sports are a problem because they redirect intellectual activity from more important social, cultural, and political activity and engagement. While fans commonly critique and analyze management decisions and athletic performances with great degrees of vigor, insight, and creativity, few make similar efforts when it comes to politics, international affairs, or community problems. Many cultural studies theorists argue that sports are an "opiate of the masses" distracting the "mindless public" away from the systematic failures of capitalism and democracy.[39] A representative view comes from political commentator Noam Chomsky:

> I sometimes turn on the radio and I find very often that what I'm listening to is a a a discussion of sports. These are telephone conversations. People call in and have long and intricate discussions, and it's plain that quite a high degree of thought and analysis is going into that. People know a tremendous amount.... These are ordinary people, not professionals, who are applying their intelligence and analytic skills in these areas and accumulating quite a lot of knowledge and, for all I know, understanding. On the other hand, when I hear people talk about, say, international affairs or domestic problems, it's a level of superficiality that's beyond belief.[40]

On the one hand, while it may be easy to dismiss Chomsky's comments as a typical and elitist commentary from an intellectual class that often detests sports and other forms of mass culture, they do have a degree of merit. On the other hand, these observations miss the all-too-obvious fact that contemporary American culture is bombarded with other "unworthy" distractions: the obsession of youth with social media, on-demand television that encourages "binge watching," and

Two. The Sports Gaming Culture

the often-infantile fascination with celebrity culture and its tabloidesque gossip industry. One could argue that sports are hardly the worst of these distractions. More important here, the new model of fandom provided by fantasy sports and its attendant insider knowledge economy risks separating fans from athletes in almost adversarial terms. The fact that one's level of fandom is based on such managerial-based knowledge yields and reflects an alienation of fans from sports.

*****

To be sure, the relationship between fans and athletes is, and has often been, a contentious one. On the one hand, fans admire the physical feats and sporting accomplishments of professional athletes yet commonly complain about their escalating salaries, lack of loyalty and commitment, and sometimes brash and arrogant behavior. Many fans reminisce about a "golden age of sports" when players played for the love of the game, respected ownership, and displayed a degree of honor toward the fans who paid to see them play. Today, sports coverage is often beset with stories of athletes mired in scandal, reinforcing the cynicism fans feel toward sports while intensifying the mythological "purity" by which the past is often imagined. In his controversial book *Ball Four*, former major league pitcher Jim Bouton claimed that the athletes of yesteryear were hardly innocent: many baseball players drank excessively, took performance-enhancing amphetamines (or "greenies"), cheated on their wives, despised ownership, and were overly concerned with money. The only difference between then and today was that sports journalists were less likely to report these unsavory details, believing it was necessary to promote the myth that players adhered to the "importance of clean living."[41] As a consequence of Bouton's book shattering the all-American purity associated with major league baseball, he was blacklisted by his former team, the New York Yankees, vilified by the commissioner, and scorned by many players. However, scandal reporting today in sports has become normalized, in part due to the need to provide content in a 24/7 sports media machine often struggling for something interesting to talk about, especially during a sport's off-season. Equally influential is that scandal sells, prompting sports fans to tune into national sports television and radio shows to consume the spectacle of athletes, coaches, and management having done wrong. Each iteration of this charade merely confirms an already-held opinion among fans; athletes, while physically exceptional, are often "bad" people corrupted by high salaries, ego, and free agency. Certainly, as the narrative goes, players are not who or what they used to be.

In respect to free agency, which provides players the opportunity to negotiate with other teams once their current contract expires, fans commonly view it as a system that is ruining sports. A common critique is that because of free agency, players are no longer loyal to their teams and are only motivated by the money that the highest bidder will pay them. The narrative commonly goes that players placed their allegiance to their team above money before free agency corrupted this relationship. Of course, this argument overlooks the role of the reserve clause in professional sports that essentially tied players to the teams that drafted them. At the time, players routinely signed one-year contracts with their teams and could only negotiate a subsequent contract with the team that "owned" them, thus limiting player salaries by barring their ability to negotiate a deal elsewhere. The only way players could technically become free agents under the reserve system was by being released by their teams.

In the early years of professional baseball "free agency" actually did exist. Owners developed the reserve clause in 1879 over concerns that players were making too much money and, thus, could threaten the financial health and integrity of professional baseball in its untested infancy.[42] The players, on the other hand, believed the rule not to be in the best interest of the game but a rather calculated and lopsided arrangement to increase ownership profits through a mechanism that treated players as their exclusive property. Led by John Montgomery Ward, who was the president of the Brotherhood of Professional Baseball Players—the first players' union in any sport in the United States—several players in 1890 formed the Players' League, which operated without the reserve clause. While the league folded after the season, it represented "the final significant challenge to professional sports as we know them."[43] Meanwhile, the reserve clause (with minor variations) was adopted in the NFL, the NBA, and the NHL and is still operating in Major League Soccer today.

Several challenges to the merits of the reserve clause would occur later, led most famously by major league baseball outfielder Curt Flood, who wrote a letter to Commissioner Bowie Kuhn asking for his free agency after refusing to accept his trade from the St. Louis Cardinals to the Philadelphia Phillies in 1969.[44] Not only did he express his reservations about playing in a city known for its notoriously racist culture; he also argued that the reserve clause treated players like property and was akin to modern-day slavery. After Kuhn refused to grant him the free agency he asked for, Flood retired and later filed an antitrust suit against the commissioner challenging the legality of the reserve clause. While Flood would eventually return to baseball, having signed with the Washington Senators in 1971, his case in the lower courts did not prevail, ultimately leading to an appeal within the Supreme Court. There the court upheld baseball's antitrust exemption by a 5-to-3 margin, yet Justice Harry Blackmun, who authored the opinion of the court, stated that baseball's exemption was "an exception and an anomaly" and an "established aberration."[45]

The ambiguity between the decision and the Court's opinion created enough of an opening that welcomed further challenges to baseball's antitrust exemption and its heralded reserve clause. In 1972, Major League Baseball witnessed its first-ever player strike, which lasted 13 days and ended with the Players' Association successfully bargaining for the right to salary arbitration. After the season was over, negotiations continued between the union and the league, resulting in owners agreeing to the principle of free agency as long as players met certain criteria. First, a player could only become a free agent once he had earned five years of major league experience and only if his existing team offered him a contract under $30,000. Meanwhile, players with eight years of experience could only declare free agency if their team made an offer under $40,000. The Players' Association rejected these conditions yet reached an agreement with Major League Baseball to postpone the issue of free agency for later bargaining sessions.[46] While some may suggest that this was greedy and uncompromising on the part of the players, their objections were not without merit. Players could only earn free agency if they were essentially unwanted by their teams, while owners would still be able to retain their superstars without having to pay them the kind of money they would otherwise command on the open market. In essence, the proposed plan for free agency would still accomplish what the reserve clause was originally designed to do by limiting salaries of the best players.

In 1974, Catfish Hunter signed a two-year deal with the Oakland

American Sports in an Age of Consumption

Athletics that included a stipulation that half of his salary would be deposited into an insurance company fund. Team owner Charles Finley did not make the promised payments and Hunter filed a grievance against the Athletics claiming the team had violated the terms of their agreement. The case went before an arbitration panel that decided in Hunter's favor, releasing him from his contract and allowing him to become major league baseball's first legitimate "free agent" since the reserve clause was implemented. After Hunter signed with the New York Yankees to a multiyear deal, further attempts to challenge the reserve clause occurred in the National League. In 1975, pitchers Dave McNally of the Montreal Expos and Andy Messersmith of the Los Angeles Dodgers refused to sign the contracts offered by their respective teams, claiming that they were being underpaid. However, both teams picked up an option year on each player, which allowed them to renew the contracts for another year without McNally's and Messersmith's signatures. After the season, both players claimed they were no longer contractually bound to their teams because they had already exercised their options on both players. Their argument was based on a loophole within the option rules that provided an unprecedented challenge to the reserve system. Their case was heard before an arbitration panel that not only ruled in McNally's and Messersmith's favor but added further that *any* player could become a free agent after the conclusion of his contract, regardless of how much major league service he had attained.[47]

As one could imagine, Major League Baseball owners were furious and subsequently fired Peter Seitz—who headed the arbitration panel for Dave McNally and Andy Messersmith as well as in the case of Catfish Hunter—and filed an appeal within federal courts, who later rejected it. Owners then padlocked the doors of their facilities to begin Spring Training in 1976 and forced a lockout on the players. Commissioner Bowie Kuhn ended the standoff before the end of the preseason and, at the conclusion of the season, owners finally agreed to the players' right to free agency only if they had six years of major league service.

This was not the first example of free agency in professional sports, as it existed in the early beginnings of professional baseball. Moreover, the NFL instituted it in 1947, although it was not until 1962 that a free agent actually changed teams when R.C. Owens moved from the San Francisco 49ers to the Baltimore Colts.[48] In 1963, the "Rozelle Rule"—named after NFL commissioner Pete Rozell—was put into place that compensated teams who lost a free agent financially or with draft picks taken from other teams. In the 1976 court case *Mackey v. NFL*, the Rozelle Rule was removed and replaced by a free agency/reserve clause component that allowed owners to protect 37 of their players "with the right of first refusal."[49] This was a forerunner to the "franchise tag" and "restricted free agency" currently in place in the NFL, although former NFL Pro Bowler Frank Minnifeld's successful lawsuit against the league in 1992 led to unrestricted free agency.[50] Meanwhile, in professional basketball, the existence of two rival leagues, the National Basketball League (NBL) and the Basketball Association of America (BAA) provided players with leverage similar to free agency by the ability to jump to the other league if unsatisfied with their contract. After the 1948–1949 season, the two leagues merged into the National Basketball Association (NBA), allowing a reserve system to be more effective.[51] However, the formation of the American Basketball Association (ABA) in 1967 reintroduced the upward pressure on salaries created by rival leagues that the merger of the NBL and the BAA was supposed to guard against.

With NBA superstars Rick Barry, Billy Cunningham, and Zelmo Beaty moving to the ABA as well as the league's success at signing top college prospects such as Mel Daniels and Spencer Haywood, the NBA began discussions with the ABA regarding a possible merger.[52] In response, players filed an antitrust lawsuit to block any proposed merger and to eliminate the reserve clause, even suing for past damages created by it. One outcome of the suit was that players gained the right to restricted free agency, while the ABA would eventually merge with the NBA in 1976.[53] While NBA players would later be allowed to become unrestricted free agents as part of their 1988 collective bargaining agreement with owners, the salary caps created by an earlier agreement would serve to limit salaries and player movement between teams.[54] These were deemed necessary due to franchises such as Cleveland, Denver, Indiana, Kansas City, San Diego, and Utah suffering significant financial losses during a time in which the NBA's popularity was embarrassingly dismal.[55] While this makes sense, the issue has remained a contentious one between owners and players, as evidenced by the 2011 lockout as owners bargained for, among other things, a "hard cap" to replace the "soft cap" that had a multitude of exceptions and loopholes.[56]

While a complete treatment of labor history in professional sports is beyond the scope of this chapter, it is beyond dispute that free agency is regarded as an abomination by many sports fans who believe it is responsible for the outrageous ticket prices that price many of them out. To a degree, this is both somewhat true and understandable, as team owners often pass the cost of lucrative free-agent contracts to the fans themselves. At the same time, such sentiments risk simplifying the complex reality of free agency. A reasonable counterargument is that the often-mind-blowing amounts being paid to today's professional athletes in the four major sports is proof of these sports' profitability and the massive amounts of revenue being generated through their labor. For example, Time Warner Cable negotiated an $8.35 billion, 25-year television deal with the Los Angeles Dodgers for the right to broadcast the team's games.[57] In 2013, the NFL and its 32 franchises generated approximately $1.07 billion in sponsorship revenue alone, not to mention the four-year $4 billion deal with DirectTV that allows fans to watch every out-of-market game being broadcast.[58] These are only a few examples of significant revenue streams beyond high ticket prices and outrageously priced concession items, which are more noticeable only because they are experienced more directly and immediately by fans themselves. One could argue that with such significant amounts of money flowing through the ownership coffers, players are entitled to the contracts they demand. After all, they are whom fans pay to see in person or watch on television, which cannot be said for the owners themselves.

However, such arguments are not all that rhetorically effective at a time in which workers who provide more socially necessary labor, such as teachers, firefighters, and law-enforcement officers, are struggling financially. For the average sports fans troubled by the widening economic chasm between themselves and the players they root for (and, historically, identified with), a reasonable amount of cynicism and anger is justified. Thus, fantasy sports do provide some degree of compensation by restoring a feeling of control to many fans jaded by the perception that athletes no longer feel accountable or obligated to them. With the ravaging of the working and middle classes due to the effects of postindustrialism and globalization, the infusion of capitalist

Two. The Sports Gaming Culture

logic in deeper facets of everyday life, and the further corporatization of democracy, professional athletes become a convenient scapegoat upon which to project fan anger caused by their own financial precariousness. Thus, the athlete's transformation into a commodity through fantasy ownership and control is merely another realm where fans can reclaim a privileged status and where athletes perform and labor on their behalf. In other words, if athletes are believed to trivialize the role fans plays in paying their salaries by not demonstrating loyalty and thankfulness fans can return the favor by reducing athletes to a mere commodity traded and released at will.

*****

As mentioned earlier in the chapter, fantasy sports are seen as an effective strategy by professional sports league to grow their popularity among younger fan demographics. This is especially the case on fantasy sports sites where fans can wager money to test their sports knowledge against that of other players. Such monetary incentives, as league officials and owners realize, compel participants to take fantasy sports more seriously, thus compelling fans to watch more games, download more apps to their phone, and consume insider information more regularly and vigorously. Thus, fantasy sports sites where participants can play for money create a more rabid market for products that already exist, such as mobile phone applications, league and fantasy Web sites, and season-ticket television and streaming packages that allow fans to watch out-of-market games. A consequence of all of this is that fantasy sports create a different kind of fan, less swayed by loyalty to a particular team and more concerned with monitoring their fantasy team's progress. Evidence of this can be found in the way that sports media coverage has been transformed to cater more to fantasy sports themselves.

For example, MLB TV is a video streaming service available on MLB.com that allows subscribers the opportunity to watch every out-of-market baseball game being televised on a given day, even archiving games –similar to other on-demand television programming—for fans to watch later at their convenience. For fantasy sports participants who subscribe to the service, they can set a "lineup" of players they want to follow on a given day, receiving an alert when a selected hitter is up to bat or a selected pitcher is on the mound. By clicking on the alert tag, viewers are taken to that particular game's televised broadcast, where they can watch a selected player before receiving an alert that directs them to another broadcast. In this way, fantasy sports participants can dispense with the "filler" by focusing their viewing habits only on the players of one's team. Lost is the compelling narrative of a close game, a pennant chase, or a milestone achievement, replaced by the more efficient and fragmented experience provided by mindlessly jumping from one game to another. Similar to neoliberalism, in which hyper-individualism and self-interest are regarded as beneficial, this viewing experience dispenses with more collective considerations such as team performance in favor of one's fantasy performance centered on the isolated performances of one's selected players without the narrative drama that makes team sports compelling. One study found that almost half of fantasy football participants (41 percent) preferred their fantasy team to win over their favorite real-world team and speculated that this "could have major implications on ticket sales, team merchandise sales, and sponsorship sales."[59] As fantasy "gambling" sites such as FanDuel and DraftKings become regarded as a more acceptable and engaging way of participating in fantasy sports, the "fantasy sports lens" will become more dominant in how fans watch and talk about sports.

Some argue there are graver ethical principles at stake when major professional sports leagues align themselves with sites such as FanDuel and DraftKings. Historically, the leagues have made significant efforts to distance themselves from gambling culture in order to alleviate possible suspicion from fans that games could be fixed. Yet there is ample evidence that allowing fans to gamble on sports increases the likelihood that they will watch and take interest in sports. According to the American Gaming Association (AGA), an estimated $2 billion was wagered on the 2012 NCAA Men's Basketball tournament, including $240 million in Las Vegas casinos alone, where sports betting is legal.[60] According to AGA president and CEO Geoff Freeman:

> Sports betting has played a major role in making March Madness the big-time event it is today. With more people filling out brackets than casting a ballot for President Obama—who makes his NCAA predictions in the Oval Office each year—it's clear that Americans embrace gaming.[61]

Moral and ethical considerations of sports gambling, not to mention the addictive and financially disastrous effects for many related to gambling in general, are regarded as irrelevant within a political culture

Two. The Sports Gaming Culture

that regards an individual's right to profit as a significant quintessential embodiment of democracy and freedom in general. Under conditions of neoliberalism, citizenship is reduced to consumerism and individuals are increasingly encouraged to think only of themselves and getting ahead. Furthermore, social awareness and selfless community-mindedness are devalued. The self-serving nature of contemporary citizenship creates an inner void that serves corporate capitalism generally. It supplies a ready supply of "ambitious" people who will sacrifice personal relationships in the pursuit of upward mobility and, likewise, create a culture convinced, yet endlessly betrayed, that money and material objects constitute happiness. It creates both the ideal worker and consumer and the model subject for corporate capitalism to continuously thrive and profit. The acceptance of the gambling culture that many fantasy sport sites are a part of is a visible example of the degree to which pursuing self-interest by any means necessary has become common sense. Individuals, even in their capacity as fans, are called upon to think of themselves as capitalists where making bets in the pursuit of profit is how the economic game is played. Greed was once the exclusive province of the rich, but now it flows generously throughout the entire social body.

As the "reformed" Gordon Gekko, having served a lengthy prison sentence for insider trading, lectures students in the movie *Wall Street: Money Never Sleeps*:

> Someone reminded me the other day that I once said greed is good. Well, it appears that greed is not only good; it is legal. We are all drinking the same Kool-Aid. But it is greed that makes my bartender buy three houses he cannot afford with no money down. And it is greed that makes your parents refinance their $200,000 mortgage for $250,000. Now, they take that extra $50,000 and go to the shopping mall so they can buy a new plasma TV, cell phones and an SUV. And, hey, why not a second home while we are at it.[62]

While fantasy sports participants have many motivations, most of which are both innocent and harmless, there still remains an ideological residue that conforms to the logic of neoliberal capitalism and the entrepreneurial spirit that all citizens are told they should embrace.

Three

Does It Have to Be in the Game?
Sports Video Games and Sponsorship

We live in a culture virtually drowning in advertising, illustrated by the estimated $180 billion companies spent in 2014 in the United States to market their products and services, a number projected to reach $220 billion by 2018 as ever-popular mobile phone applications promise more effective and direct ways to engage consumers.[1] Advertising not only dominates traditional media fare such as television, radio, and magazines but also is becoming more prominent on college campuses, in city transportation such as buses and trains, and in sports stadiums whose names and architecture often invoke an explicit sales pitch. And the more it can be found in one place, the more that advertising "clutter" becomes a problem. Companies pursue virginal space in other places and when successful are followed by others, thus reproducing more clutter that leads to an ambitious pursuit to find untapped advertising space elsewhere. Today, the popularity of video games make them a lucrative target for companies as the effectiveness of traditional advertising platforms, such as television commercials, is declining. In the United States alone, an estimated 150 million Americans play video games, spending approximately $15.4 billion on video games and related accessories in 2014.[2] Like any other recreational and cultural activity that produces such a sizeable audience share, companies are swooping in to transform the popularity of video gaming into advertising gold.

According to the Entertainment Software Association, four of the top-twenty-selling video games in 2014 were sports video games, a

Three. Does It Have to Be in the Game?

major feat in an industry now dominated by a repetitive supply of first-person shooters like the popular Call of Duty series.[3] As a matter of fact, the first commercially successful video game, *Pong*, was a "sports simulation game" offering, by today's standards, a graphically crude and simplified imitation of table tennis.[4] Early home gaming consoles such as the Magnavox Odyssey and the Atari included a large library of sports video games in such sports as baseball, tennis, basketball, and football. Today, with the graphical sophistication and computing power of gaming consoles such as the Xbox One and PlayStation 4, sports video games provide a level of sports simulation unimaginable in the early years of the industry. Many gamers go so far as to conclude that these games seem almost as "real" as live sports themselves, featuring players who look, behave, and perform like their real-life counterparts, stadiums and arenas in which every concourse and nuance is replicated, and "season" modes that track not only wins and losses but detailed statistical analysis as well. Equally involved in the notion of sports video game "realism" are advertisements that feature official league sponsors. When *MLB 15: The Show* was released in March of 2015, the message board community was awash with buzz because apparel and equipment companies such as Nike and Louisville Slugger would finally be included in the game. In summary, companies looking to purchase advertising in sports video games found that doing so would be an easy sell. After all, sports fans had become so accustomed to the near-endless bombardment of advertising messages on sports broadcasts and inside stadiums, that official league sponsors are considered as much a part of the game as anything else.[5]

Of course, many may object that video games are deserving of such academic scrutiny because they offer little more than a little fun and diversion from the nagging commitments of everyday life. While it is undoubtable that video games offer a form of pleasure and recreation, this does not mean that they do not have particular effects on their audiences in terms of how they see the world. As Thomas P. Oates and Robert Alan Brookey note, video games feature "better graphics and complex narratives" and are, thus, more "culturally expressive," meaning they have become more important in defining the culture we are and claim to be.[6] Video games, like television programs and movies, shape our values and attitudes while reflecting the kind of society we inhabit. The popularity of first-person shooters is not an accident or a coincidence but mirrors America's obsession with actual and mediated forms of violence. Yet attempts to analyze the ideological overtones of video games have been met with significant resistance, as evidenced by the well-documented and admittedly confusing "Gamergate" scandal.

Dubbed the "Internet culture war," Gamergate started after indie game designer Zoe Quinn was accused by an ex-boyfriend on his blog of sleeping with several industry insiders, including a writer for the prominent gaming site Kotaku who wrote a favorable review for her new game, *Depression Quest*.[7] Quinn received enough rape and death threats after a group of anonymous hackers posted her home address online that she left her home and contacted law enforcement. Initial reports writing on the scandal suggested that the anger was merely about ethics in journalism, but it became clear shortly thereafter that Gamergate was a right-wing backlash against the "intrusion" of women in gaming culture. Even after the journalist from Kotaku, along with Quinn herself, denied their having a sexual relationship, the controversy morphed into a larger argument of whom gaming culture rightfully belonged to. Feminist writer and media critic Anita Sarkeesian became part of the Gamergate saga after posting a series of YouTube videos discussing the stereotypical representation of female characters in video games. The response was typical—feminists and other leftists were now trying to ruin video games in the name of political correctness by assaulting an innocent male pastime. Sarkeesian, like Quinn, received a barrage of death threats and had to change addresses. Milo Yiannopoulous, writer for the conservative Web site Breitbart, iterated his "[sympathies] with the frustrated male stereotype" while accusing "feminist programmers and campaigners" of "terrorising the entire community—lying, bullying and manipulating their way around the internet for profit and attention."[8] Justifying the backlash against Quinn and Sarkeesian, Yiannopoulous played the conspiracy card, suggesting "there is no evidence that any violent threat against a prominent female figure in the media or technology industry has ever been credible."[9] Thus, according to Yiannopoulous, Sarkeesian and Quinn made the threats up in order to forward their feminist, anti-male agenda. Yet evidence uncovered by *The Washington Post* suggests the contrary.[10]

Fortunately, most critical research on video games has not experienced this kind of backlash, largely because it is confined to academic journals and books that are mostly read by other academics. However,

Three. Does It Have to Be in the Game?

as the Gamergate scandal suggests, attempts to read video games critically are not welcome by the traditionally male gaming community, especially when such work is viewed as a threat to the kind of games that could be made in the future. Yet there is no denying that video games have garnered an increasing and influential stake in the pop cultural imagination, nor is it reasonable to assume they have no effect on how gamers view the world.[11] Of course, this may be overstating the denial, as media coverage of mass shootings is followed by the familiar trope of how much perpetrators loved their violent video games and music.[12] Such conclusions may be too simplistic and, furthermore, confront us with the "chicken or the egg" dilemma: Do violent video games cause people to be violent or are already-violent individuals attracted to these games because they allow the individuals to play out disturbing violent fantasies whose causes lie elsewhere? While there is no denying that playing violent video games has an effect on cognition and behavior, studies are inconclusive regarding what exactly the effect is. Some studies have actually found no link between playing violent video games and behavior while others have found only limited, short-term effects related to elevated levels of rude behavior following playing a game that gradually dissipate.[13]

The focus of this chapter is how advertising in sports video games encourages a consumerist worldview that normalizes the relationship between sports and commercialism. This is not to suggest that exposure to ads in games will have the same effect on everyone, nor will it always have the desired effect that programmers want. However, there is an ideological message implicit in the inclusion of advertisements in sports video games that reveals a specific intention. Specifically, that being a "real" sports fan requires both consumer thinking and behavior and, through the claims to realism that modern sports video game titles make, league sponsors are inseparable from live sports themselves. This analysis will also include how ads made themselves into sports video games in the first place, as well as a discussion regarding how sports video games are used to public relations purposes by leagues to fashion a desired image among the gaming and fan public and why the consumerist worldview being promoted within video games is so important to them.

*****

American Sports in an Age of Consumption

Before discussing the history of advertisements in sports video games, it is necessary to explore how advertising actually works.[14] It is widely accepted that the most effective advertising appeals to our private and culturally informed desires—the need for recognition and esteem from others, love and companionship, and the urge to "stand out" among others—and channels them through the market on the implicit promise that certain consumer brands can fulfill these needs. Yet according to T.J. Jackson Lears, advertising legitimatizes certain values over others in order to serve and valorize the market as a fundamental democratic institution.[15] This involves the notion not only that capitalism expands and delivers personal freedom and liberation but also that consumption is necessary to achieve happiness in society. Advertising, far from merely offering information on products and services, appeals to our most basic emotions, vulnerabilities, and insecurities. It also generates and builds an image for products and services increasingly indistinguishable from one another in our vast consumer marketplace. There is nothing particularly unique about a Nike tennis shoe, but the millions invested by the company annually to market its product attempt to suggest otherwise. Ironically, this does not involve ads that argue *why* Nike is better but rather a composite of carefully crafted images that associate Nike with particular emotions and lifestyles. And Nike is not alone—most consumer products and services are sold on the basis of images alone that bear no relationship to the particular properties of the thing being sold. Known in advertising and marketing circles as "branding," it is viewed as necessary "within a context of manufactured sameness" where "image-based difference [has] to be manufactured along with the product."[16]

When one gives thought to this process, it does not make sense that cartoon elves are used to sell cookies (the Keebler Elves), insurance (the GEICO Gecko), and snack foods (Cheetos' Chester Cheetah). None of these bear any rational relationship to the actual products being marketed, yet they provide a series of compelling images that associate these products with favorable emotions. Of course, few would admit purchasing any of these products on the basis of cartoons or digitized wildlife with an English accent. And yet the persistence of these characters in advertising campaigns would suggest we do, at least subconsciously. Each creates a series of memorable images that operate to prime consumer choice toward the brand. Of course, this means

Three. Does It Have to Be in the Game?

that much of our consumer behavior is completely irrational. While few people may actually compare insurance quotes from competing companies to find the best deal, many unconsciously choose GEICO on the basis of the familiarity and emotion generated by the talking gecko. Edward Bernays, the father of modern public relations and nephew of Sigmund Freud, understood that companies could sell more products by targeting the irrational impulses that his uncle theorized influenced much of human behavior.[17] Bernays developed advertising campaigns that did not focus on the properties of the product being sold—like traditional advertising had largely being doing up to that point—but on the basis of attractive images whereby consumers would associate a product with being more than what it actually was.

In 1929, Bernays was hired by George Washington Hill, the president of the American Tobacco Company, to develop an advertising and marketing campaign to expand the market for his Lucky Strikes cigarettes by appealing to women. At the time, it was considered taboo for women to smoke in public and those who did were often assumed to be sexually promiscuous. Bernays sought to challenge this convention with his "Torches of Freedom" campaign that took place during New York's Easter Parade, where several high-society women recruited by *Vogue* magazine smoked Lucky Strike cigarettes on Fifth Avenue, where they would attract the most attention. Because Bernays had alerted the press beforehand that the spectacle would take place, several local, national, and international newspapers arrived to cover the event. The message of the "Torches of Freedom" campaign was simple: convince women that smoking cigarettes in public was a symbol of liberation from an oppressive male culture. Of course, the association between smoking and sexual equality was an entire fabrication, but it did convince large throngs of women to start smoking cigarettes, which was precisely what Bernay's Lucky Strikes campaign was designed to do. Convincing people that a cigarette was not *just* a cigarette but a tool of female independence transformed the advertising paradigm entirely, and his ideas are still in use in most modern advertising campaigns today.

Meanwhile, sports are used today in company's branding efforts to build a desirable image for their products. Perhaps the most famous example is Michael Jordan's endorsement of Nike, which successfully convinced millions of American youths that the company was not *just* an athletic shoe company but partially responsible in making Jordan a basketball god. Although he retired from professional basketball after the 1997–1998 season, sales of his Air Jordan basketball shoe line topped $2.5 billion in 2012, representing 58 percent of all basketball shoes sold in the United States and an astounding 77 percent of all kids' basketball shoes sold during that year.[18] Jordan serves as an ideal spokesperson for not only Nike but also companies and products such as Gatorade, Coke, Hanes underwear, MCI telephone service, Ball Park Franks hot dogs, Bijan cologne, McDonald's and also Rayovac batteries.[19] So lucrative were these partnerships that in 1998 Jordan actually made more money in endorsement deals ($45 million, including $16 million from Nike alone) than he did actually playing basketball ($34 million) that year.[20]

Part of Jordan's appeal was certainly related to his unbelievable and mythic basketball skills but also his the way in which he embodied the post-racial discourse of the New Right during the Reagan era. Jordan assuaged white guilt toward poverty in African American communities by serving as "proof" that these inequities were merely "problems of individual pathology and deviance" rather than structural or social inequalities.[21] If Jordan, a black man, could achieve economic success in America, this supported the New Right's narrative that the United States was truly a color-blind society and that opportunity was available to everyone, regardless of race. Jordan's Cosbyesque image fit into the backlash politics of the conservative movement toward 1960s era reform presumed to be responsible for America's moral and cultural decay.[22] In order for this to work, Jordan had to disavow himself from taking particular stances toward racial inequalities in America to solidify his status as the "good black" palpable to the mainstream and his corporate sponsors. In 1990, when Jordan was asked why he did not endorse African American North Carolina Democrat Harvey Grantt in his Senate campaign against Republican Jesse Helms—known for being an old-time racist—he responded, "Republicans buy sneakers, too."[23]

Jordan was certainly not the first athlete to endorse products, but he is arguably the most memorable. So successfully did Michael Jordan and the Nike brand fuse in the cultural imagination, that every gravity-defying dunk, fadeaway jumper, and team championship during Jordan's tenure with the Bulls was a ringing endorsement of Nike itself.

Three. Does It Have to Be in the Game?

As mentioned before, since advertising largely appeals to an audience's emotions, it is no surprise that sports and high-profile athletes become marketing fodder for companies aiming to sell a product through endorsements and sponsorships. Without question, fans can become so heavily emotionally invested in their favorite teams and players—not to mention the emotional intensity of watching sports themselves—that sport as an institution is considered an appropriate platform through which to advertise and market. This fact, along with sports' ability to capture and deliver large audiences including the often-elusive 18–49 male demographic, makes them ideal for commercial exploitation. While being a sports fan can often be an emotional roller coaster characterized by exuberant highs and depressing lows, overwhelmingly the experience of being fan is characterized as a positive. Thus, companies that advertise and market through sports are hoping that the positive emotions that people have of sports themselves will transfer to the products and services being marketed and advertised through them.[24]

Before delving specifically into the issue of sports video games and advertising and its intended effects on audiences, it is necessary to discuss why sports video game advertising is occurring in the first place. While this is related to the expansion of advertising in more facets of everyday life, along with the popularity of sports video games in general, it also is connected to the diminishing impact of advertising in traditional platforms such as television and radio commercials among others. With the advent of the remote control and, years later, technology such as the digital video recorder (DVR) it became possible for audiences to skip commercials while watching television. This posed a threat to a long-standing broadcasting formula: commercial advertising pays for the television program in exchange for the right to advertise to audiences. Under this traditional paradigm, networks could charge higher amounts for companies to advertise during highly rated programs that commanded the highest viewership. If, however, these same audiences could skip the commercials, this consequently lowered the value and effect of advertising itself.

Today, however, networks have largely abandoned this long-standing formula, as few programs can generate a large mass audience due to the abundance of networks and channel options available on cable and satellite television. Rather, channels are created to cater to

American Sports in an Age of Consumption

niche audiences, or smaller segments united by demographics or shared interests, who are sold to companies attempting to reach that particular audience. For example, G4 TV and its programming content are geared largely toward males whose interests are video games and technology. Thus, G4 TV sells this audience, via selling commercial time, to video game and technology companies aiming to reach them. This makes the advertisements more effective despite pitching to a smaller audience—it is easier to sell video games to those who love video games rather than those who do not with networks like G4 TV serving to capture them. In the industry, "broadcasting" has become a dinosaur term, replaced by the ubiquitously used "narrowcasting," which captures this emerging philosophy.[25] While specific television programs have always been used to deliver a specific audience to advertisers seeking to reach them, it is now entire networks that do so as well.

With audiences being able to easily skip commercials (often very willingly), through channel surfing and fast forwarding through pre-recorded and on-demand content, it is clear that audiences, for the most part, choose to avoid advertising if possible. The only exception to this can be found in the world of sports. The Super Bowl is not only one of the few remaining cultural television "events" able to generate a large mass audience; it is also the only time when viewers actually *want* to see the commercials.[26] Super Bowl ads are not regarded as a nuisance like commercials found in other programs but instead are regarded as fascinating and important and—some would contend—more important and more fascinating than the "big game" itself. For the 2014 Super Bowl between the Seattle Seahawks and the Denver Broncos, more than 112 million Americans tuned in for the game, with ratings actually increasing during the commercial breaks.[27] Unsurprisingly, companies pay lavish sums of money to reach such a large and attentive audience, not only in the Hollywood blockbuster production quality of the ads themselves but also the $4.5 million asking price for a 30-second spot during the Super Bowl.[28] While this is astounding, there is much value added if a company produces a memorable spot, as there is much free advertising to be had. Commercials are deconstructed and evaluated for their popularity, creativity, and entertainment value (judged largely on their humor) on televised news, company Web sites, and cultural repositories like YouTube and Facebook days after.[29]

Three. Does It Have to Be in the Game?

This is only part of the commercial spectacle, as the Super Bowl is now branded as a license to consume without apology or guilt. As a matter of fact, consumption is considered an almost obligatory fan ritual to properly celebrate the event, as the ubiquitous phenomenon of Super Bowl parties will attest. According to the National Retail Federation, fans spend approximately $12 billion on food, drinks, and game merchandise in "preparation" for the big game. This includes the sale of not only 7.5 million new televisions but also 1.2 billion chicken wings, 79 million pounds of guacamole, 32 million slices of pizza, 11.2 million pounds of potato chips, and 50 million cases of beer.[30]

Even though other less popular sporting events do not yield the commercial returns of the Super Bowl, they are one of the remaining types of televised events in which traditional commercial advertising remains effective. While most television programming can be streamed online and on demand on Internet Web sites—some commercially supported but to a lesser extent—sports continue to attract a significant television audience. To be sure, streaming services are also available for sports; however, there are many rules that force these sites to enforce various blackout restrictions to ensure the integrity of traditional television commercial advertising. In major league baseball, for example, these restrictions prevent fans from watching games on MLB.com or cable "season ticket" channels that take place during nationally televised games on Fox and ESPN. Fans who want to watch their local teams online are prevented from doing so and are forced, instead, to view the game on their cable regional sports network. In both cases, these blackout restrictions are designed to preserve the advertising revenue of these regional and national networks by guaranteeing an audience by limiting their options to watch games elsewhere. Given the astronomical sums these networks have to pay to secure the rights to broadcast live sports in the first place, these blackout restrictions are considered necessary to ensure that advertisers are gaining the exposure they are paying for. According to Dave Zirin:

> It's a distorted marketplace: one where the financial value of American football, men's basketball, and baseball has never been higher, as witnessed by the bacchanalia of max contracts being tossed around the NBA. Yet this value is not a function of their exploding popularity but of the fact that they have become the tentpole that keeps the multibillion-dollar basic-cable industry upright: the last programming in our streaming DVR'd universe that people will still endure commercials to watch.[31]

American Sports in an Age of Consumption

Elsewhere, traditional television commercial advertising is yielding diminishing returns—companies are realizing people are skipping the commercials—forcing networks to develop alternative strategies to combat the problem. Perhaps, the most common is product placement, whereby companies pay money for their products to appear within a show itself. According to Bloomberg Business writers Ronald Glover and Tom Lowry, "as the cost of making TV shows escalates—at a time of declining ad sales—television networks are scouring Madison Avenue for partners that want to give their products a little screen time."[32] Historically, product placement was only common in movies, but increasingly television shows themselves have become their own "product placement bonanzas" especially within so-called reality TV.[33] *Survivor*, *The Apprentice*, *Extreme Home Makeover*, and *The Biggest Loser* are hardly more than commercials pretending to be television shows, with just enough dramatic and narrative pretense to blur the lines between the two. The singing contest that is *American Idol* is virtually overshadowed by host Ryan Seacrest's urging viewers to download contestants' songs on their Apple iPods, music videos in which corporate products like Ford are prominently displayed, and judges sipping happily and enthusiastically from their red Coke cups.[34]

Of course, it is not just reality television shows that are turning into long-form commercials but also drama and comedy programs as well. The producers and writers of the widely popular pseudo-documentary *The Office* were known for writing advertising within character dialogue itself. For example, in the Season Two episode "Christmas Party," office Machiavellian Dwight Schrute is heard discussing the "awesome" capabilities and cost of the Apple iPod with his colleagues.[35] Other episodes feature office manager Michael Scott professing his love for Chili's restaurants, employees eating at Hooters, and Dwight himself taking a job as Staples after being fired by Dunder Mifflin, the fictional paper company that is the focus of the show. Writers and advertisers love product placements because they do not appear to audiences to be advertisements at all but rather are misconstrued as innocent narrative elements that contribute to the realism and authenticity of these shows.[36] Yet none of these product placements are coincidental; rather, they are the product of the waning effectiveness of traditional television advertising in general.

This is not to suggest, however, that sports are completely immune

Three. Does It Have to Be in the Game?

from these processes. The pressure that sports networks face in generating enough advertising revenue to offset the escalating costs of securing the rights to broadcast live sports has led to increasing amounts of product placements and mentions in television and radio offerings. In 2014, the NBA negotiated a nine-year $24 billion television deal, which, while unbelievable, paled in comparison to the NFL's $7 billion a year deal with national networks.[37] Regional networks such as the YES Network—80 percent of which is owned by Rupert Murdoch's News Corporation—are currently involved in a 20-year deal with the New York Yankees estimated to be valued at $7.7 billion.[38] Media consultant Chris Bevilacqua, who was involved in the Texas Rangers' deal with Fox Sports Southwest, stated that "live sports are holding together the $150 billion cable industry."[39] While people typically record shows on their DVRs to watch later at their convenience, sports remains one of the few types of programs people insist on seeing live. However, by doing so viewers are denying themselves the freedom to skip the commercials, a luxury not possible during a live broadcast. Consequently, ad spending during live sports increased by 33 percent over a three-year period leading up to 2012 at $11 billion annually.[40]

For these reasons, the money generated through television accounts for more than half of the revenue in many professional leagues.[41] It also is a significant factor in the increasingly bloated salaries in the four major professional sports, such as Miami Marlins outfielder Giancarlo Stanton's 13-year $325 million contract he signed prior to the 2015 season, the largest contract in the history of professional sports.[42] However, the expense associated with these television contracts is already being referred to as a "bubble" that is unsustainable.[43] When networks such as ESPN pay such vast sums for the right to televise live sports, they try to offset these costs by charging cable companies such as Comcast and Time Warner more money to be able to carry their networks in their packages. As a consequence, these companies then pass the costs to their subscribers, resulting in higher bills, hidden costs, and disgruntled customers. For example, the average cable and satellite customer pays $6.10 a month for ESPN, which, according to *Forbes*, "is far and away the most expensive network."[44] As cable and satellite companies contemplate a move toward "a la carte" television—where customers would pay only for the channels they want—subscribers would pay an estimated $36.30 for ESPN alone.[45]

American Sports in an Age of Consumption

Unsurprisingly, cable television subscriptions have been steadily decreasing in recent years—as a matter of fact, 10 percent since 2009—and are now outpaced by the number of high-speed Internet subscribers.[46] Yet the major professional sports organizations such as the NBA, the NFL, and MLB know that these cable companies need them to attract many of their subscribers as well as the regional and national sports networks such as ESPN and Fox Sports, whose brands depend on live sports, especially the most popular variety. As *Slate* journalist Felix Salmon states, "For the cable companies, even if they pass on all the costs, live sports are not a way to lose subscribers—they're a way to *retain* subscribers."[47]

While traditional advertising remains, for the most part, effective because "live sports are the one thing that will glue a nation to a single channel for hours,"[48] networks have adjusted to their inflated costs by inserting more advertising within sports broadcasts. Referred to in the industry as "drop ins,"[49] they are the extension of product placement in sports already occurring elsewhere apace in the media culture. In short, these involve selling game happenings and occurrences to sponsors who are mentioned by announcers every time an occurrence takes place. On the Yankees' radio network, for instance,

> the first Yankees walk prompts, "Just walk into any of CityMD's six convenient locations." The announcement of the game's umpires is brought to you by Levy Philips & Konigsberg, a law firm specializing in asbestos cases. The personal injury firm Cellino & Barnes gets a plug when the announcers explain the broadcast's copyright violation policy. A call to the bullpen comes with a nod to one of three sponsors: Aamco Car Care, Hyundai, and the Tri-State Ford Dealers. The postgame wrap up show? That's brought to you, naturally, by Reynold's Wrap.[50]

While "drop ins" have long been a part of sports radio broadcasts, never before have they been so prominent. And the sponsoring companies who purchase them find them more valuable than 30-second commercials because they are inescapable. However, some announcers have begun to grow weary at the sheer number of sponsorship mentions, which they feel creates "clutter" in their broadcasts. Current Los Angeles Dodgers radio announcer Charlie Steiner states that "they're not tough to do, but does it feel like it slows the pace of the game? Of course it does. From an announcer's point of view, less is more."[51] Philadelphia Phillies radio announcer Scott Franzke laments, "You realize that they're there to pay for the broadcast. So I'm certainly not

Three. Does It Have to Be in the Game?

begrudging that. But you still want some integrity in the broadcast."[52] According to *New York Times* journalist Richard Sandomir, "in this ecosystem, a walk is not only as good as a hit. It's a sales opportunity."[53]

Television sports broadcasts have also been the victim of the "drop in" glut while at the same time charging more of a premium for them due to their visual nature. This allows networks more advertising flexibility, including implanting "virtual ads" overtop signage areas and stadium arena scoreboards that can only be visible to the viewers at home. Beyond the profits, it also solves the problem of stadium sponsors receiving advertising they did not pay for while blocking out companies that are competitors with official league sponsors. Virtual ads are more common during marquee sporting events that command larger audiences, such as the Super Bowl, World Series, and MLB All-Star Game.

Sports sponsorship is obviously not new, and for a time in the early years of professional sports it fulfilled a philanthropic, rather than self-serving, purpose. The first evidence of a sporting event being sponsored by anyone occurred in 1887 when the French magazine named *Velocipede* financed an auto race.[54] The purpose of early sponsorships such as these was to bankroll an event that otherwise would not have been possible. And companies and entrepreneurs did not expect to yield a financial return for doing so. Today, however, the purpose of sponsorship is to increase a company's visibility and financial bottom line for events that could, in most cases, occur without sponsors. In many cases, the sponsorship culture of sports so heavily borders on the ridiculous that it could easily be mistaken for satire due to the control that sponsoring companies have regarding what athletes do and say and how their respective brands appear on television, in stadiums, and elsewhere.

Perhaps the most famous sponsorship nightmare occurred during the 1992 Summer Olympics when the "Dream Team" made up of NBA All-Stars—who previously were denied the opportunity to compete in the Olympics due to their professional status—won the gold medal. Michael Jordan, the poster child and darling of Nike, refused to wear the official United States Olympic Committee awards ceremony garb because it featured the logo of Nike's competitor Reebok on the right shoulder.[55] He then convinced all 11 of his teammates, half of whom were sponsored by Nike, to unzip their jackets for the ceremony so as to obscure the Reebok patch. This occurred after several attempts over the course of two years to resolve the sponsoring issue between USA Basketball and the United States Olympic Committee. Sparing any degree of humility, Jordan celebrated the sponsorship "protest" by saying, "When you hire 12 Clint Eastwoods to come in here and do a job, don't ask them what bullets they're putting into the gun."[56]

Meanwhile, after the Detroit Tigers were eliminated by the Boston Red Sox in the American League Championship Series in 2013 Tigers outfielder Torii Hunter was less than enthused with having to watch yet another World Series from home. Addressing the national media, he stated, "I see this all the time, guys jumping up and down on the field at the end of the season. And I'm sitting on the couch and having a Coors Light." The moderator for the session, realizing the MLB's beer sponsor was Budweiser, not Coors, corrected Hunter immediately by saying, "Torii, of course, you meant a Bud Light."[57] Sponsorship deals have become such a serious business that even off-the-cuff remarks such as Hunter's are viewed as enough of a threat to jeopardize them. Jeffery Cohen, MLB's vice president of corporate sales and marketing, states that "when we sign a deal, we sign a long-term, all-inclusive deal and we mean business and they mean business."[58]

This means that during MLB's "jewel events," such as the All-Star Game and the entire postseason, the league ensures the integrity of its sponsorship deals by intensely policing its stadiums and effacing any ads of its sponsors' competitors and those of companies whose deals extend only to a particular team, not the league itself.[59] As Cohen explains:

> It's not antagonistic. We work very closely with the clubs. This starts with a preliminary email in July to the clubs in contention. In August the clubs all send us materials with images of their ballpark and (sign) rotations and that kind of thing. We get on the phone with them at the end of August and we start telling them what needs to be switched, what can stay.[60]

At Fenway Park, this means that the Dunkin' Donuts logos in the dugout have to be covered and the grounds crew have to switch to a backup tarp because its normal tarp is sponsored by locally owned L.L.Bean, whose logo emblazons the top. This means that in every stadium hosting a postseason game teams must drink Gatorade in the dugout regardless if the host team has a different drink sponsor during the regular season. And this also entails hiring staff to ensure that

Three. Does It Have to Be in the Game?

players are not wearing or carrying anything into the postgame media session from non-official sponsors who comprise what MLB colorfully refers to as "[its] other list of banned substances."[61]

The totalitarian thrust of these policies is most evident during mega international sporting events because those sponsorship deals are more expensive. The fact that companies are purchasing exclusive marketing and branding rights not only escalates the cost of being an "official sponsor" but consequently requires leagues and organizing bodies to become hypervigilant in protecting the privileges these agreements guarantee. During the 2012 Summer Olympics in London, branding teams went so far as to remove or tape over manufacturer logos in each venue's bathrooms if the manufacturers were not "official" Olympic sponsors.[62] Once the Games began, these same groups were instructed to target fans wearing clothing and accessories bearing the logos of non-Olympic sponsors.[63] These so-called brand protection measures were so aggressive that they even extended beyond the Olympic venues themselves. Alan Tomlinson, a professor at the University of Brighton, orchestrated a series of lectures on the Games as part of the school's sports studies program but had to avoid using the phrase "London 2012" in the titles of these lectures "because we would have been pounced on."[64] This was because of the International Olympic Committee's rules that prohibited any marketing activity "[creating] an association in the mind of consumers between a non-sponsor and the Olympics."[65] The rules also specified that nonsponsoring companies could not use any two of the following words at the same time in their marketing and advertising campaigns: "games," "two thousand and twelve," "2012" and "twenty-twelve," while prohibiting any of those words being paired with "London," "medals," "sponsors," "summer," "gold," "silver," or "bronze."

While a complete and thorough analysis of the magnitude of sports sponsorship and its corresponding effects is beyond the scope of this book, these examples attest to how sports are often trivialized in the process. So blurred have the lines between sports and commercialism become that it is increasingly difficult to enjoy the former and its incessant barrage of sponsorship logos and announcer mentions that increasingly clutter and interrupt the action. It is here that people are addressed more as consumers than fans through an elaborately contrived corporate marketing spectacle celebrated by leagues and networks as the deserving "star" of the show. While sports sponsorship is nothing new, never before has it insisted on having so much of the fan's attention, nor has it claimed a divine right to command center stage. As a consequence, sporting events feel all the more hollow and superficial, further alienating fans from sports by marketing and advertising practices that increasingly mediate that relationship almost every step of the way.

*****

Given the all-too-visible nexus between sports and advertising, it is unsurprising that sports video games would eventually become targeted as another platform for sponsors to reach the fan public who often play them. In fact, advertisements for real-world products in video games are becoming the norm regardless of which genre they are classified into. According to the Entertainment Software Association, an organization that researches trends in the video game industry, the market for in-game advertisements is projected to reach $7.2 billion by 2016.[66] An exploding trend is "advergaming," in which a game is designed around the concept of promoting a particular product, brand, or service, such as the Home Shopping Network's Today's Special Puzzle, which features items being promoted by the network that day on its television channel. As video gaming becomes more popular across a wider spectrum of the public, companies are using advergames and in-game advertising to reach their targeted demographics.

The first instance of this practice being used in a video game occurred with the release in 1978 of *Adventureland*, which included an advertisement for *Pirate Adventure* from programmer Scott Adams, who developed both titles.[67] This was followed by Anheuser-Busch purchasing advertisements in Bally Midway's 1983 release *Tapper*, where players served Budweiser to an impatient throng of beer drinkers while also collecting the empty mugs being thrown at them before they hit the floor. While the trend of in-game advertisements was slow to develop, it completely halted with the infamous "video game crash" of 1983. The explosive sales of home gaming systems, led by Atari, led to unimpressive copycats flooding the market while shortening development and production cycles for games to keep pace with the demand.[68] The most cited example believed to seal the fate of the industry's downfall was Atari's 1982 release *E.T. the Extra Terrestrial*, for which the

Three. Does It Have to Be in the Game?

company paid $22 million for the licensing rights in anticipation that it would not only become the "can't miss" video game for the holiday shopping season but outshine Atari's competitors.[69]

Atari had paid too much for the *E.T.* license, so it would require selling all five million of the cartridges produced just to break even.[70] While this was easily dismissed as a bad investment, the company believed it was necessary in order to restore and solidify its reputation as the industry leader. With the holiday shopping season rapidly approaching, programmer Howard Scott Warshaw only had six weeks to produce *E.T.*, well short of the "normal" six-month development cycle for a typical game.[71] The final product was such a disaster that not only did the game fall short of its sales projections, but many of those who did purchase *E.T.* returned to the stores demanding their money back. While the video game industry bubble was already demonstrating signs of bursting before the release of *E.T.*, its status as the "worst video game ever" has been mythologized as the industry's undoing in 1983.[72] Atari laid off many of its workers en masse as the company's stock plummeted earthward, even going so far as to bury 14 truckloads of unsold games from its El Paso warehouse in a landfill in nearby Alamogordo, New Mexico. At the time, it appeared that video games would be consigned to the dustbin of other consumer fads that appear periodically within the culture at large. While other console companies such as Coleco and Mattel momentarily filled the void, none inherited Atari's dominance and market share until late in 1985 when the Nintendo Entertainment System was released, which not only resuscitated the industry but even made "Nintendo" a household word.[73]

Once the video game industry achieved a degree of financial stability, in-game advertising not only became more commonplace, but the strategies devised to enhance their impact and effectiveness became more sophisticated. Traditionally, in-game advertisements were "static," meaning that they consisted of unchanging virtual billboards or product placements programmed directly into a video game.[74] However, in 2002 the South Beach Beverage Company (SoBe) paid Ubisoft Entertainment to have its product integrated into the actual gameplay for its *Tom Clancy's Splinter Cell: Double Agent* release. Players could "consume" SoBe through the game's main character, black ops agent Sam Fisher, in the company's hope that "[gamers] would do the same" in the real world.[75] Subsequently, the paradigm shifted as the focus moved from ensuring that gamers saw the ad to providing opportunities for these same gamers to interact with the ad instead. This would increase the likelihood the gamers could remember and recall the brands featured in games, a necessary prerequisite for influencing their purchasing behavior toward the advertised products.

In recent years, video game consoles have been developed with Internet capabilities, allowing gamers to compete with one another online, purchase games and upgrades, and, often unknowingly, advertise products themselves for free.[76] These capabilities also allow video game companies to make more money from selling advertising space in their products. A recent trend has involved the move toward "dynamic" advertising, which, because of the online capabilities of newer consoles, allows companies to change the ads embedded in games over time. This allows the companies to not only accommodate "time-sensitive" campaigns such as movie releases but also tailor them according to the time of day gamers are playing and the geographical location at which they connect online. For example, in the months leading up the 2008 presidential election candidate Barack Obama purchased dynamic ads in the arcade racer *Burnout Paradise* as well as the latest incarnation of the *Madden* football series.[77] These ads featured virtual billboards reminding gamers to register to vote early, followed by the address for Obama's Vote For Change Web site, and were only visible to gamers who connected online in swing states. With more gamers connecting and playing games online, programmers are able to track data on the ads themselves, as well as a gamer's habits. These include "time spent looking at advertisements, the most-viewed advertisements and viewing angles," which could be used in order to "determine the most successful ads, which provides valuable insights for future campaigns."[78] The Orwellian impulse behind quantifying the effectiveness and reach of in-game ads seems shocking and for good reason, but few gamers are actually aware that it occurs.

It perhaps goes without saying that in-game ads are common in sports video games, which allow leagues and their sponsors another platform to reach and market to fans. However, in-game advertising serves an additional purpose: to further fuse the relationship between leagues and sponsors so as to make them appear inseparable.[79] Referred to some in the industry as "incremental affinity," the goal is to present

Three. Does It Have to Be in the Game?

sponsors as being just as much a part of sports as the athletes and teams themselves.[80] So strong has the association already become in many fans' experience of televised sports that the inclusion of official sponsors in their video game counterparts is regarded as essential to bolster game developers' claims that they offer a "real" and simulated experience of the sports titles they offer. Elizabeth Hart, Senior Vice President of Global Media Sales for Electronic Arts—a prominent sports video game company—states that "fans have grown to expect that the game experience mirrors the real world." She adds that "part of the authenticity that is embedded in the game ... includes the finer details like in-stadium and in-arena signage."[81] In other words, gamers expect that the advertising found in real-world sporting venues is replicated in sports video game simulations in order for them to feel "authentic." As video games in general have become more graphically sophisticated, gamers have higher expectations in regard to how much visual detail they expect companies to deliver in their products. In the sports video game market, gone are the days in which gamers merely wanted a title that included actual players and teams—this alone was enough make the experience feel "real" enough. Today, however, official sponsors have become such a visible part of live sports that many gamers will claim a title falls short of feeling real and authentic unless they are included.

For official league sponsors, video game advertising offers other advantages compared to televised sports: gamers cannot escape them. Robert Fox, Executive Director of the ESPN Sports Poll, argues that "when a person is engaged in [a sports video game], there is no channel surfing."[82] The same poll found that approximately three out of four sports fans claimed that sports video game advertising "[reinforces] a company's real-world sponsorship of that sport."[83] While some people who play sports video games may not actually be fans of the sports they are playing, video game developers and marketers are using these games as an additional avenue to target avid fans of real sports. And the sponsoring companies are not only hoping that the ads translate into profit in the short term but also hope that the ads reinforce the feeling that they are also "a part of the game." Thus, when fans think of baseball, football, basketball and other sports they are also imagining the likes of Nike, Reebok, Gatorade, and so on. The goal is that the positive emotions fans experience toward these sports will transfer to the sponsors who are associated with them, creating a legion of lifelong devotees to these respective brands with the same degree of loyalty they demonstrate toward the sports they love.

However, the ads not only include the all-too-obvious message that fans should buy a particular product; they also encourage fans to consistently embody the role of the consumer.[84] Given the vast commercial scope of modern sports, this is considered essential in order for leagues and their sponsors to maximize the returns their relationship is expected to bring. In some respects, being considered a "real" fan of a sport is often dependent on one's willingness to spend in order to demonstrate one's fandom toward others. This mirrors, in many significant ways, the redefinition of citizenship in contemporary American democracy itself. As large corporations gain political influence over elected officials and public decision-making, several theorists have noted how notions of democracy have become reduced simply to the freedom to buy things.[85] This is far removed from the idea that a functioning democracy provides citizens both a stake and a voice in the institutions that govern them, not to mention important freedoms that protect speech and the press. Unfortunately, these liberties pertaining to citizenship are too often regarded as irrelevant in a society where "free-market wisdom" is presented as a savior toward society's problems, inefficiencies, and shortsightedness. As moneyed influences are increasingly able to direct the political system in a way advantageous to their own ends, they benefit from the dilution of citizenship to the mere level of consumerism. It not only prompts more consumer spending but also contributes toward undermining the checks and balances necessary to holding those in power accountable, which would otherwise be the case with a more engaged public. The role of the sports fan is being reshaped within this context, as similarly predicated on one's consumer habits. To further demonstrate how and why this is the case, I will explore two sports video games—the *Madden* and *MLB: The Show* series—and how they influence what a "real" fan is supposed to be.

Without question, the *Madden* football franchise is regarded as the undisputed king of sports video games. In 2014, *Madden NFL 15* was the second-highest-selling video game across all consoles, only bested by the military-style first-person shooter *Call of Duty: Advanced Warfare*.[86] Featuring the endorsement of former NFL coach and broadcaster

Three. Does It Have to Be in the Game?

John Madden, the annually released football simulation has sold over 100 million copies since it was first released on the Apple II, Commodore 64, and DOS computer systems in 1989.[87] Generating over $4 billion in revenue for Electronic Arts (EA)—the company that develops and produces the game—*Madden* is the blockbuster release for the company. While these numbers may be unsurprising given the popularity of the NFL in general and the fact that Electronic Arts pays $50 million for the exclusive rights to produce the game,[88] it is also the result of the cross-marketing spectacle that accompanies each annual release of *Madden*.

In 2005, EA negotiated a 15-year partnership with ESPN, who agreed to integrate the game into its coverage of NFL football, including using Madden to break down plays and strategies and even using the Madden simulation engine to predict outcomes of upcoming games.[89] Such a visible endorsement by the self-proclaimed industry leader in sports seemed to attest to the realism of the Madden franchise in its treatment as an authority and informative resource for ESPN's football commentary. The network even produced its own show around the video game called *Madden Nation*, which was hardly more than a thinly veiled commercial for EA's crown jewel. Premiering in December of 2005, the show featured the top *Madden* gamers competing in an elimination-style tournament with the winners facing off in a live competition in Times Square for a $100,000 grand prize. While the show is no longer on the air, it was responsible for further cementing *Madden*'s status in the sport's cultural psyche while legitimizing its gambling culture online. The quest to become a top *Madden* player is driven by not only the pursuit of masculine esteem and bragging rights but also its heavy monetary stakes. One professional *Madden* gamer noted that "my dad would use me to hustle guys. I was 12 playing 30-year olds. One time I lost $2,500 in a single night. My dad was disappointed."[90]

There is also the prerelease hype surrounding the upcoming *Madden* release perhaps best illustrated by the *Madden* cover vote—where fans can vote for which player will grace the cover—with the final results being announced on ESPN's *SportsCenter*.[91] As a matter of fact, the cover vote now operates on the level of superstition, as evidenced by the "Madden curse" based on the high number of players who performed poorly or had seasons shortened by injury after appearing on the Madden cover.[92] The curse is so widely believed that some fans even go so far as to "[campaign] to keep their teams' stars off the game's cover."[93] Regardless of one's perception regarding whether the "*Madden* curse" is real, it lends itself to copious amounts of online banter that solidify the game's mythological reputation while further driving sales.

Perhaps more interesting is the fact that *Madden*'s simulation of NFL football is taken to be so real that the player ratings—which define how "good" an NFL player will perform in the *Madden* universe—are often regarded as gospel and beyond question. Posted on EA's Madden Web site prior to the game's release and regurgitated and critiqued on sports Web sites elsewhere, the player ratings are taken to be the definitive measurement of athletes' skill not only in the game but also in real life. Based on a 100-point scale, the ratings assess an athlete's various skills in passing, blocking, and speed and also their overall talent. In an online video titled "Rookies React to Madden 16 Ratings," the most prestigious of the incoming rookie class are interviewed and asked to predict what their overall Madden score is. At one point, Jameis Winston, the first overall pick in the 2015 NFL draft, responded, "82 or 84. I hope so. If it's not, I'm going to be mad."[94] After being told what their actual overall score was, most players had estimated their ability too high, leading to several disappointed responses and reactions.

But all of this prerelease and ritualistic buzz, such as the cover release press conferences and the "leaking" of player ratings, not only generates anticipation for the upcoming *Madden* game, it also provides value for the companies whose ads are included within it.[95] The latter certainly benefit from all of the celebratory fanfare surrounding a video game where their logos can be found. It also guarantees that the NFL and its licensee EA can charge a premium for the advertising embedded in *Madden* and can use this anticipatory hype as a kind of leverage to negotiate higher advertising rates. In-game advertising in *Madden* is also seen as necessary for official NFL sponsors to cement their relationship with the league in a game not only notably popular but also highly esteemed as offering an NFL experience regarded as being as real as the real thing. Furthermore, since sponsorships are already so visible in NFL television broadcasts and stadiums, the inclusion of ads in the league's video game counterpart appears natural, inevitable, and even necessary for the game to feel "real." Noted blogger Andy Rosenberg, who writes about in-game advertising, states that "the point is

Three. Does It Have to Be in the Game?

advertising is everywhere in professionals sports. The fact that it is now included in sports video games only makes the sports video gaming experience that much more authentic."[96]

In *Madden NFL 15*, the advertising appears minimal, and many of the leagues official sponsors, such as Pepsi and Anheuser-Busch, are absent.[97] However, logos and mentions of General Motors Company (GMC), Gatorade, Papa John's, and Nike, as well as NFL.com, which provides updates for news and information occurring throughout the league on a ticker tape that periodically flashes at the bottom of the screen during game play. For the most part, the ads of sponsoring companies appear where they would normally appear in a television broadcast, such as in the halftime report ("GMC Half-Time Report"), the postgame report featuring the play of the game ("GMC Never Say Never Moment"), and time-outs between quarters (Papa John's). Meanwhile, players on the sidelines can be seen sipping from cups emblazoned with the Gatorade logo while the Nike logo is featured on team jerseys and apparel. Given the popularity of the *Madden* franchise, it on the one hand may be surprising that there are not more sponsors being featured visibly in the game. On the other hand, this may be due to the fact that too much advertising leads to clutter, making it harder for the sponsors' messages to "stand out" on their own. Perhaps sponsors are willing to pay more money on the condition that *Madden* does not include too many ads from other companies in order to render their own more effective.

At the same time, by extending the definition of what constitutes an advertisement from the presence of official sponsors and their logos to a more general worldview promoting consumption as necessary to solidify one's status as a "real" fan, *Madden* advertises more than what is immediately visible upon first glance. In the game itself, the overwhelming majority of virtual spectators are seen wearing official team merchandise—everything from replica jerseys to hoodies—sending the message that this is what real fans do. Of course, one could argue that this contributes to the authenticity and realism of *Madden* itself; after all, many fans sport their favorite team's colors and style at real-life sporting events. However, given that the game features not only NFL.com, but also the Web sites for every NFL team, the purpose is to direct fans toward these Web sites in the hope they will visit the online "shops" where they can purchase officially licensed merchandise—

much of it advertised in *Madden*. As the game is heralded as offering a real-life simulation of NFL football so close to the real thing, then outfitting virtual fans in official merchandise normalizes this as a reality. Through these carefully crafted rhetorical pleas that consistently engage gamers as consumers—in a league where team merchandise is a major revenue source—the linking of fandom and consumption in this way is "necessary" to sell more officially licensed jerseys, hats, sweatshirts, and so on.

It should be noted at this point that everything included in *Madden* is the result of programmers and the NFL deciding not only what should (or should not) be included in the game but also how the league should be represented. If, in fact, "it's in the game," as the EA slogan suggests, it is put there for a reason. Without question the NFL is very concerned about the image it portrays to the public, and it is reasonable to assume that *everything* included in the game has to be in accordance with that image. In 2003, ESPN produced a drama series called *Playmakers* about a fictional football team named the Cougars in a fictional professional football league. The show was an instant hit, as viewers were fascinated with a compelling and intelligent storyline in which several of the major characters struggled with drug use, brushes with the law, and accusations of homosexuality. The NFL, however, was not amused and was concerned that the show's fictional league could be mistaken by viewers as really being the NFL itself. Commissioner Paul Tagliabue met with Disney—which owns ESPN—and complained to CEO Michael Eisner that *Playmakers* was harming the reputation of the league. According to ESPN executive vice president Mark Shapiro, "the major issue was that ... [*Playmakers*] lacked redeeming characters and redeeming qualities," and he added that "[Tagliabue] just didn't like the inevitable comparisons being drawn to [the NFL]."[98] Concerned that *Playmakers* could jeopardize ESPN's opportunity to renew its television contract with the NFL—at the time set to expire in 2006—the network dropped the show amidst pressure from the league.

As evidenced by the *Playmakers* example, the NFL is especially concerned with how it is represented, and there is no reason to assume that this is not the case with video games as well. Meanwhile, EA is the only company allowed to produce an official NFL game, due to its exclusive licensing agreement with the league and the NFL Players Association, estimated to cost them $50 million.[99] Because much of

Three. Does It Have to Be in the Game?

EA's revenue depend on the sales of the annual *Madden* release, it is clear that the company has to follow the NFL's wishes regarding how the league is presented in the video game, lest EA jeopardize its exclusive rights deal. Thus, when *Madden* is heralded as being a real NFL experience it is a reality defined within the contours of the NFL's wishes. As Meredith M. Bagley and Ian Summers note, "sponsors or licensees exert influence of the aspects of 'reality' simulated in their games."[100] So while sports video game simulations such as *Madden* are celebrated for their purported reality, it is a heavily filtered reality that conforms to how the leagues wish to be seen. In other words, it is interesting to examine not only which aspects of reality are included in games, but also which aspects of reality are left out.[101]

A good example can be found in EA's *NCAA Football* series, which long provided gamers the opportunity to coach and recruit a championship Division I football team. While the series is now defunct, stemming from a series of lawsuits pertaining to the use of player likenesses and attributes of actual college players without compensation, *NCAA Football* for a time challenged the hegemony of *Madden* in the football video game market. The 2006 version of the game included a unique feature as part of its "dynasty mode" where gamers had to make decisions regarding whether or not to discipline players for various infractions, including academic ineligibility. Gamers were prompted to "maintain the integrity of their program…. Keeping close tabs on your team discipline will result in a clean program that attracts other outstanding student-athletes."[102] Ignoring these disciplinary issues, however, could result in NCAA sanctions within the game. Shortly after the game was released NCAA pressured EA to pull the game from the shelves due to these game-play elements, and today a "kill order" still exists preventing used video game stores from selling the game. While infractions such as academic ineligibility constitute a reality that college coaches have to address, its inclusion in NCAA Football 06 "would hurt [the NCAA's] image as a pure, 'amateur' athletic institution."[103]

In *Madden*'s version of "real" NFL football, gamers do not have to address steroid use, spousal abuse, and other public relations nightmares that have hampered the league recently. Rather, the NFL is portrayed as clean, honest, and reputable. While the game's dynasty mode allows players to manage and coach a team across multiple seasons— including drafting and signing college players, negotiating contracts with free agents, and setting depth charts—gamers do not have to deal with disciplinary issues simply because they are not programmed into the game. Perhaps in the saddest irony, gamers are given the option to relocate their teams if their home cities vote against a new stadium proposal. It is portrayed as just a cost of doing business in the NFL while minimizing the controversial nature of this decision in real life. It is clear that *Madden*, much like other sports video games with official licenses, offers a narrative that aligns with how the NFL wishes to be portrayed. Thus, the inclusion of sponsorship ads and virtual fans donning official merchandise in the stands is part of that desired image. The effect is that gamers are consistently addressed as consumers as much as fans, which is the mentality the NFL and its associated sponsors want. With so many products and services being hawked in stadiums, online, and on televised games, not to mention all the official merchandise fit to sell, *Madden* perpetuates the already-well-repeated message to fans that their purpose is to consume. With so many marketing and advertising agendas to fulfill between the NFL and its sponsors, this is seen as a mechanism to maximize the value and financial return of these relationships by constantly reminding fans to be consumers.[104]

Meanwhile, *MLB 15: The Show* is a Major League Baseball simulation game and has been celebrated for its lifelike graphics and innovative attention to detail. While there are other officially licensed baseball games on the market, such as the revitalized arcade classic RBI Baseball, *MLB: The Show* is the only baseball simulation available on a "next gen" console—the PlayStation 3 and the PlayStation 4.[105] The game itself bears many resemblances to Madden in terms of its in-game advertising strategy, such as virtual fans seen wearing officially licensed merchandise, as well as advertisements and logos for several of MLB's sponsors. More interesting, however, was that the latest version of *MLB: The Show*—released in March of 2015—was heavily marketed on the basis of its new advertising content.[106] The game's press release boasted that "for the first time ever *MLB: The Show* will include licensed equipment from some of the most recognisable brands in baseball." While this did not represent an entirely new innovation in sports video games—the Tiger Woods golf simulation has included licensed equipment for years—the inclusion of bats, gloves, and shoes bearing the logos of Nike, Franklin, Louisville Slugger, Rawlings, and Mizuno

Three. Does It Have to Be in the Game?

was celebrated as a testament to *MLB: The Show* "getting closer to the real thing."[107] While actual MLB players certainly wear equipment from these manufacturers, it would also serve to reach a desirable demographic that these companies are trying to reach. According to industry research, fans who play sports video games tend to be more physically active than sports fans who do not.[108] Thus, sports equipment manufacturers would be able to use *MLB 15: The Show* to drive gamers' purchasing behavior toward their desired brands.

One way that this is accomplished would be to plant suggestions that the equipment from these manufacturers contributes to *actually playing better*, not only within the video game but in real life as well. While there may be some validity to the argument that the quality of one's equipment can impact performance, this point is often exaggerated within *MLB 15: The Show*. One of the game's most popular gameplay options is "Road to the Show," where gamers design their own players and control them through the minor leagues on the path to and through the major leagues. Gamers not only earn experience points that allow them to improve their players' overall skill but can also "unlock" licensed equipment upgrades that enhance performance by meeting particular objectives. For example, gamers can earn the Rawlings Excellence Pro batting glove, which increases a player's plate discipline a full 10 points (on a 100-point scale). Rhetorically, the message suggests that this brand of batting gloves will actually help gamers—as well as real-life athletes—keep from swinging at bad pitches outside the strike zone.

Of course, with the inclusion of licensed equipment comes the opportunity to promote a player's real-life endorsements with one or more of these companies as well as the product lines bearing their name. One upgrade that "Road to the Show" gamers can earn is access to All-Star Mike Trout's signature line "Nike Lunar Vapor Trout" cleats, which improve one's speed (14 points) and ability to read a ball defensively (10 points) as well as increase one's strikeouts per nine innings as a pitcher (8 points). In 2014, Trout became the first MLB player to have his own line of cleats since Ken Griffey, Jr., with Nike boasting in it ads that the "Lunar Vapor Trouts" are "designed for the directional speed needed to steal more bases, get to more balls in the outfield, and get out of the batters box more quickly."[109] Without quantifying how much Trout's performance would be enhanced by the Nike Trouts, consumers would be led to question whether the difference maker in Trout making a spectacular defensive play, beating out an infield hit, or stealing a base was somehow the cleats themselves. In fact, the very vagueness of this language, without any degree of evidence, could be exploited by Nike, whose Trouts were seen as providing the edge that makes him an elite athlete. This despite the fact that his already-present baseball greatness got him the shoe deal in the first place. The item description of the Trouts in *MLB 15: The Show* is virtually taken word for word from Nike's own marketing language on the cleats. And while it could be said that these and other similar items make The Show's game play more compelling—even when it makes no sense to say that cleats could induce more strikeouts—it does coincide with the narrative of Nike and the other featured equipment providers that they are responsible for making real players great.

Many may remember Nike's television marketing campaign for the Air Jordans in the early 1990s that featured director Spike Lee pondering the quasi-existential question of whether Michael Jordan's greatness was due to his Nike shoes. In one of these commercials, Lee, portraying a fictional character named Mars Blackman, asks Jordan, "What makes you the greatest player in the universe?"[110] Blackman asks him if it is "the vicious dunks," "the low-cut socks" and, on several occasions in the ad, "the shoes." Jordan, feigning embarrassment and humility, responds "no" to Blackman's questions against a backdrop of highlight-deserving dunks and repeated close-ups of a pair of Air Jordans. The commercial ends with the message that "Mr. Jordan's opinions do not necessarily reflect those of Nike, Inc.," allowing the company to mock the suggestion that Nike helped make Jordan great while suggesting exactly that at the same time. While some of the advertising strategies by Nike and its competitors could be excused—after all, what claims can you make regarding athletic equipment other than improving performance?—to suggest that one's product *is* what makes great players great is a bit manipulative and misleading. Meanwhile, *MLB 15: The Show*, in its licensed equipment upgrades available to gamers, perpetuates this oft-repeated marketing narrative that having the "right" equipment can significantly elevate one's game, rather than enhance it on a more modest scale.

Perhaps more interesting is the fact that *MLB 15: The Show* includes a bevy of advertisements for non-profit companies and organ-

Three. Does It Have to Be in the Game?

izations, including the Boys & Girls Clubs of America, Welcome Back Veterans, and Stand Up to Cancer, each of whom enjoys a sponsorship relationship with Major League Baseball. At first glance, their inclusion seems noble and selfless. However, the rhetorical effect is that the league and its for-profit sponsors are able to manufacture an image of being good corporate citizens by aligning themselves with charitable organizations. And without attempting to sound too cynical, this relationship is often exploited for the purpose of increasing their bottom line. In 2009, Major League Baseball sponsors State Farm, Bank of America, and Pepsi each announced that they were going to increase their charitable giving as a demonstration of their humble sensitivity during the economic recession. Meanwhile, Major League Baseball would highlight its sponsors' goodwill during television broadcasts in order to bolster its own claims as a socially responsible organization concerned with giving back to the community. During the 2009 Home Run Derby in St. Louis, Missouri, many of the event's sponsors, such as MasterCard and General Motors, boasted about not only their charitable sensitivities but also how profitable these were at the same time. General Motors claimed that each dollar spent toward its sponsorship with Major League Baseball equaled five dollars in sales. Ray Bednar, the head of global sponsorship marketing at Bank of America, stated that "I can completely understand the cynicism and understand the questions about philanthropy and investment in sports." However, this had nothing to do with whether exploiting charitable causes for profit was ethical, but rather the "cynicism" he mentioned was related to critics' questioning whether charitable giving could be financially lucrative. In response, Bednar contended that "we make money at this, and *that's the most important message to get out.*"[111]

In recent years, companies within and outside of sports have regarded charitable sponsorships as an almost obligatory marketing strategy to send the message that companies care about more than just money. Known as "cause-related marketing," it involves the promise to donate a percentage of the sales that a product or service generates to a charitable organization or cause.[112] It is a popular strategy, as many consumers not only support companies who appear to have a social conscience but also enjoy the convenience of helping those in need without having to take on any additional commitments—such as volunteering—beyond purchasing the product itself. When a cause-related marketing campaign is successful, the added sales more than compensates for the cost of the promised donation. And while many will argue that such considerations are irrelevant as long as needy organizations gain more money to fund scientific research and awareness campaigns, others fear that the commercialization of charitable giving undermines the message and the seriousness of the cause itself.

A good example can be seen in the breast cancer awareness movement, which has enjoyed the support of major sporting organizations such as the WNBA, MLB, the NBA, the NHL, the NFL, and the NCAA. Perhaps the most visible symbol of this movement has been the pink ribbon, originally inspired by the peach-colored ribbons created by 68-year-old Charlotte Haley, whose granddaughter, mother, and sister each passed away from breast cancer.[113] Haley herself, in fact, was a breast cancer survivor, but her inspiration for the ribbon was not the number of people similarly affected but the small amount of the National Cancer Institute's annual budget going toward breast cancer prevention. Each ribbon originally included an attached card that read: "The National Cancer Institute annual budget is $1.8 billion, only 5 percent goes for cancer prevention." After Haley started gaining media attention for her handmade creations, she was approached by cosmetic giant Estée Lauder, which wanted to make her ribbons the official symbol of breast cancer, including placing them for sale in its stores. Haley refused, stating that Estée Lauder was more interested in exploiting the breast cancer movement for profit than serving the message her ribbons represented. According to Haley, "[Estée Lauder] said all we have to do if we want it is to change the ribbon [to pink]," which they did.[114]

Ravida Din, the producer of the documentary *Pink Ribbons, Inc.*, inspired by the research and work of professor Samantha King and journalist Barbara Ehrenreich, chronicles the use of the pink ribbon to market products by companies while contributing little of the money generated to actual breast cancer prevention and research. Din stated that "the question I was intrigued by was 'how did we get this kind of breast cancer culture that privileges shopping [as a solution] as opposed to getting angry and asking for a change?'"[115] Din's work also criticizes the positive and cheerful tenor of breast cancer rallies and campaigns that, while well intentioned, tend to minimize the pain, suffering, and impact of the disease behind a veneer of optimistic slogans, empowerment

Three. Does It Have to Be in the Game?

rhetoric, and smiling, happy faces. Furthermore, critics of this kind of breast cancer movement contend that it minimizes the relationship between the disease and certain environmental factors, such as many of the synthetic chemicals used in cosmetics having been linked to breast cancer.[116] As a matter of fact, many companies that manufacture products with similar carcinogenic compounds correlated with breast cancer often support the breast cancer movement to improve their image with the public.[117] Given their undoubtable funding influence, it is unsurprising that discussion regarding these environmental factors is often downplayed or ignored while little money goes toward research into prevention that would otherwise implicate some of these products. Meanwhile, the rates of breast cancer diagnoses have remained steady over the last 60 years while the treatment options available are virtually the same as they were 40 years ago.[118] The arguments here, however, are not intended to discourage individuals from donating money to breast cancer awareness and research, nor are they suggesting that such contributions have no impact or influence. Rather, the focus is how many companies and organizations claiming to support a worthy cause are being disingenuous when they market their efforts as being mobilized by social conscience, not profit.

The criticism of how the breast cancer movement is being used as a marketing strategy design foremost to sell products has implicated sports leagues and teams themselves. As mentioned previously, MLB began partnering with non-profit organizations after the 2008 recession to highlight its "dedication to giving back" during troubling and uncertain economic times. Within this context, MLB and other professional sports organizations jumping on the charitable bandwagon perhaps were afraid that many fans would refuse to support an apparatus of millionaire athletes and billionaire owners unless they demonstrated an adequate dose of sympathy, humility, and goodwill as many Americans struggled from the impact of the recession. As mentioned before, several prominent sports leagues have audibly advertised their endorsement of the breast cancer movement, from holding symbolic tributes where athletes don pink-colored gear during select games to donating money from the sale of this same gear in stadiums and on team Web sites. Recently, however, these seemingly noble efforts have come under scrutiny as evidence has surfaced that leagues are using cause-related marketing as a more clever way to sell products and merchandise while promoting their official sponsorships.

The NFL, for example, is known for its month long "NFL Pink" initiative "that paints everything from players' shoes to fields to penalty flags pink," including peddling pink-colored merchandise to fans on the promise that money will be donated to the American Cancer Society (ACS). However, the campaign has been criticized as misleading, especially the league's claim on its web site NFL.com. that 100 percent of the league's proceeds from the sales of pink products during the month will go to the ACS.[119] In actuality, the NFL only contributes approximately 5 percent of the proceeds from the sale of pink gear to the organization.[120] According to Ken Berger, CEO of Charity Navigator—an independent and non-profit organization that evaluates charitable campaigns for the purpose of transparency—any company that donates 25 cents or less on every dollar made through a charitable sponsorship is given a negative rating (actually 0 on a 100-point scale). According to Berger, "if people knew that only 5 percent of what they are giving was going to charity, I think people would seriously reconsider giving their money."[121] And while this would be justifiable if the league were more transparent and honest regarding its actual charitable donations—which is the case with companies involved in similar campaigns—Berger notes that "you have no way of knowing with NFL branded merchandise."[122] Actually, the NFL's average annual donation to ACS is $1.1 million, which, while appearing significant, accounted for only .01 percent of the $10 billion in revenue the league generated in 2013.[123]

Also under increasing scrutiny is the NFL's Crucial Catch breast cancer campaign accompanied by the slogan that "Annual Screening Saves Lives." According to Karuna Jaggar of the Think Before You Pink organization, a watchdog group for the breast cancer movement, "screening doesn't save lives and screening mammography ... is different from diagnostic mammography. The NFL has no business providing medical advice to women that is outdated, unproven, and misguided."[124] Worse yet, none of the money donated by the NFL actually funds any cancer research but, instead, goes toward the ACS's CHANGE program, which provides grants to community health facilities located within 100 miles of an NFL city to provide breast cancer and health information to women.[125] Not only does this exclude a vast majority of women, but the NFL makes no mention regarding how its donation is

Three. Does It Have to Be in the Game?

allocated by the ACS in its marketing and advertising campaigns. And, finally, the NFL's breast cancer initiative became "particularly important" after Commissioner Roger Goodell's initial apathy toward the Ray Rice domestic violence case and the NFL's poor handling of similar cases at the time pending in the league.[126] After companies began to question whether or not to sever their sponsorship with the NFL was beneficial regarding its treatment toward domestic violence—including Procter & Gamble, which broke off its sponsorship with the league— the breast cancer awareness campaign became a tool used to send the message that the NFL cared about women. This was not only important since 45 percent of the NFL's fan base are women[127] but also to refashion its image among the corporate public concerned that remaining affiliated with the league would render them guilty by association when it came to the issue of domestic violence.

The NFL is not the only league whose breast cancer awareness campaign has been denounced as a misleading and covert strategy to simply increase profits. MLB, for example, goes pink on Mother's Day in the name of breast cancer research and awareness and, in 2013, it became apparent that highlighting its sponsors was more important than the cause. Orioles outfielder Nick Markakis and Twins third baseman Trevor Plouffe ordered custom black bats featuring pink logos from manufacturer MaxBat to honor their mothers, who are breast cancer survivors. Since Louisville Slugger already had an exclusive agreement with MLB to provide the pink bats that players would use that day, Markakis and Plouffe were told they would not be allowed to use their own personalized bats. In response, Plouffe posted on Twitter that he was "seriously disgusted that a company would block awareness for Breast Cancer research so their brand can stand out."[128] Meanwhile, Markakis provided a more subdued and reserved response, stating that "it would mean a little more to me with my mom being a breast cancer survivor and be able to support her in that way. But I guess the rules are the rules right?"[129]

Returning to *MLB 15: The Show*, the presence of advertisements for non-profit organizations provides evidence that even sports video games are used to manufacture a particular image of the league. In this case, this involves supporting the MLB's mission to fashion itself as a socially conscious organization to rally public favor and attract consumer dollars to bolster its bottom line. This is not to suggest, however, that the MLB—or the NFL for that matter—has no concern for the various charitable causes it supports. Rather, the evidence suggests that these sponsorship relationships are motivated more by financial considerations than goodwill and sympathy.

Likewise, while the existence of sponsorships in professional sports may be economically necessary to a degree, the purpose here was to also highlight the significant amounts of control that sponsors have—and often demand—in their relationships with leagues, teams, and players. This is an important observation, especially within a political and cultural moment in which many citizens believe that companies, and consequently the free market, are more "democratic" and care more about "freedom" than government itself. Furthermore, as sponsors have leveraged more sports "screen time" to pitch their products and services, fans are regarded and treated as little more than consumers who matter only in their willingness to buy something. This has implications in terms of not only the relationship between fans and sports but also the integrity of sports themselves, which have become secondary to their capacity to sell.[130] And the effects extend beyond the world of sports into the political culture at large. Matthew P. McAllister, an expert on marketing and advertising and their effects on culture, argues that "the continued acceptance and visibility of advertising practices in sports helps to normalize commercial intrusion not just in athletics, but in ... other domains as well."[131]

The market may have a place in a democratic society, but the prevailing notion by some politicians and pundits is that *it should be everywhere*, including schools, universities, and the curriculums and majors they offer, the criminal justice system and privatized prisons, and the entire sports experience itself. And in the democratic culture at large, the increasing control of the "free market" is celebrated as a "moral" solution designed to save the United States from its perceived decadence and increasing "mediocrity." And while earlier generations would have thought of democracy more broadly—freedom of speech, the freedom to assemble, to vote, and otherwise be effective players in the political system—contemporary citizens increasingly can only think of shopping. And it does not help that they are constantly reminded, via politicians on the left and right, by advertisers and marketers, and even in cultural institutions such as sport itself, that this is all that really matters and is really left to do.

Four

"It's Not How You Play, but How You Look"
Sports Merchandising and Consumer Spectacle

When the University of Maryland football team upset the University of Miami (FL) in September of 2011, the game generated significant "buzz" on social media sites such as Twitter and national sports networks such as ESPN. According to Google Trends, the "University of Maryland" was the number one search term on Google following the school's surprising victory over the Hurricanes.[1] However, much of this had nothing to do with Maryland's triumph over its more esteemed ACC foe or its potential bowl opportunities at the end of the season but was about the "Maryland Pride" uniforms that the team wore on the field. For Under Armour, the company that designed the entire outfit, that was the point. The jerseys sported a bizarre and unsettling amalgamation of the Maryland black and yellow state flag interspersed with the school's colors—maroon and yellow—in a dizzying spectacle fit for a Twitter culture. Shawn Nestor, spokesman for the University of Maryland, remarked that "[Under Armour's] trying to increase their visibility and so are we."[2] And the ploy worked to great effect, as the "Maryland Pride" uniforms became the main story on NBC's *Today Show*, ABC's *Good Morning America*, and ESPN's *Outside the Lines*.[3] Even NBA All-Star LeBron James tweeted: "OH GOSH! Maryland uniforms#Ewwwwww!" while ESPN sports commentator Michael Wilbon called them "brilliantly ugly."[4]

Inspired by the bold uniform designs of the University of Oregon football team, the so-called "trailblazers of the unorthodox,"[5] outrageous uniforms are used to attract recruits, media attention, and generate revenue through merchandising. And not only are they becoming the norm in college sports; they are increasingly prevalent in the world of professional sports as well, especially in the minor leagues. The Florida Everblades, an affiliate with the NHL's Carolina Hurricanes and Tampa Bay Lightning, once wore kiwi-colored jerseys to celebrate the upcoming holidays that were deemed so ugly they could "[serve] as a suitable substitute for coal if you were looking to punish anyone."[6] Other examples included the Toledo Mud Hens sporting Chewbacca-themed uniforms for "Star Wars Night," the Lowell Spinners donning "ugly sweater" threads for its "Christmas in July" celebration, the Fresno Grizzlies and their Teenage Mutant Ninja Turtle–inspired jerseys for a night devoted to the movie, and the Kalamazoo Growlers wearing uniforms composed of fans' "selfies" for its "Salute to Selfie Night." While minor league sports often have to be more inventive to lure fans to games, major league sports are increasingly turning to similar promotions centered on a spectacular jersey design. For the upcoming NBA season, for example, the Indiana Pacers announced that they are going to wear "Hickory throwback jerseys" as a tribute to the film *Hoosiers* for select games throughout the year.[7] In a culture, especially among younger demographics, defined increasingly by a sense of irony and "lazy cynicism,"[8] so-called ugly uniforms have become not only "cool" but also a lucrative consumer fad.

As we will see, outrageous uniform designs are used to tap into a cultural ethos defined by the clichéd slogan that "life is a joke" in order to sell jerseys and other merchandise by pandering to the apathy and narcissism of youth consumer culture. Rhetorically, these uniform designs are used as a means of identifying with the values of a younger sports audience whose consumer habits are often sparked by a desire to express their edginess, individuality, and sense of rebelliousness. "Ugly" jersey designs and colors, by rejecting the aesthetic norms of good taste—however it may be defined at the moment—garner cultural currency with younger sports audiences attracted to their sense of playful nihilism. However, what is often lost is the degree to which rebellion has lost its political edge, reduced to a set of harmless consumer choices believed to express it. In other words, there is nothing particularly rebellious when it comes to "ugly" jerseys and designs; rather, they are part of a marketing ploy to sell more jerseys and hats in a way that further feeds the machine, not rages against it.

Four. "It's Not How You Play, but How You Look"

Traditionally, fans have purchased licensed merchandise as a sign and a gesture to express their loyalty to a particular team or sport.[9] Team owners also understood that anything worn on the field by players proved popular in merchandising shops, and many teams started introducing new uniform designs and colors, along with alternate jerseys and equipment worn on select game days, to increase sales. "Real" fans, knowing their status and die-hard loyalty to a team depended on keeping up with these latest fashions, constituted a significant market. However, teams and leagues also realized the added profitability that could come from reaching a wider consumer base of casual sports fans and non–sports fans alike. Many leagues began selling licensed merchandise in a near-infinite multitude of colors and designs, which, in many cases, significantly departed from a team's signature look. Thus, one could sport a red Yankees cap, as made famous (perhaps embarrassingly so) by Limp Bizkit lead singer Fred Durst, a pink Detroit Lions jersey, or camouflage Chicago Bulls warm-up pants. In the process, a team logo was being transformed into a brand, similar to Abercrombie & Fitch and Levi's. As Ron Bishop notes, "creating a brand means more to sports marketing executives than any real connection that fans have to their team."[10] Meanwhile, the athletes on the field, court, and ice would be used to market many of these variations as they donned alternate jerseys and retro garb. By expanding the variations of a team's look, owners and their merchandise machine could create a vast cornucopia of possible options in an effort to target the widest consumer base possible, whether they were fans or not.

It is important to emphasize that alternative jerseys are not an entirely new trend, even if they are more common and visible in today's sporting landscape than in decades past. Major League Baseball experimented with them beginning in the 1970s, led by infamous Oakland A's owner Charlie Finley, who was the first to introduce a mix-and-match combination of uniform styles and colors. These included green and gold jerseys and pants as well as a more traditional white uniform that the A's would wear for Sunday home games.[11] At the time, Finley realized he was starting a trend, correctly predicting that other teams would eventually follow his initiative. Of course, the motivation was not to sell jerseys—the merchandising market did not really exist outside of selling souvenirs—but to create uniforms that would look good on color television.[12] While these uniforms were offensive to baseball purists, many of whom assumed they represented another rude encroachment of the 1960s counterculture in sports,[13] the colorful duds created some of the most memorable, and at times infamous, uniforms in sports history. Even so, several players considered them effeminate and unmanly, a token betrayal of the entrenched masculine culture of baseball. For example, New York Yankees outfielder Mickey Mantle, the veritable symbol of boyish innocence and all-American sporting heroism, joked that "[the A's] should have come out of the dugout on tippy-toes, holding hands, and singing."[14]

By the 1980s, expressing one's status as a true fan had taken a decidedly commercial route, as one's loyalty or devotion to a team became dependent on one's willingness and ability to own licensed merchandise and apparel. This shift was influenced by similar trends occurring outside of sporting culture. The rock band Kiss virtually perfected the branding of its makeup, and lipstick, wearing look, putting their comic book likenesses on nearly everything, including board games, pinball machines, lunch boxes, and trading cards.[15] The purchasing of Kiss memorabilia was seen as solidifying one's membership into the "Kiss Army," the band's own fan club. Elsewhere, movies and television shows that targeted young children and adolescents, such as the *Star Wars* franchise, produced a near-endless array of action figures and branded memorabilia. The fact that many of these were toys designed to be played with created a vast collector market years later as die-hard *Star Wars* enthusiasts were paying top dollar for unopened action-figure packages, a rarity given that they were produced for kids.

During the same time period, the sports memorabilia and merchandising market grew, albeit on a modest and less commercially visible scale. American filmmaker Spike Lee began making public appearances wearing a Brooklyn Dodgers cap during the late 1980s, sparking a nationwide trend among African American youth and hip-hop artists drawn by the hat's retro appeal and authenticity.[16] Furthermore, it signified the possibility that sports merchandise bearing a throwback design could appeal to wider consumer audience, not just sports fans seduced by the ability to own a piece of history. At the time, the attraction of vintage-style hats and jerseys had, at best, a niche allurement. Their popularity was mostly limited to a small number of aging and nostalgic fans looking to collect remnants from a "lost age"

Four. "It's Not How You Play, but How You Look"

of purity and innocence believed to be forgotten in modern culture, while allowing them to relive their youth. Ted Spencer, former curator for the National Baseball Hall of Fame and Museum, remarked that "all the baby boomers have grown up. The [retro] hats are part of a childhood fantasy being fulfilled."[17] Meanwhile, Pete Capolino, the owner of Mitchell & Ness—which was producing the majority of retro style jerseys and hats at the time—indicated that "I figured my market was 35- to 75-year-old, conservative, college-educated, suburban white men. Somebody like me."[18]

As a sporting goods store located in Philadelphia, Mitchell & Ness once outfitted the Philadelphia Phillies and the Philadelphia Flyers during the 1950s but since had few other claims to prominence. When Capolino found a large abandoned supply of old flannel in a warehouse in the mid–1980s, however, he decided to use it to corner the retro market only beginning to develop.[19] Averaging $300 per retro jersey and stitched from authentic threads from the time period, the items were not only expensive; they were "uncool" in the eyes of anyone without gray hair. While it is difficult to imagine now, given the popularity of retro merchandise among a general legion of consumers, nostalgia had not yet found the right cultural vehicle to be considered edgy, trendy, or cool.

*****

The success of Universal Pictures' critically acclaimed *Field of Dreams*, which debuted in theatres nationwide in 1989, presented "Major League Baseball with a nostalgic antidote to bad publicity over sagging ratings ... [the] player lockout and the fallout from the Pete Rose and George Steinbrenner scandals."[20] While Rose's lifetime suspension from then MLB commissioner A. Bartlett Giamatti for placing bets on his team while managing the Cincinnati Reds is well known, less remembered was George Steinbrenner's own punishment. The Yankee owner was also handed a suspension, not for placing bets but for hiring the Mafia-connected Howie Spira to spy and dig up "dirt" on outfielder Dave Winfield, who signed a then-unprecedented 10-year contract with the Yankees in 1980. By the end of the 1980s, Winfield was ritualistically scapegoated for not delivering Steinbrenner a coveted World Series title. At one point, the fiery owner told the press, "I let Mr. October [Reggie Jackson] get away, and I got Mr. May, Dave Winfield. He gets his numbers when it doesn't count."[21] Major League Baseball's loss of integrity among its fan base amidst these scandals, not to mention their resentment toward escalating player salaries, signified a legitimate crisis for the national pastime.

Thus, *Field of Dreams* was released at a pivotal moment, spinning an emotional narrative that would renew faith in the "American game" and its cultural claims to innocence and purity.[22] Relying heavily on pastoral imagery, *Field of Dreams* centers on an Iowa corn farmer named Ray Kinsella who plows his crop to build a baseball field after a ghostly voice tells him to do so. Facing potential financial ruin, not to mention the questioning of his sanity by his wife, her brother and even himself, Kinsella eventually receives some degree of validation when the apparition of Shoeless Joe Jackson appears mysteriously in the outfield. Jackson is soon followed by other long-deceased players, including several members of the infamous 1919 Chicago White Sox who, like Jackson, received lifetime suspensions for their alleged involvement in throwing the World Series against the Cincinnati Reds. Kinsella later receives another message from the ghostly voice, which he interprets as meaning that he must travel to Boston to bring back author Terrance Mann to his farm in Iowa. However, the players on the field are only visible to those seemingly "pure" at heart—Ray Kinsella; his wife, Annie; their daughter; and Mann himself. And when Annie's brother appears with bankers, urging Ray to sell the farm due to his mounting debt, Mann urges Ray not to, stating:

> The one constant through all the years, Ray, has been baseball. America has rolled by like an army of steamrollers. It has been erased like a blackboard, rebuilt and erased again. But baseball has marked the time. This field, this game: it's part of our past, Ray. It reminds us of all that once was good and it could be again. Oh ... people will come Ray. People will most definitely come.[23]

The film ends with Kinsella's estranged father, a former minor league catcher, appearing in the outfield at an age seemingly prior to Ray having been born. After a few emotional exchanges, Ray and his father agree to play catch as the camera zooms upward to reveal a traffic jam several miles long of people making their journey to the field. The closing scene suggests American culture's yearning to return to a time of innocence and simple living, which, as Mann claims in his monologue, can be experienced most authentically through baseball. The game itself, as *Field of Dreams* attests, not only provides a connection to this romanticized past but also yields the only remaining hope that "all that once was good ... could be again."

Field of Dreams certainly was not the first baseball film that invited audiences to return to the game's mythic past in search of cultural renewal and redemption, but it was hard to imagine a baseball movie more popular. Major League Baseball, inspired by the film's resonance with audiences through nostalgia, found an effective public relations and marketing strategy designed to rehabilitate its image among fans. In one instance, Bonneville Media Communication produced a television ad featuring pitcher Nolan Ryan, then with the Texas Rangers, playing catch as a young boy with his father on their farm.[24] The ad, clearly inspired by *Field of Dreams*, reinforces baseball as a refuge for family values and innocence, symbolized through a game of catch between father and son in the proverbial Heartland. Similarly, MLB Properties marketed its Cooperstown Collection of retro jerseys and apparel with commercials featuring a father and son playing baseball foregrounded by black-and-white images of the game's great players and memorable moments.[25] The choice to use archival footage located the essence of baseball within its past before it was corrupted by free agency, ego, and, ironically, the same commercialism that MLB Properties was using to sell its jerseys. While neither *Field of Dreams* nor these marketing campaigns were the first to invoke nostalgia to a beleaguered public disenchanted with the culture wars and the demands of modern life, they did serve to "repaint the sport's image as an experience, an institution, to woo the busy family of the 1990s"[26]

Despite organized baseball originating in the city—the first organized game took place in June 1846 in Hoboken, New Jersey, located across the river from Manhattan—it has long occupied "the broad discursive field of pastoralism and America."[27] In other words, baseball signifies in the cultural imagination the expansive open fields of the American countryside characterized by its slow passage of time and quiet, tranquil lucidity. So central is this association that Cooperstown was chosen as the site of the National Baseball Hall of Fame, because the area embodied the agrarian purity attributed to the national game. Baseball officials even insisted that Abner Doubleday invented the game in Cooperstown, despite well-documented evidence that neither Doubleday nor Cooperstown was ever involved in the creation of the game.[28] Regardless, visits to the National Baseball Hall of Fame and the *Field of Dreams* baseball field, located in Dyersville, Iowa, are often described as "pilgrimages."[29] The rural confines of both not only reinforce "hegemonic narratives about country, family, and history"[30]; they also symbolize the conservative politics that contemporary nostalgia often invokes: an idealized past located before the 1960s, which were defined by the Civil Rights Movement, second-wave feminism, and the widespread protests of the Vietnam War.

Meanwhile, the Chicago White Sox made a concerted effort to "pitch the pure experience of historical baseball" by scheduling Saturday home games with postgame fireworks at an earlier time of 6:00 p.m. to attract families.[31] They were also the first major professional team to wear "throwback jerseys" during a regular season game as part of a "Turn Back the Clock" night during the club's final season at historic Comiskey Park.[32] Given their centrality in *Field of Dreams*, this seemed appropriate. In a July matchup against the visiting Milwaukee Brewers, the White Sox took the field in pin-striped uniforms modeled after those worn in 1917, while similarly styled replica caps were being sold for $38 apiece. White Sox first baseman Ron Kittle remarked, "It's not how you play the game but how you look. I look good in these. I'd like to wear them on the road, but they didn't make a set of greys."[33] Brewers outfielder Robin Yount commented that "if they can put people in the stands by doing this, great."[34] Fans in attendance were even encouraged to dress in period garb as part of the festivities, which included a monkey and an organ grinder to greet fans, slick-haired barbershop quartets, and bargain-priced popcorn at five cents a bag. With the help of cheap tickets, some priced as low as fifty cents, the game drew 40,666 fans to watch an otherwise hopelessly mediocre White Sox club struggling to fill seats at Comiskey Park during its final season.[35] So successful was the White Sox's "Turn Back the Clock" night that it was imitated by several major league clubs the following season, each aiming to capitalize on the lure of nostalgia to sell tickets.

The 1990s also witnessed a wave of kid-themed baseball movies such as *Rookie of the Year* (1993), *The Sandlot* (1993), *Angels of the Outfield* (1994), and *Little Big League* (1994). Each was a wondrous celebration of the purity and innocence associated with American childhood while suggesting that baseball appropriately embodied its character and spirit. While the films were clearly targeted to kids, they also resonated with adults because they stoked nostalgic remembrance

Four. "It's Not How You Play, but How You Look"

of one's own youth, its unapologetic capacity to dream big, and its unbounded enthusiasm. Unlike *The Bad News Bears* (1976) which dared to question whether children or baseball were as necessarily "innocent" as commonly believed,[36] these kid-friendly films generated a dose of Disneyfied rejuvenation designed to restore faith in American youth, the American Dream, and the national pastime. They also provided a momentary, yet effective, counterweight toward growing fan disillusionment toward baseball and other professional sports believed to be bastardized by free agency, greed, and selfishness.

All of these examples proved that the public had a voracious appetite for nostalgia that was not only profitable but also effective in rehabilitating the image of professional sports themselves through symbolic and actual tributes to the past. In 1992, the opening of the first "retro" ballpark, Oriole Park at Camden Yards, instantly transported fans back to a mythical past and was so popular, other major league teams lobbied to have a stadium just like it. Of course, the degree to which the past was truly as utopian as believed depended on who you asked. For African Americans and other racial minorities, not to mention women, it represented a time of open and legalized discrimination, unveiled prejudice, and secondary citizenship. This irony was not lost on Major League Baseball, which had its own past of organized discrimination to contend with. In an attempt to reconcile these competing narratives, the league simultaneously acknowledged its historical prejudice while celebrating its "progressive" commitment to change and equality.

On April 15, 2004, Major League Baseball celebrated Jackie Robinson Day for the first time to mark the anniversary of his major league debut in 1947.[37] Players took the field wearing Robinson's number 42, which had previously been retired by Commissioner Bud Selig in 1997 to commemorate the 50th anniversary of Robinson's historic feat. Meanwhile, the Chicago White Sox became the first team to honor the Negro Leagues in 1992 when they wore replica caps of the Chicago American Giants, a now annual tribute for the White Sox and other teams around the league. While the contributions of African Americans to baseball were certainly deserving of such recognition and commemoration, both celebrations were responses to the declining numbers of African Americans on the field and in the stands. For a nation that considered Robinson's breaking of the color barrier a significant civil rights achievement, declining black patronage and participation was an issue that needed to be addressed. Rob Galas, former vice president of the Chicago White Sox and creator of the first Negro League tribute, stated that "for years, people in baseball have asked where are all the black fans. Hopefully, this is a baby step toward the right direction of attracting more African American fans to enjoy our total entertainment package."[38] The nostalgia movement in Major League Baseball was only perpetuating one of the attributed causes of the declining numbers of African Americans involved in the sport, namely, that it was being perceived as a "white man's game."[39]

Of course, baseball was not the only sport having gone retro, as other professional leagues sought to capitalize on the profitability of nostalgia by sporting old-style uniforms. In 1996, ten NBA teams wore retro jerseys to commemorate the 50th anniversary of the NBA, while the NHL and NFL both celebrated their 75th anniversaries with teams wearing throwback uniforms during the 1991 and 1994 seasons, respectively.[40] Christopher Arena, the NBA's senior director of apparel, boasted emphatically that "we look at this as theatre ... there's a stage and the players are wearing costumes. Wearing the same uniform 41 times in a row can get a little boring."[41] Without question, the goal of these retro-infused gestures was to offer fans "memories for sale" in order to sell more licensed merchandise, especially of the vintage variety.[42] The players, meanwhile, would be used to model and advertise the merchandise during games.

*****

Retro jerseys had not yet acquired the cultural capital to become a seismic consumer trend, even in these early instances where throwback uniforms were part of a carefully crafted nostalgic experience. It was not until they had entered the world of hip-hop culture that retro jerseys and caps earned the near-unanimous reputation of being "cool." Even until the late 1990s, the market for vintage gear and apparel was largely confined to aging, college-educated white men who saw them as a means of reliving their past. This changed in 1998 when the rap duo Outkast appeared in music videos sporting retro-style jerseys such as the 1980s red, yellow, and orange "tequila sunrise" Astros jersey deemed by some to be one of the ugliest uniforms of all time.[43] Meanwhile, hip-hop artist Fabulous wrote a song appropriately named

Four. "It's Not How You Play, but How You Look"

"Throw Back" describing his retro jersey collection, which included a Jordan-era Bulls jersey that he noted hailed the days "when Mike [Michael Jordan] had hair and a gold chain."[44] By 2001, hip-hop and throwback style had fully collided, the latter becoming an almost obligatory aesthetic in rap music videos, concerts, and television appearances. Reebok even went so far as to sign endorsement deals with hip-hop titans Jay-Z and 50 Cent to promote athletic shoes that featured their names. Russ Bengston, editor in chief of *Slam Magazine*, claimed that "what Reebok figured out was that personality was more important than performance when it comes to athletic shoes. So who needs Shaq [Shaquille O'Neill] or Kobe [Bryant] when you have an unathletic rapper? It's all about image."[45]

Indeed, image was becoming the defining standard of personhood and individuality not only in hip-hop but elsewhere in an American culture increasingly drawn to the superficial and spectacular. Yet the retro jersey becoming a tangible symbol of mainstream consumer "cool" was due to two other notable forces: the crisis of authenticity in hip-hop and the marketing efforts of Mitchell & Ness. By the late 1990s, rap music had attained mainstream respectability, as evidenced by Lauryn Hill becoming the first hip-hop artist to win the "Album of the Year" category at the 1999 Grammy Awards.[46] This was followed by Hill appearing on the cover of *Time* magazine—a relative staple in doctors' offices throughout the country—as part of its "Hip-Hop Nation" issue, accompanied with the caption noting how rap had "changed America."[47] Such accolades polarized the hip-hop community as underground artists lamented that such cultural acceptance betrayed rap's countercultural ethos while those who had achieved commercial success insisted they were not selling out.[48] The slogan of who, in fact, was "keeping it real" became the measurement in the battle taking place over how hip-hop should be both represented and defined.

When *The Source* magazine ran a cover story on Puff Daddy (renaming himself later P. Diddy), a hip-hop artist whose music videos had become standard fare on MTV, critics were outraged by his comments citing M.C. Hammer as a musical influence. Hammer, hip-hop's version of *Leave it to Beaver*, was viewed as a prepackaged phony used by the music industry to reach younger music fans through hip-hop without offending the sensibilities of their parents. Adults, many of whom were frightened by the possibility of their kids listening to "gangsta rap," found Hammer a suitable compromise with a musical genre becoming increasingly popular among American youth. Hammer's "hits," including "(U) Can't Touch This" and "Too Legit to Quit," were deemed family friendly enough that even Grandma would approve. The irony, however, was not lost on M.C. Hammer, who would later try to cultivate a more aggressive image in an attempt to win over a growing audience gravitating toward the more hard-core leanings of gangsta rap. While he achieved a modicum of success with his later works, his reputation remained shackled by the trappings of his earlier recordings. The fact that Puff Daddy apparently loved Hammer communicated the message that perhaps he understood nothing of rap music to begin with.

The only hip-hop artist arguably to enjoy a worse fate at the time due to his commercial success was Vanilla Ice, whose lyrics were laced with references to his "white boy" status in a predominately African American rap culture. Viewed as an attempt by the music industry to put a white face on a black musical art form in order to be palatable to mainstream audiences, Ice, too, became a joke. Even preschoolers knew the lyrics to "Ice, Ice Baby" by heart and, while the song references a drive-by shooting, Ice's credibility had as much edge as Disney and Mickey Mouse. Like Hammer, Ice was seen as too soft to have the street credibility to be considered an authentic hip-hop artist. Bemoaned by purists as lacking the necessary life experiences to be considered a real rapper, Ice began touting to the press that he was a "rough and tumble" bad boy from the "mean streets of Miami."[49] When it was found out that Vanilla Ice was born Rob Van Winkle in an affluent Dallas suburb, Ice firmly cemented his place in hip-hop's Hall of Shame.

However, by the late 1990s hard-core rap artists such as Ice Cube, Ice-T, Dr. Dre, and Snoop Dogg were even becoming household names. However, the fact that they were still able to incite moral panic among parents and politicians indicated perhaps that commercial success did not necessarily compromise authenticity. Nonetheless, *Time*'s acknowledgment of hip-hop's cultural force was enough to prompt questions regarding whether rap music had strayed too far from its roots and whether its subversive character was mere image or fact. Originating in the Bronx during the 1970s, rap music was the voice of African American culture, detailing its experiences with racism, discrimination, economic disenfranchisement, and alienation from the

Four. "It's Not How You Play, but How You Look"

white mainstream.[50] Even Chuck D of the rap group Public Enemy referred to it as the "CNN for black people" that spoke of issues largely ignored by the mainstream media.[51] As hip-hop became increasingly acceptable, many within the hip-hop community feared that commercial success meant loss of control to the corporate suits in the music industry. When artists began wearing retro apparel, mostly drawn from the 1970s and 1980s in music videos, it represented a symbolic homage to hip-hops roots from the same era. Tacitly, throwback jerseys suggested that one could be a famous rap artist without forgetting the roots from which hip-hop sprang—a conviction largely expressed through style, if not always substance.

Yet this was not an organic trend of hip-hop artists suddenly deciding that what was once old was cool but rather a part of Mitchell & Ness'—the leading manufacturer in retro apparel—marketing strategy. In 2000, the company hired Reuben "Big Rube" Harley based on his connections with the hip-hop community, which he reasoned Mitchell & Ness could exploit to sell more product. Harley, a longtime customer of the company, approached its owner, Peter Capolino, with a bold proposition to help him increase sales, remarking, "You hire me, and I'll make sure your garments are on all the right people," adding that rap artists "don't know about you. They think you some old white guy from Philly."[52] As the company's new marketing director, Harley understood that persuading hip-hop artists to wear throwback uniforms and hats would be a guaranteed sell:

> When I get something in, I determine how big a video is going to be, then I provide the garment for that person. Like J' Lo's [Jennifer Lopez's] new video with LL Cool J. I put that lime-green 1934 White Sox jacket on him; now everybody wants it.[53]

Harley's plan worked, and according to Capolino, "in 2000 and 2001, my jerseys started popping up on MTV, BET, and VH1. I think I had them in 41 stores nationally as of 2001. I now have over 1,000 stores nationally."[54] In 2000, Mitchell & Ness had revenues in excess of $2.8 million, which increased to $23 million by 2003, while the sales of competitor Hardwood Classic witnessed a 300 percent increase between 2002 and 2003, "making ... [retro apparel] one of the fastest-growing revenue streams in the [sports merchandising] business."[55] What also became apparent was that the market for retro apparel was not limited to sports fans alone but a broader consumer base often motivated by keeping up with a trend, rather than expressing themselves as sports fans. In 2004, while television ratings for the NBA were on the decline, sales of licensed merchandise increased by an astounding 154 percent, which topped the even more popular NFL.[56] Much of this new revenue was generated by the sale of throwback jerseys, which, through their connection with hip-hop culture, were seemingly becoming the most sought-after licensed merchandise available.

However, while retro apparel was arguably becoming a fashion trend, it comprised only 10 percent, for example, of the NBA's merchandising revenues at the height of their popularity.[57] Much of this may have had to do with how expensive throwback jerseys and hats were rather than a lack of demand, which, by Capolino's own account, had reached a fever pitch. Even institutional players in professional sports were acknowledging throwback attire's popularity and cultural impact. Howard Smith, Major League Baseball's Vice President for Merchandising, claimed, "I'm telling you, ... [retro jerseys are] such an explosion. We haven't witnessed a trend this far-reaching in our business in a long time."[58] Bruce Jennings, NHL Group Vice President of Consumer Products Marketing, noted that retro apparel "was still a niche program. But it's also something that's very, very consumer driven."[59]

As mentioned previously, uniforms and hats worn by players are big sellers in souvenir shops and on online websites, so in the aftermath of the retro "explosion" teams found that they could further fuel demand for them—and simultaneously interest in their sport—by having their teams were throwback jerseys more often. In 2002, Major League Baseball teams wore retro uniforms for an entire week, perhaps hoping that their popularity might gain the league a few more fans. Shortly thereafter, the NHL urged its teams to wear throwback gear—which it acknowledged was an urban fashion staple—for some of their games during the 2003–2004 season in hopes that more African Americans would watch hockey.[60] And, of course, the NHL speculated that it would be a useful strategy for boosting its own merchandising sales by capitalizing on the popularity of vintage NBA and MLB uniforms and hats, "which have been deemed fashionable."[61] Meanwhile, the NBA teams in 2002–2003 wore "Hardwood Classics Jerseys" for designated games following the positive response the Los Angeles Lakers received after sporting vintage Minneapolis Lakers uniforms for a matchup the

Four. "It's Not How You Play, but How You Look"

previous season.[62] Not to be left out, NFL teams playing in the annual Thanksgiving football doubleheader also went retro, perhaps to market the gear the day before the biggest holiday shopping day of the season.[63]

Mitchell & Ness, the company at the forefront of the retro phenomenon, maintained its allegiance to sports history rather than capitalizing on a fad it helped create. In 2002, owner Peter Capolino insisted that "I do not create sports fashion. I'm not Nike or Reebok. What I do is re-create totally accurate history."[64] Yet, in a later interview after retro style had become a visible symbol in popular culture, he iterated that "we're not making money because of history. It's because of hip-hop."[65] As retro sports apparel led the way in pioneering the belief that licensed merchandise could be considered "fashionable" capable of reaching a broader consumer market, wearing a team hat or jersey was no longer a reliable symbol of fandom. It could merely be a matter of wanting to "look good" for people who knew little, if not nothing, about sports. Art Bowser, assistant manager of a Mitchell & Ness store in Philadelphia, recounted, "I had a kid looking at a Boston Celtics jersey and he asked me, 'Who's this guy?' It was Larry Bird's jersey. I felt kinda old."[66] For other consumers hopping on the trend-driven bandwagon, the "uglier" the retro jerseys, the more popular and sought after they were by young consumers. Capolino noted that his top sellers were a Dave Winfield San Diego Padres jersey from the 1970s, claiming, "It's that ugly mustard and brown, but the youth of America loves it," while Nolan Ryan's 1980s Astros jersey, "one of the ugliest jerseys ever made," was Capolino's most popular offering.[67]

At risk of overly analyzing the point, retro jerseys were popular not only because popular hip-hop artists wore them but also because, in many cases, they were in fact deemed ugly and tacky. Thus, they tapped into the zeitgeist of youth culture well noted not for its propensity for irony and detachment, which a *New York Times* writer noted "is the primary mode by which daily life is dealt."[68] It is a grand refusal seemingly against the Establishment but marked by the inability and even unwillingness to take much of anything seriously. Even advertising practices increasingly mock their own conventions, gaining credibility among their audiences by first announcing, ironically, that they have no credibility. Some adolescents wear Justin Bieber T-shirts not because they like his "music" but because, ironically, they do not. It is often a culture of style without substance, opinions without convictions, and rebellion without a clearly defined target. And while it could be a rational response to the overexposure of popular culture courtesy of the Internet and social media, the ironic ethos of youth culture represents the values of consumerism being carried to their logical endpoint. In the world of retro apparel, it meant manufacturers scouring the annals of sports history to find "uglier" and more regrettable-looking uniforms to reproduce for sale.

Today, professional teams' wearing retro jerseys is no longer an "event" but part of the commonplace cycling through of alternate jerseys that they undergo during the course of a season. Doing so can be quite profitable when it comes to selling the "what players wear during the game" merchandise in team shops: the more options, the more money. And while the retro apparel fad has noticeably waned over the years, it continues to influence the design of team uniforms and styles in the contemporary moment. The ideology of the ugly uniform was used to identify with younger fans—who as mentioned before are less interested in sport than previous generations—make money, attain national visibility, and eventually be used for teams to go "viral" on social media.

*****

The most telling example of this new value system can be found in college football after the University of Oregon gained national prominence not from winning games but from sporting bold and daring uniforms on the field. After the university negotiated a licensing deal with Nike—whose co-founder is Oregon alum Phil Knight—to outfit the school's athletic teams in 1996, the modern uniform makeover had begun.[69] Since the establishment of the University of Oregon in 1894, its football program had a reputation for mediocrity, even after appearing in the Rose Bowl in 1995 and the Cotton Bowl in 1996. After the university's licensing deal with Nike, its creative director, Todd Van Horne, noted that "nothing [was] off the table" when it came to uniform designs, including football helmets with glass beads retailing at $2,400 a gallon.[70] Nike's football design also included a dizzying array of uniform combinations such as neon yellow, gray, green, and white jerseys, helmets, socks, and shoes. The initial reception by the fan public included everything from shock, embarrassment, and wonderment to

Four. "It's Not How You Play, but How You Look"

cheers and disgust. Regardless of the tenor of individual opinion, Oregon teams were regarded as the "undisputed champions of the 21st century's attention economy."[71] Without question, Nike had transformed the reputation of Oregon's football team through a commitment to unapologetic flair and image. And while the retro movement had not fully matured in sports, nor was its association with hip-hop yet made, Oregon's bold uniforms anticipated a trend that would remain clear years later through the throwback trend: bold, perhaps ugly, uniforms are a "hit" with younger fans.

Nike and the University of Oregon's marketing plan was designed to slice through the visibility clutter of college football while appealing to a younger generation of recruits and fans through the attention-grabbing effect of bold uniform designs. Journalist Mike Tanier wrote that "these uniforms, if they make traditionalists wince and sportswriters snicker, do seem to excite recruits and move younger fans to break out their credit cards."[72] And as the University of Oregon became the center of the national sporting public's attention, the school was able to sign recruits who years previously would have gone elsewhere. Within a few years after finalizing its deal with Nike, the University of Oregon had emerged as a college football powerhouse largely due to their uniforms. Michael Smith of the *SportsBusiness Journal* noted that Nike's strategy was "to build football into a national power largely on the strength of marketing and branding."[73] For some, the University of Oregon uniforms signified the crass commercialism increasingly overtaking sports, sacrificing integrity for spectacle in order to sell products. Others suggested that Oregon was merely tapping into the ethos of a younger demographic, who value almost any gesture designed for attention-grabbing effect. One journalist wrote that "if no one knows your product exists, there is no demand for your product, and at the end of the day it's about 18 year old kids. The uniforms are the key ingredient to getting bodies there, and the bodies are what win you football games."[74]

The outrageous uniform trend that began with the University of Oregon altered some of the criteria by which football teams would be judged. While the traditional variables such as wins and losses, national rankings, conference prestige, and the difficulty of one's schedule would remain important, universities would also be measured by their status and reputation *as a brand*. According to a 2010 ESPN sports poll that asked Division I football players to rank the school with the best uniforms, the University of Oregon topped the list with 53.7 percent of the vote.[75] One Big Ten football player, speaking anonymously, stated that "I don't even have to think about that one. I almost wanted to transfer to [the University of Oregon] just for those uniforms."[76] Boise State linebacker Derrell Acrey, meanwhile, claimed "every team wants to be like … [the University of Oregon]. If we could, we'd change uniforms every year."[77] As evidenced by these comments, the branding mentality initiated by Nike and the University of Oregon had become part of the discourse of college football. Team uniforms not only had become a fashionable commodity designed to sell but also were part of a school's recruiting pitch to prospective players. Dave Sheinin, a columnist for *The Washington Post,* contended that "such a thing would have been absurd just a few years ago, when most teams had two uniforms—home and away—and all anyone needed was a pocket schedule to know which would be worn on a given Saturday … if they cared at all."[78]

Indeed, uniforms had become validated as a legitimate part of the entire sporting spectacle, equally newsworthy as the action taking place on the field. In 2010, Nike held a press conference where they unveiled its new uniforms for Ohio State, the University of Miami, Boise State, Alabama, and Oregon State.[79] During the carefully orchestrated "pseudo-event," the company also announced its line of "one-off uniforms" that would be worn for specific games only. For its November matchup against Mississippi State, Alabama sported uniforms with houndstooth-shaped numbers to honor former coach Paul "Bear" Bryant. Meanwhile, the November meeting between West Virginia and Pittsburgh would feature both teams in "Backyard Brawl" jerseys to signify and celebrate their rivalry. And while Nike claimed it was honoring tradition, it was actually branding tradition in order to sell more replica jerseys and other kinds of apparel. And Nike was not alone, as Under Armour and Adidas found that creating uncanny and outrageous uniforms for the teams they outfitted not only pleased many universities and fans but also was an effective means by which to advertise themselves. But in a sport that often purports to respect tradition by uniting alumni and current students through the comradeship of homecoming weekends, school pride, and storied rivalries, some contended that Nike, Under Armour, and Adidas were betraying that spirit for the sake of profit.

Four. "It's Not How You Play, but How You Look"

In September of 2011, Notre Dame and the University of Michigan faced off wearing "throwback" jerseys. Critics quickly pointed out, however, that the Michigan uniforms "resembled nothing the team had worn in the past."[80] In other instances, schools such as the University of Georgia, Navy, Army, and Michigan State had taken the field in so-called futuristic uniforms, arguably to justify bold uniform styles that deviate from their traditional look. Even sports journalists, many of whom regard criticizing the institutional powers of sports as a betrayal of their job description, were writing that college football uniforms had become too "outrageous."[81] Yet, by 2015, college football uniforms have become part of the preseason hype for the upcoming season, as teams' daring designs become fodder for either criticism or celebration. And while historically team uniforms were hardly ever scrutinized by the mass media, much less the subject of public fascination, they are increasingly *the* story. And as uniform press conferences become part of the annual ritual of college football, covered all too willingly by a complicit sporting press, outrageous uniforms are incentivized through attention. And as teams additionally compete through uniform styles and consequently are rewarded for doing so by getting the sports coverage they want, the uniforms become more outrageous.

For 2015, the University of Oregon teased the possibility of wearing glow-in-the-dark uniforms for the upcoming season while Notre Dame announced it would be donning "Green Monster" uniforms for its game at Fenway Park.[82] But in an era of the increasing and evolving commercialism of sports, and the primacy of the image in our media-saturated culture, outrageous uniform designs signify the values and attitude of the contemporary moment.

The retro phenomenon in sports and hip-hop validated the "importance" of image as an effective strategy for achieving visibility in a cluttered sports media marketplace. As a matter of fact, "people today are the most media-saturated and media-engaged people in history."[83] Not only are there more media options available for audiences to consume, but the Internet has allowed them to become active producers of media content courtesy of personal blogs, social media outlets such as Twitter, and video sites like YouTube. Even the "selfie" serves as evidence of a culture poised to always think of itself as a performer before an audience of its own. Within this context, the currency of an image is not determined by any degree of substance but rather its ability to attract the attention of an increasingly elusive audience. So, while professional and college teams regularly alternate uniform designs to boost merchandising sales, they are also conforming to the logic of what Thomas H. Davenport and John C. Beck refer to as the "attention economy."[84]

*****

In 2014, the San Diego Padres selected Heisman Trophy winner Johnny Manziel in the 28th round in the June Major League Baseball Draft after he made an appearance at Petco Park for batting practice.[85] While major league teams had previously signed football players for public relations purposes—such as Seattle Seahawks quarterback Russell Wilson's acquisition by the Texas Rangers in the 2013 Rule 5 Draft—all were considered legitimate prospects, unlike Manziel, who had not played since high school.[86] Several sportswriters speculated that the Padres' drafting of the former Texas A&M standout was motivated to sell team merchandise and attract media attention for a team that, at the time, had no star players:

> What is clear is that the Padres organization made a decision to bet on merchandise rather than gamble on talent. Manziel already has the most popular NFL rookie jersey and he had the most popular NFL jersey overall for several weeks after the draft. If he can move some San Diego units, that would represent a victory for a team with few charismatic stars (Seth Smith anyone?). The choice also makes the club part of the baseball conversation, an achievement for the guys in the front office.[87]

Other writers, in equally celebratory tone, applauded the Padres' decision to draft Manziel as a "ready-made business opportunity" and that "even if he doesn't intend on playing baseball in the future, start printing those Manziel t-shirts and jerseys anyway! We smell money."[88] Unsurprisingly, the story went viral through social media, including a photo that circulated around Twitter of Padres' 2011 first-round draft pick Travis Jankowski wearing a Manziel customized jersey with the Heisman winner's name and number on the back.[89]

Meanwhile, the Padres were accused of making a mockery of the baseball draft in picking a player whom, aside from one batting practice appearance at Petco Park, the team had never seen play baseball. General manager Josh Byrnes countered by claiming that players taken that late in the draft are merely filler "so that you can have teams that help

Four. "It's Not How You Play, but How You Look"

your prospect play," adding that "there's a lot of favor drafts, family members, etc., so I'm the last person to make a mockery of the draft."[90] While Padres president and chief executive officer Mike Dee admitted the Manziel "brand" had some "cachet to it," he and Byrnes insisted that drafting Manziel was legitimately motivated by the possibility of him playing professional baseball.[91] Unsurprisingly, Manziel did not sign a contract with the Padres and his lackluster performance with the Browns since then, coupled with a stint in rehab, meant that the merchandising gravy chain expected to flow from his association with the Padres never reached fruition.

In an age in which social media is king and value is determined in the currency of Facebook "likes" and Twitter "retweets," teams become more desperate to break through the clutter well evident within a media-saturated culture. Creating more bold and daring uniform designs, even regularly revisiting retro chic, caters to the value system of this modern environment. In doing so, teams are relating to younger fans—and a good many adults as well—who identify with the branding logic behind the attention-seeking motivations clearly expressed in these gestures. As critic William Deresiewicz states:

> The camera has created a culture of celebrity; the computer is creating a culture of connectivity. As the two technologies converge—broadband tipping the web from text to image; social networking sites spreading the mesh of interconnection ever wider—the two cultures betray a common impulse. Celebrity and connectivity are both ways of becoming known. This is what the contemporary self wants. It wants to be recognized, wants to be connected: It wants to be visible. If not to the millions, on *Survivor* or Oprah, then to the hundreds, on Twitters or Facebook. This is the quality that validates us, this is how we become real to ourselves—by being seen by others. The great contemporary terror is anonymity. If Lionel Trilling was right, if the property that grounded the self in Romanticism was sincerity, and in modernism was authenticity, then in postmodernism it is visibility.[92]

In an age in which everyday individuals see themselves increasingly as their own "personal brand"[93]—goaded undoubtedly by the norms of social media to do so—the length to which sports organizations will go to gain attention is something that fans relate to because they are often doing the same themselves. By doing so, these institutions are embracing this ethic in order to persuade them to buy the product, by either watching the games, purchasing sponsorship products, or consuming licensed merchandise. Kenneth Burke's theory of identification is pertinent here in which he explains "you persuade a man only insofar as you can talk his language by gesture, speech, tonality, order, image, attitude, idea, *identifying* your ways with his."[94] As sports organizations learned through the retro movement that exploded in the late 1990s, embracing the ethos of popular culture is effective in selling team merchandise. Sports, long believed to be counterweights to the "moral ravaging" of popular culture, have instead embraced it for the interests of profitability and relevance.

Five

Sports, Consumer Culture and the Prospects for Change

The purpose of this book was to expose the shallowness and superficiality of the increasing commercialization of the major professional sports and how it impacts their relationship with fans. Without question, the consumer culture ethic found in sports both reflects and influences social, political, and cultural changes occurring in the contemporary moment, specifically the further transformation of American democracy into a "consumer's republic."[1] The fusion of economics and politics, not to mention the political influence that large moneyed interests wield in elections and legislation, has led to the reduction of citizens to mere consumers. As the spirit of shopping has come to define notions of "freedom" and "democracy" as their fulfillment par excellence, an ideology for the benefit of capitalism is not only created but also naturalized as common sense. It has become so embedded in the cultural psyche that even suggesting the conflation between democracy and consumerism as a problem is regarded as preposterous, perhaps even elitist.[2]

Yet, in the world of sports, this union demonstrates that it leads to several undesirable outcomes, namely, the trivialization of sports themselves as fans are reduced to the status of consumers. Specifically, this means new stadiums that most cannot afford to attend, emblazoned with advertisements that clutter the landscape, more expensive and exclusive amenities, and stadium names referencing a company that often could care less about sports except to exploit their popularity for profit. This also means fantasy sports taking on the character of gambling as a sports-marketing tactic and sports video games being used to naturalize the relationship between sports and their sponsors. Meanwhile, the constantly changing uniforms that teams were on the field, court, or ice are used to advertise themselves in merchandise shops and shopping malls and, hence, are ultimately disposable when a new look must be developed to replenish demand for jerseys and hats. While no pre-commercial utopia has ever existed in professional sports, it certainly does *feel* that way when the past is contrasted with the present, the latter resembling a virtual wasteland of commercial messages persistently bombarding fans with the imperative to consume. Fans today, seemingly, have no other usable or productive purpose than to be a willing audience and a complicit actor to these messages.

Meanwhile, there are organizations dedicated to reforming professional sports, their relationship to fans, and their contribution to public life. The League of Fans (LF) was created by political activist Ralph Nadar and its stated mission is to "encourage social and civic responsibility in the sports industry and culture."[3] At the foundation of their ideological and policy commitments is a belief that professional and amateur sports constitute a public trust that should embrace a broader purpose other than mere profitability. Recently, the LF has challenged the NCAA to replace the current one-year-renewal athletic scholarship policy with a five-year guaranteed scholarship while urging universities to better align college sports with the academic principles of higher education.[4] They have also advocated for the elimination of public taxpayer subsidies for new stadium construction as well as the creation of a regulatory body known as the National Sports Commission (NSC) to encourage access and participation in sport for all citizens.[5] The NSC's motive would be to reverse a larger cultural trend in which an increasingly number of Americans are engaging sports more as spectators rather than as participants. The fact that a record number of 82 million Americans are estimated to be physically inactive leads to escalating health-care costs and diminished life expectancies because of the general lack of exercise in our sedentary culture.[6] Without question, professional and amateur organizations prefer the spectator engagement with sports because it better fulfills their commercial and marketing objectives. If more fans were actually playing sports rather than watching them, this would possibly, on the one hand,

Five. Sports, Consumer Culture and the Prospects for Change

diminish the audience that sports organizations are expected to deliver to their corporate sponsors. On the other hand, one could argue that encouraging more people to play sports would subsequently create more sports fans likely to follow sports in which they are actively engaged.

While encouraging more physical activity seems common sense, the current commercial model of professional and amateur sports requires a relatively inactive culture encouraged to spend more of its time immobilized in front of a television screen, iPad, or smartphone. These are the primary communication systems used by sports organizations to deliver their commercial messages in furtherance of their marketing and advertising strategies. Thus, every effort is made to intensify fans' engagement with these systems. In 2013, the NFL announced that all stadiums had to comply with newly minted standards for Wi-Fi capabilities set forth by the league by the end of the 2014 season.[7] With this applauded as a "fan-friendly" gesture designed to cater to a cell phone–addicted culture, the NFL claimed it would provide fans with more bandwidth to upload photos and videos, check fantasy stats, provide more access to instant replays, and "offer fans in-stadium the same technological connectivity they enjoy at home."[8] Of course, the primary reason for the Wi-Fi upgrade in NFL stadiums would be to track fans' data usage patterns to sell to current or potential sponsors while sending stadium-specific advertising directly to their phones. Michelle McKenna-Doyle, the NFL's chief information officer, stated that the policy gives the NFL "analytics for what our fans our doing, which leads us to more marketing."[9] Meanwhile, Chuck Berger, CEO of Extreme Networks, which would be the major provider of in-stadium Wi-Fi, claimed that "the franchises in the NFL are doing this not only to allow you to upload selfies, but to take advantage of the commercial opportunity to send you promotional information" such as "Tom Brady just threw a touchdown pass. Twenty-five percent off his jersey at the logo wear store. Things like that."[10]

There are no penalties for team's not upgrading their Wi-Fi capabilities before the proposed deadline and several have postponed doing so in order to either honor existing contractual agreements with wireless providers or use the NFL policy as a justification for a new facility.[11] Regardless, the league "expects that by implementing these standards, teams in municipally owned stadiums will be able to use those benchmarks as leverage in talks over upgrading Wi-Fi."[12] In other words, the cost of upgrading NFL stadiums to meet the league's new Wi-Fi standards would not be covered by team owners but rather the taxpayers. As a matter of fact, not only are public dollars being used to finance the construction of most sports stadiums, but some teams have leases that additionally charge the public to finance upgrades if enough teams have them elsewhere—known as the "state of the art" clause.[13]

In Cincinnati, the Bengals have a lease with Hamilton County that states that if 14 other NFL teams have a "state of the art" amenity or technology then taxpayers are *required* to pay for it to be installed in Paul Brown Stadium.[14] This even includes the city being tasked with purchasing a "holographic replay system" for the Bengals should it ever be invented. Currently, the team is installing a new $10 million scoreboard with Hamilton County residents financing three-quarters of the cost. This is added to the already-escalating debt service for new Paul Brown Stadium, which accounted for 11 percent of the county's general fund in 2008, which increased to 16.4 percent in 2010. In St. Louis, stadium financing expert Neil deMause estimated that it would cost the city $36 million a year to keep the Edward Jones Dome—the home of the Rams—a "first tier facility."[15] Owners claim that unless their stadiums are routinely upgraded to include the latest technological innovations, fads, and gadgets, ticket sales will be negatively impacted. As the NFL has stated in reference to its Wi-Fi policy and the consequences if teams do not comply, "if they don't do this, there will be poor-performing ticket sales. They will suffer enough consequences by not doing this."[16]

All of this is driven by the imperatives of consumer culture, and the consequences reduce the status of sports from something more meaningful and compelling to a mere vehicle used for teams and their sponsors to extract more revenue from fans by constantly treating them as consumers. As a matter of fact, the individuals, companies, and organizations that are increasingly purchasing teams are not doing so because of any sentimental love of sports but rather because the popularity and visibility of sports translates into easy profit. For them, sports are merely another business within their thick portfolio of corporate holdings and stock options and they are only motivated by generating as much revenue through sports as possible. Despite the

Five. Sports, Consumer Culture and the Prospects for Change

pervasive rhetoric that greedy athletes are ruining sports by virtue of their astronomical salary demands, the fact that owners manage to meet these demands is evidence of how much revenue they are generating in the first place. Even teams that are supposedly "broke" can be sold to an interested ownership group for a significant amount of profit. In 2011, Los Angeles Dodgers owner Frank McCourt filed for bankruptcy and, after receiving a loan from Commissioner Bud Selig to allegedly cover his operating expenses, managed to then sell the team to the Guggenheim Group for a *record* $2.15 billion. As part of the negotiated deal, McCourt would make $1.5 billion in profit from the sale while transferring $412 million of debt to the new ownership group—not bad for a team McCourt had been claiming was "going under."[17]

Far from Shakespeare's famous observance that "all the world's a stage," contemporary economic thought conceives of the entire world as simply a market and all of us as "merely consumers." Of course, team owners, despite the greed that drives their worldview, are hardly to blame, because they operate within a social and political context that fosters their behavior by elevating the status of the market and its ethos as an unquestionable good.[18] Neoliberalism presumes that capitalism should operate without constraint, and the subsequent penetration of the market into ever more intimate facets of everyday life is the outcome of this ideology. Thus, it should not be surprising that in fans' engagement with sports, more of that experience is mediated by commercialism and the imperative to buy something sold by someone somewhere. As a matter of fact, an economic system whose players desire greater degrees of profit would eventually create a situation, seemingly arrived at in the contemporary moment, where the logic of market thinking would dominate the entirety of cultural, social, and political life.[19] And it is without question that the *Citizens United* Supreme Court decision is a reflection of this new, all-encompassing reality and the further shattering of limitations of the market in the political system.

This book was not designed to vilify the act of buying goods and services, to make consumers feel guilty or ignorant, or to suggest that sports have no redeemable character worth watching, loving, or supporting. As far as capitalism goes, there is a significant difference between a small, locally owned business connected to a community and its people and a large corporation operated by a rabid business-class coalition who will probably never visit the towns in which most of their companies operate. Rather, the purpose was to understand, through sports themselves, how reducing the vast meaningfulness of life to the mere pursuit of money and consumer goods is an ultimately self-defeating proposition. In their modern commercial form, the experience of sports that owners and other institutional players are delivering to fans is founded exactly on this vision. As a matter of fact, the version of democracy hawked daily to citizens is a hypercommodified world in which the only "meaningful" choices people have are between Coke and Pepsi, Nike and Reebok, and Sprint and Verizon. Reacting to Frito-Lay's sponsorship of the 2007 Tostitos BCS National Championship football game between Ohio State and Florida, media expert Matthew McAllister noted that "Frito-Lay's definition of the good life, as well as that of other advertisers, commercially influenced media organizations, and sports organizations, is not the same definition of the 'public good' that we should embrace in a vibrant and balanced democratic society."[20] If the rampant commercialism of sports makes them feel hollow and superficial, it is precisely because the very ethos of consumer culture itself offers a world that promises much more than it ever delivers, defined by image rather than substance, and converts being into the pursuit of having. In relation to democracy, earlier generations certainly did understand that while the market should have a place, they were also keenly aware of the perils that befall when it becomes every place. And however imperfectly democracy has fulfilled its goals, especially in its treatment toward the poor, the working classes, racial minorities, women, and so on, it rested on a definition of the public good that certainly had more in mind than simply shopping.

One way to counter the rampant commercialization of sports and its corresponding negative effects would be to transfer ownership of teams to the public. This is similar to the recommendations of sportswriter and critic Dave Zirin, who advocated the drafting of a "fan bill of rights" where local municipalities through eminent domain could seize control of a team if it is operated against the public's interest.[21] For those who may argue that such a solution is impractical and that the public is incapable of operating a team as effectively as a private owner, the case of the Green Bay Packers proves otherwise. Currently,

Five. Sports, Consumer Culture and the Prospects for Change

they are the only publicly owned, non-profit sports franchise operating within the United States. When the team faced bankruptcy in 1923, the city of Green Bay took control of the team and sold ownership shares to the public while limiting the number of shares any individual could own to 200. Today, over half of the concession stands at Lambeau Field are operated by charities while 60 percent of the revenues generated through the sale of the famous "cheese head" are invested in cause-related organizations. Of course, to preserve the private ownership model, the NFL would later write into its bylaws prohibitions on other communities' owning or operating franchises similar to Green Bay. As a matter of fact, similar rules operate in other major professional sports as well. When Joan Kroc, widow of McDonald's founder and San Diego Padres owner Ray Kroc, attempted to transfer ownership of team to the community after her husband's passing, Major League Baseball owners blocked the deal from happening.[22] Globally, on the other hand, there are several dozen Association Football soccer teams that are either completely or mostly owned by the fans of those respective clubs.

Under the current private ownership model, one of its more negative and damaging legacies can be seen when team owners threaten to relocate their franchise unless the public commits tax dollars toward building the team a new facility. First, for obvious reasons, such threats would be nonexistent within a public ownership model in professional sports because control of a team would ultimately reside within the community itself. Second, a portion of the team's revenues could then be reinvested toward funding essential city services such as hospitals and schools or, perhaps, a charitable organization committed to a pressing social or health issue. Even though professional sports teams are considered the property of the individual or group who paid for them, fans believe that they, too, own their teams due to their emotional investments in them. As Nick Trujillo and Bob Krizek suggest, "the [local] franchise is not just another bank, department store, or amusement park; it is experienced as a public trust that engenders a powerful sense of identification and identity for fans and franchise employees alike."[23] Their research on how White Sox fans dealt with the closing of Comiskey Park in 1990 illustrated that the ballpark not only was a place where games took place but also symbolized a connection that united generations. Many indicated they remembered their first game in the ballpark with a family member since passed and how attending Comiskey Park was a way of keeping memories of these people alive. Thus, when the ballpark finally closed, some fans experienced a powerful since of grief and mourning not only for the stadium itself but also for having to confront saying good-bye to lost relatives whose spirit was connected to Comiskey. Thus, when fans complain that sports have indeed become too commercialized by owners and sponsors aiming to monetize the entire experience, the real issue stems from sports being treated as simply another business and consumer product. For many fans, the fact that following a team provides a unique sense of belonging and connection, not to mention some degree of "compensatory fulfillment" for the often-dull rigors of everyday life, means that sports embody something greater than commercialism and product hawking.[24]

Thus, sports are seemingly being corrupted by these forces precisely because they already operate elsewhere, specifically in respects to their influence on how public life and democracy are viewed and realized. Yet sports are hardly a mere reflection of these shifts but rather have the constitutive effect of normalizing them.[25] Today, the very idea of the "public" carries a negative connotation, often conceived as parasitic, overfunded, underperforming, dirty, unaccountable, freeloading, and wasteful. As a matter of fact, when political pundits and officials rhetorically celebrate the wonders of "small government" they are actually calling for the elimination of regulatory oversight in business, a reduction in investments in education and other essential public services, and the privatization of these services. In essence, cutting public spending that often helps regular people often funds tax breaks for the wealthy without creating more debt while freeing additional capital to subsidize big business and the material infrastructure necessary for it to generate more profit. As noted economist David Harvey notes, appeals to "small government" are dishonest, as many of its proponents want big government when it comes to subsidizing—or in some cases saving, as the 2008 Wall Street bailout attests—large corporate interests. Thus, appeals to "small government" are a populist ploy to dismantle government spending that financial elites do not want.[26]

A perfect example of this dynamic can be found in the funding mechanisms for the new arena for the NBA's Milwaukee Bucks to

Five. Sports, Consumer Culture and the Prospects for Change

replace their current home, the BMO Harris Bradley Center. According to team president Peter Feigin, when the team was purchased by Wesley Edens and Marc Lasry for $550 million in 2014 the purchase agreement contained a stipulation by which the NBA would buy back the team for $575 million if a new arena was not completed in time for the 2017–2018 season.[27] As the team struggled to gain public taxpayer approval to finance part of the proposed facility's cost in time to meet the contracted deadline, it seemed as if the league would have to purchase the team. However, reports surfaced that if the NBA did so they would then resell the team to "the highest bidder in either Seattle or Las Vegas for as much as $1.6 billion," good for a $1 billion profit that would be shared by the league's other 29 owners.[28] If the current owners decided to keep the team and relocate elsewhere—presumably in a city promising a new arena—they would then have to pay a "relocation fee" of several hundred million dollars that would again be shared by the rest of the NBA owners. Meanwhile, Bucks ownership, relocation threats notwithstanding, began lobbying for $250 million in public funds to finance part of the cost of their proposed $500 million facility. As with a hedge fund, owners Edens and Lasry were guaranteed to make a profit regardless of the outcome.

Then, Wisconsin governor Scott Walker, a self-proclaimed fiscal conservative, signed a bill passed by the state assembly in August of 2015 to allocate up to $250 million—projected to include an additional $200 million after calculating interest—in public funds that the Milwaukee Bucks were seeking.[29] The most controversial part of the stadium deal was that Walker had just signed a state budget that called for $250 million in budget cuts for the University of Wisconsin education system, money that would then be handed over to the Bucks ownership group for their new arena.[30] In this example of "welfare for the wealthy," the effect of Walker's draconian education cuts is expected to result in faculty layoffs, cutting courses, merging degree programs, larger class sizes and, ultimately, "students taking longer and spending more money to graduate."[31] Meanwhile, the *International Business Times* later revealed that John Hammes, part of the Bucks ownership group, was leading fund-raising efforts for Walker's presidential bid in 2016 and that the stadium deal was Walker's effort to return the favor.[32] The governor, meanwhile, justified his decision to embittered and angry Wisconsin residents that the new arena "protected state revenues" and "was really about protecting the taxpayers of the state," citing the economic stimulus the Bucks' new home would provide to Milwaukee and the state of Wisconsin.[33] However, Walker's projections contradicted the vast amount of research conducted by sports economists that has repeatedly shown that a new stadium contributes little to nothing in terms of economic and income growth, tax revenues, and job creation.[34]

Other examples abound in which government investments in public institutions and programs are being reduced, presumably in the interest of fiscal conservatism and eliminating debt, while massive subsidies are provided to large financial interests at the taxpayers' expense. Government seemingly only exists to benefit the wealthy minority and, as a consequence of the *Citizens United* Supreme Court decision, this class can spend without limit on elections to influence public policy by ensuring that the "right" candidates get elected to further their economic objectives. This is not a conspiracy theory but rather the ethos of neoliberalism, in which the only role of government is to facilitate a favorable business climate, regardless of the negative effects accruing to the public and the institutions they rely on.[35] It is within this context that citizens are treated as merely "consumers" whose only meaningful purpose presumably in life is to shop in search of "empowerment" and "self-fulfillment" in whatever the market takes them to mean. Thus, it is unsurprising that in sports we find an appropriate intersection with this now dominant belief where fans similarly only matter as consumers and little else. This is obvious for anyone who has visited a "new" sports stadium or watched a game on television. The former sells an "experience" designed to get fans to spend more money at the ballpark while the latter increasingly exists to influence fan spending habits when they are home or elsewhere.

Those who insist that sports are not political are guilty of substituting idealism and wishful thinking for truth, for sports have and always will be a political institution. Jackie Robinson's breaking of major league baseball's color barrier provided hope and inspiration for the emerging Civil Rights movement, Billie Jean King's victory over Bobby Riggs in the "Battle of the Sexes" legitimatized Title IX, while taxpayer subsidies for new stadiums illustrate the convergence between government and economics. For as this book I hope has made clear, sports both mirror and shape our contemporary political culture. More

Five. Sports, Consumer Culture and the Prospects for Change

important, sports hold forth the possibility of changing our democratic culture for the better by offering, at their essence, a more empowered and emboldened model of citizenship beyond that of the consumer to which democracy is so often reduced. As Grant Jarvie remarks, sports "may be part of a progressive hope in keeping alive different versions of the world we both live in and could live in."[36] Sports, while far from perfect, offer reminders of the importance of community, the value of attachment to others, and, most important, that the human condition should embody something greater than the spirit of the market. As fan culture becomes reduced to consumer culture, sports become reduced to the status of the ever-interchangeable commodity, inseparable from anything else being offered for sale at the moment, and branded with one corporate logo after the next. While sports have long been a business, there was felt to be a time when fans could pretend otherwise without having to make much cognitive effort to delude themselves.[37] Unfortunately, in today's sporting world the business logic of the games we follow has achieved such visibility that fans are understandably disenchanted and alienated from sports as they increasingly take on the emptiness of the consumer culture they are called upon to serve. To restore the integrity of sports, however, requires, first, a change in the political context in which they operate and, second, a devaluation of the consumerism that so problematically drives it.

Chapter Notes

Introduction

1. As cited in Stuart Miller, "Memories of Eight Great Moments in Baseball History," *Baseball Digest* 50 (1991): 75.
2. See Sut Jhally, "Advertising as Religion: The Dialectic of Technology and Magic," in *The Spectacle of Accumulation: Essays in Culture, Media, & Politics*, ed. Sut Jhally, 85–97. (New York: Peter Lang, 2006).
3. Thorstein Veblen, *The Theory of the Leisure Class* (Mineola, NY: Dover, 1994).
4. Lizabeth Cohen, A Consumer's Republic: The Politics of Mass Consumption (New York: Random House, 2003), 10.
5. Ibid.
6. Benjamin Barber, Consumed: How Markets Corrupt Children, Infantilize Adults, and Swallow Citizens Whole (New York: W.W. Norton, 2007).
7. Cohen, A Consumer's Republic.
8. Alain de Botton, *Status Anxiety* (New York: Random House, 2004).
9. Sut Jhally, "Cultural Studies and the Sports-Media Complex," in Jhally, *The Spectacle of Accumulation*, 136.
10. Ibid., 137.
11. Ibid.
12. Ibid.
13. Matthew P. McAllister, "Hypercommercialism, Televisuality, and the Changing of College Bowl Sponsorship," *American Behavioral Scientist* 53 (2008): 1476–1491.
14. Sponsors Pay Big Bucks to Join College Bowl Games," *Associated Press*, December 19, 2014, available at http://www.nytimes.com/aponline/2014/12/19/us/ap-us-college-bowls-name-game.html?_r=0.
15. Darren Heitner, "The March Madness Advertising Business Is Booming," Forbes.com, March 17, 2015, available at http://www.forbes.com/sites/darrenheitner/2015/03/17/the-march-madness-advertising-business-is-booming/.
16. "Last Week Tonight with John Oliver: The NCAA (HBO)," YouTube Video, 20:53, posted by *LastWeekTonight*, March 15, 2015, https://www.youtube.com/watch?v=pX8BXH3SJn0.
17. Ibid.
18. Josh Boyd, "Selling Home: Corporate Stadium Names and the Destruction of Commemoration," *Journal of Applied Communication Research* 28 (2000): 330–346.
19. Kate Macmillan, "What's In a Name?," Forbes.com, September 11, 2008, available at http://www.forbes.com/2008/09/10/nfl-stadium-naming-biz-sports-nfl08_cz_km_0910rights.html.
20. Jim Bentubo, "Colleges Forgoing Million in Naming-Rights Deals" *Sports Business Daily*, August 31, 2007, available at http://www.sportsbusinessdaily.com/Daily/Issues/2007/08/Issue-236/College-Football-Preview/Colleges-Forgoing-Millions-In-Naming-Rights-Deals.aspx.
21. As quoted in Rich Thomaselli, "This MLB Promotion Won't Mess with the Bases" *Advertising Age*, April 22, 2009, available at http://adage.com/article/madisonvine-news/mlb-movie-promotion-g-force-spider-man/136200/.
22. Naomi Klein, *No Logo* (New York: Picador, 2000).
23. The quote is from ibid., 68.
24. Ezra Galston, "Death to Dinosaur Brands: How Millennials Are Redefining What It Means to Be Loyal," Forbes.com, June 3, 2015, available at http://www.forbes.com/sites/samanthasharf/2015/06/03/death-to-dinosaur-brands-how-millennials-are-redefining-what-it-means-to-be-loyal/.
25. See Michael Butterworth, Baseball and Rhetorics of Purity: The National Pas-

time and American Identity During the War on Terror (Tuscaloosa: University of Alabama Press, 2010).

26. John Dunbar, "The 'Citizens United' Decision and Why It Matters," The Center for Public Integrity, October 18, 2012, available at http://www.publicintegrity.org/2012/10/18/11527/citizens-united-decision-and-why-it-matters, para. 7.

27. David Harvey, *A Brief History of Neoliberalism* (Oxford: Oxford University Press, 2007).

28. Rudy Abramson, "'Turn the Bull Loose,' Reagan Says on Exchange Floor: President Gives Bullish Wall St. Pep Talk," *Los Angeles Times*, March 29, 1985, available at http://articles.latimes.com/1985-03-29/news/mn-20409_1_wall-st-pep-talk.

29. Robert Reich, *Aftershock: The Next Economy and America's Future* (New York: Alfred A. Knopf, 2010).

30. Alanna Petroff, "'The Trickle Down Theory' Is Dead Wrong," CNN Money, June 15, 2015, available at http://money.cnn.com/2015/06/15/news/economy/trickle-down-theory-wrong-imf; Reich, *Aftershock*.

31. Harvey, A Brief History of Neoliberalism, 2.

32. Ibid.

33. Reich, Aftershock.

34. Center on Budget and Policy Priorities, "Years of Cuts Threaten to Put College Out of Reach for More Students," CBPP.org., May 13, 2015, available at http://www.cbpp.org/research/state-budget-and-tax/years-of-cuts-threaten-to-put-college-out-of-reach-for-more-students.

35. Alain de Botton refers to this as "status anxiety" and has written extensively about its hold on contemporary America. For more, see de Botton, *Status Anxiety*.

36. See Shama Hyder, "7 Things You Can Do to Build an Awesome Personal Brand," Forbes.com, August 18, 2014, available at http://www.forbes.com/sites/shamahyder/2014/08/18/7-things-you-can-do-to-build-an-awesome-personal-brand/.

37. Cork Gaines, "The NBA Is the Highest-Paying Sports League in the World," *Business Insider*, May 20, 2015, available at http://www.businessinsider.com/sports-leagues-top-salaries-2015-5.

38. James Quirk and Rodney Fort, *Hardball: The Abuse of Power in Pro Team Sports* (Princeton, NJ: Princeton University Press, 1999).

39. Melia Robinson, "Jay-Z's 10 Best Endorsement Deals," *Business Insider*, July 12, 2013, available at http://www.businessinsider.com/jay-zs-product-endorsement-deals-2013–7.

40. Ibid., para. 6.

41. Ibid., para. 10.

42. "Quotes by Charlie Finley," *ESPN Classic*, November 19, 2003, available at http://espn.go.com/classic/s/finleyquotes000817.html.

43. Dave Zirin, Bad Sports: How Owners Are Ruining the Games We Love (New York: Scribner, 2010).

44. Ibid., 5.

Chapter One

1. As quoted in Joe Frisaro, "Homer Feature Emblematic of Artistic Miami Park," Mlb.com, March 31, 2012, para. 21, available at http://m.marlins.mlb.com/news/article/27785486/.

2. "Miami Marlins Stadium Designed and Built by Fort Lauderdale–Based Living Color Aquariums," MSNBC.com, March 12, 2012, para. 3, available at http://www.msnbc.msn.com/id/46707805/ns/business-press_releases/t/miami-marlins-stadiumaquarium-designed-built-fort-lauderdale-based-living-color-aquariums/.

3. I say that the Clevelander was branding itself as a yuppie hangout for the club-hopping faithful in Miami because of the pictures posted on the Web site replete with what appear to be young, upwardly mobile urban professionals enjoying a "day at the ballpark." For more, see "The Clevelander," Marlins.com, n.d., available at http://miami.marlins.mlb.com/mia/ballpark/clevelander.jsp.

4. "AT&T Stadium Tours," AT&TStadium.com, n.d., available at http://attstadium.com/tours/tourInfo.cfm; "Cowboys Stadium to Be Renamed AT&T Stadium," *USA Today*, July 25, 2013, available at http://www.usatoday.com/story/sports/nfl/cowboys/2013/07/25/cowboys-stadium-at-t-stadium/2586977/.

5. Mike Davis, "AT&T Stadium—the NFL's Must See Stadium," Stadiumjourney.com, n.d., available at http://www.stadiumjourney.com/stadiums/at&t-stadium-s64/.

6. See "Cowboys Stadium to be Renamed AT&T Stadium."

7. Ibid.

8. Andrew D. Smith, "Cowboys Thinking Big Picture Stadium to Have World's

Chapter Notes—One

Largest Video Displays, Thousands of Monitors," *Dallas Morning News*, June 12, 2008, 1A, available at http://web.lexis-nexis.com/universe.

9. As cited in Dave Zirin, *Bad Sports: How Owners are Ruining the Games We Love* (New York: Scribner, 2010).

10. Jason Sickles, "Fans Get the Big Picture—Clearly Without $40 Million Giant Diplay, 'You'd Miss a Lot,' One Says," *Dallas Morning News*, September 21, 2009, 16A, available at http://web.lexis-nexis.com/universe.

11. Zirin, *Bad Sports*.

12. Quoted in Smith, "Cowboys Thinking Big."

13. Quoted in "Dallas Cowboys New Stadium Will Have World's Two Largest High Definition TV's," *AOL News*, June 12, 2008, para. 4, available at http://www.aolnews.com/2008/06/12/dallas-cowboys-new-stadium-will-have-worlds-twolargest-high-d/.

14. Quoted in Bruce Arthur, "Week 3 Will Live On in Ridicule; Over the Top Unveiling of New Cowboys Stadium," *National Post*, September 25, 2009, B10, available at http://web.lexis-nexis.com/universe.

15. Ibid., para. 5.

16. See Mark Rosentraub, Major League Losers: The Real Costs of Sports and Who's Paying for Them (New York: Basic Books, 1999); Mark Rosentraub, Major League Winners: Using Sports and Cultural Centers as Tools for Economic Development (Boca Raton, FL: CRC Press, 2010); Daniel Rosensweig, Retro Ballparks: Instant History, Baseball, and the New American City (Knoxville: University of Tennessee Press, 2005); Robert C. Trumpbour, The New Cathedrals: Politics and Media in the History of Stadium Construction (Syracuse, NY: Syracuse University Press, 2007).

17. Dennis Coates and Brad Humphreys, "Can New Stadiums Revitalise Urban Neighborhoods?," *Significance* 8 (2011): 65–69.

18. See Neil deMause and Joana Cagan, Field of Schemes: How the Great Stadium Swindle Turns Public Money into Private Profit (Lincoln: University of Nebraska Press, 2008); Rosentraub, Major League Losers; Rosentraub, Major League Winners; Rosensweig, Retro Ballparks; and Trumpbour, The New Cathedrals.

19. Dennis Coates and Brad Humphreys, "Do Economists Reach a Conclusion on Subsidies for Sports Franchises, Stadiums, and Mega Events?" *Econ Journal Watch* (2008): 294–315.

20. Ibid.

21. See deMause and Cagan, *Field of Schemes*.

22. Ibid.

23. Michael L. Butterworth, *Baseball and Rhetorics of Purity* (Tuscaloosa: University of Alabama Press, 2010).

24. See Rosensweig, *Retro Ballparks*, 21.

25. See deMause and Cagan, *Field of Schemes*, 6.

26. Ibid., 7.

27. Ibid., 16.

28. "Indians Record-Setting Sellout Streak Over," *USA Today*, April 5, 2001, available at http://usatoday30.usatoday.com/sports/baseball/indians/2001-04-04-sellout.htm.

29. See deMause and Cagan, *Field of Schemes*, 153.

30. Ibid.

31. Lester Munson, "A Busted Play," *Sports Illustrated*, December 4, 1995, available at http://www.si.com/vault/1995/12/04/208720/a-busted-play.

32. Ibid.

33. Mark Naymik, "Art Modell Was Offered a New Stadium for the Cleveland Browns and Passed," Cleveland.com, September 13, 2012, available at http://www.cleveland.com/naymik/index.ssf/2012/09/art_modell_gateway_stadium.html.

34. See deMause and Cagan, *Field of Schemes*, 18.

35. Cited in Rich Exner, "Decade After Being Declared Nation's Poorest City, 1-in-3 Clevelanders Remain in Poverty," Cleveland.com, September 18, 2014, available at http://www.cleveland.com/datacentral/index.ssf/2014/09/decade_after_being_declared_na.html.

36. Zirin, *Bad Owners*, 9.

37. For a more complete description of the factors facilitating population growth in American cities, see Robert Beauregard, *When America Became Suburban* (Minneapolis: University of Minnesota Press, 2006); Steve Macek, *Urban Nightmares: The Media, The Right, and the Moral Panic over the City* (Minneapolis: University of Minnesota Press, 2006); G. Scott Thomas, *The United States of Suburbia: How the Suburbs Took Control of America and What They Plan to Do with It* (Amherst, NY: Prometheus Books, 1998); and Howard Zinn, *The People's History of the United*

Chapter Notes—One

States of America, 5th ed., (New York: HarperCollins, 2003).
38. Trumpbour, The New Cathedrals.
39. Ibid.
40. Rosensweig, Retro Ballparks.
41. Ibid.
42. Ben Lisle, "William Hulbert," *The University of Virginia*, 2000, available at http://xroads.virginia.edu/~Hyper/INCORP/baseball/hulbert.html.
43. Trumpbour, The New Cathedrals, 17.
44. Heather Ann Thompson, *Whose Detroit? Politics, Labor, and Race in Modern America City* (Ithaca, NY: Cornell University Press, 2001).
45. Fred E. Harris and Thomas Wicker, cited in ibid.
46. See Zirin, A People's History of Sports in the United States.
47. Ibid.
48. Ibid.
49. The color barrier in major league baseball was an unofficial ownership agreement between team owners to agree not to sign African American ballplayers and was instituted in the early years of professional baseball. While some "light-skinned" Latino and Cuban players had previously signed professional contracts, their ability to pass as white provided them the opportunity to play major league baseball. For more on the color barrier in major league baseball and the cultural and historical importance of Jackie Robinson, see Butterworth, *Baseball and Rhetorics of Purity*, and Zirin, *A People's History of Sports in the United States*.
50. A study conducted by Saylor R. Breckenridge and Pat Rubio Goldsmith on attendance patterns during the period of racial integration in major league baseball indicates that baseball's "experiment" would have ended if attendance was negatively impacted. For more, see Saylor R. Breckenridge and Pat Rubio Goldsmith, "Spectacle, Distance, and Threat: Attendance and Integration of Major League Baseball, 1930–1961," *Sociology of Sport Journal* 26 (2009): 296–319.
51. John Paul Hill, "Commissioner A.B. 'Happy' Chandler and the Integration of Major League Baseball: A Reassessment," *NINE: A Journal of Baseball History and Culture* 19 (2010): 28–51.
52. Quoted in Chuck Johnson, "Finally, a Tribute/Black Players Carved a Niche in History," *USA Today*, August 9, 1991, 1A, para. 21, available at http://web.lexis-nexis.com/universe.

53. See Amy Bass, "Introduction: 'No Compromise with Slavery! No Union with Slaveholders,' or 'Who Was the *Last* Team to Integrate?," in *In the Game: Race, Identity, and Sports in the Twentieth Century*, ed. Amy Bass, 3 (New York: Palgrave Macmillan, 2005).
54. Zirin, Bad Owners.
55. Lizabeth Cohen, A Consumer's Republic: The Politics of Mass Consumption in Postwar America (New York: Vintage Books, 2003); Thomas, The United States of Suburbia.
56. Rosentraub, Major League Losers.
57. Sidney Fine, Violence in the Model City: The Cavanaugh Administration, Race Relations, and the Detroit Race Riot of 1967 (Ann Arbor: University of Michigan Press, 1989).
58. Kevin J. Delaney and Rick Enstein, *Public Dollars, Private Stadiums: The Battle over Building Sports Stadiums* (New Brunswick, NJ: Rutgers University Press, 2003).
59. Rosentraub, Major League Losers, 254.
60. deMause and Cagan, *Field of Schemes;* Costas Spirou and Larry Bennett, *It's Hardly Sporting: Stadiums, Neighborhoods, and the New Chicago* (Dekalb: Northern Illinois University Press, 2003).
61. Spirou and Bennett, *It's Hardly Sporting.*
62. Trumpbour, The New Cathedrals.
63. Quoted in ibid., 132.
64. Macek, Urban Nightmares
65. Robert Fishman, *Bourgeois Utopias: The Rise and Fall of Suburbia* (New York: Basic Books, 1987), 26.
66. For more on the "Disneyization" of America, see Alan Bryman, *The Disneyization of Society* (London: Sage, 2004).
67. Peter Eisinger, "The Politics of Bread and Circuses: The City for the Visitor Class," *Urban Affairs Review* 35 (2000): 316–333.
68. Elijah Anderson, The Code of the Street: Decency, Violence, and the Moral Life of the Inner City (New York: W.W. Norton, 1999).
69. Herbert J. Gans, *The War Against the Poor* (New York: Basic Books, 1995).
70. Neil Smith, The New Urban Frontier: Gentrification and the Revanchist City (London: Routledge, 1996).
71. Rosensweig, Retro Ballparks.
72. Ibid., 6.
73. Ibid.

74. See Trumpbour, The New Cathedrals.
75. See deMause and Cagan, *Field of Schemes*.
76. Ibid.
77. Ibid.
78. Tom Ziller, "Pay to Play," *SB Nation*, November 21, 2013, available at http://www.sbnation.com/2013/11/21/5129434/stadium-arena-public-funding-kings-sonics-braves.
79. "Alamodome: San Antonio," Alamodome.com, n.d., available at http://www.alamodome.com/alamodome-information/renting-the-alamodome.
80. See Neil deMause, "Sad, Deluded San Antonio People Still Think the Raiders Are Moving There," Field of Schemes.com, December 23, 2014, available at http://www.fieldofschemes.com/.
81. Neil deMause, "Spurs Could Fight Raiders Move to San Antonio, Unless They're Cut In on the Deal," Field of Schemes.com, August 12, 2014, available at http://www.fieldofschemes.com/2014/08/12/7690/spurs-could-fight-raiders-move-to-san-antonio-unless-theyre-cut-in-on-the-deal/.
82. "Arena Lease May Block Heat Move," *Palm Beach Post*, August 5, 1993, 7c, available at http://web.lexis-nexis.com/universe; Mireya Navarro, "Miami Heat Sweetens Deal to Make Case for an Arena," *New York Times*, November 3, 1996.
83. "Arena Lease," para. 1.
84. Navarro, "Miami Sweetens Deal."
85. Ibid.
86. As quoted in Navarre, "Miami Sweetens Deal," para. 13.
87. Erik Brady, "Miami Weighs In with Split Decision Heat, Panthers Get Separate Homes," *USA Today*, September 6, 1996, 19C, available at http://web.lexis-nexis.com/universe.
88. Ibid.
89. Jeff Ostrowski, "Venues Sports Green Backs; Stadium Glut Offering $$ Boom as Concert Goers Swoon," *Variety*, May 19, 1997, available at http://web.lexis-nexis.com/universe.
90. "Investor Pays $28-Million for Fading Miami Arena," *St. Petersburg Times*, August 12, 2004, 5B, available at http://web.lexis-nexis.com/universe.
91. "Heat's New Arena Is Ready," *St. Louis Post-Dispatch*, December 29, 1999, available at http://web.lexis-nexis.com/universe.

92. Barry Petchesky, "For the First Time Ever, the Miami Heat Paid Rent," Deadspin.com, November 22, 2013, available at http://deadspin.com/for-the-first-time-ever-the-miami-heat-paid-rent-1469960778.
93. Jim DeFede, "I Team: County Receives Nothing from Heat, Arena Revenue," CBSMiami.com, May 5, 2011, available at http://miami.cbslocal.com/2011/05/05/i-team-county-receives-nothing-from-heat-arena-revenue/.
94. Ibid., para. 21.
95. Trumpbour, The New Cathedrals.
96. The quote, along with the fan attendance figures cited above it, can be found in Trumpbour, *The New Cathedrals*, 20.
97. See Rosentraub, *Major League Winners*, 2010.
98. deMause and Cagan, *Field of Schemes*, 28.
99. See Eisinger, "The Politics of Bread and Circuses."
100. "Initiative, Referendum, and Recall," National Conference of State Legislators, n.d., available at http://www.ncsl.org/research/elections-and-campaigns/initiative-referendum-and-recall-overview.aspx.
101. "Seattle Court Rules in Favor of a New Stadium," *New York Times*, January 21, 1998, available at http://nytimes.com/1998/01/21/sports/plus-baseball-seattle-court-rules-in-favor-of-new-stadium.html.
102. Rosentraub, Major League Losers.
103. Quoted in Rodney Fort, "Direct Democracy and the Stadium Mess," in *Sports, Jobs, and Taxes*, ed. Roger Noll and Andrew Zimbalist (Washington, DC: Brookings Institute, 1997), 146.
104. See deMause and Cagan, *Field of Schemes*; Rosensweig; *Retro Ball* Parks; Rosentraub, *Major League Losers*; Rosentraub, *Major League Winners*; Trumpbour; *The New Cathedrals*; and Zirin, *Bad Owners*.
105. For more on the economic impact of sports franchises within local economies, see Rosentraub, *Major League Losers*.
106. Quoted in Zirin, *Bad Sports*, 10.
107. As Rosentraub notes, "Be wary of the predictions that the presence of sports teams, arenas, and stadia will result in the growth of robust restaurant and hotel structures. Will there be some level of job creation? Yes!! Will more people come downtown? Yes!! Will there be increased

Chapter Notes—One

restaurant and hotel activity? Yes!! But there will be decreases in spending at restaurants further from the stadium and less spending on other forms of recreation. A large proportion of the spending on sports, or that which results from sports, is merely a transfer of activity from one area to another. Sports are not only small potatoes, but those potatoes may have been somebody else's before the team or stadium existed." See Rosentraub, *Major League Losers*, 153.

108. Dennis Coates and Brad R. Humphreys, "The Stadium Gambit and Local Economic Development," Heartland. org, available at https://www.heartland.org/sites/default/files/4.pdf.

109. Ibid.

110. As quoted in George Ritzer, *Enchanting a Disenchanted World*, 2nd Ed. (Thousand Oaks, CA; Pine Forge Press, 2005), 20.

111. As quoted in Stephen Hawkens, "Nolan Ryan Says Fan's Widow Worried About Son," *USA Today*, July 9, 2011, para. 8–9, available at http://www.usatoday.com/sports/baseball/al/2011-07-09373146303 8x.htm.

112. As quoted in Ritzer, Enchanting a Disenchanted World, 123.

113. "Party Areas," Kansas City Royals. com, n.d., available at http://kansascity.royals.mlb.com/kc/ticketing/group.jsp?loc=party.

114. Rosensweig, *Retro Ball Parks*, 86.

115. See "NFL Intercedes in Bills Fan's Tailgate," ESPN.com, September 17, 2010, available at http://sports.espn.go.com/nfl/news/story?id=5581271.

116. "Fans Subject to Conduct Code," ESPN.com, February 17, 2005, available at http://sports.espn.go.com/nba/news/story?id=1993569.

117. For more on these "purification policies," see Rosensweig, *Retro Ball Parks*.

118. "Code of Conduct," Sun Life Stadium.com, n.d., available at http://sunlifestadium.com/code-of-conduct.

119. See Rosensweig, *Retro Ball Parks*.

120. As quoted in "NFL Intercedes in Bills Fan's Tailgate," para. 8.

121. Ibid., para. 14.

122. See Eisinger, "The Politics of Bread and Circuses"; and Rosensweig, *Retro Ball Parks*.

123. See Rosensweig, Retro Ball Parks.

124. An excellent analysis of the rampant fear in American culture can be found in Barry Glassner, *The Culture of Fear: Why Americans Are Afraid of the Wrong Things*, 10th anniversary ed. (New York: Basic Books, 2010).

125. Ronald Lee and Shawn T. Wahl, "Justifying Surveillance and Control: An Analysis of Media Framing of Pedophiles and the Internet," *Texas Speech Communication Journal* 32 (2007): 495.

126. See Glassner, The Culture of Fear.

127. Ibid.

128. Friedrich Nietzsche, *The Genealogy of Morals*, trans. Francis Golfinng (New York: Random House, 1956).

129. See Edward Blakely and Mary Gail Snyder, *Fortress America: Gated Communities in the United States* (Washington, DC: Brookings Institute, 1999).

130. Theodor Adorno, *The Culture Industry*, ed. J.M. Bernstein (New York: Routledge, 1991).

131. Zirin, *Bad Sports*, 29.

132. "Martini Bar, Other Amenities Help Drive Cost of Yankees' New Home to $1.3 Billion," ESPN.com, February 8, 2008, available at http://sports.epsn.go.com/mlb/news/story?id=3235847.

133. Quoted in deMause and Cagan, *Field of Schemes*, 202.

134. See "Martini Bar."

135. "The First Pitch," MLB.com, 2010, available at http://mlb.mlb.com/sponsors/captain_morgan/first-pitch/.

136. "Campaign Promises: The Sports Business Year in Marketing," Street and Smith's SportsBusiness Daily.com, n.d., available at http://m.sportsbusinessdaily.com/Daily/Issues/2009/12/Issue-66/2009-Year-In-Review/Campaign-Promises-The-Sports-Business-Year-In-Marketing.aspx.

137. John C. Cotey, "Farewell Old Stadium, Old Friend," *St. Petersburg Times*, October 1, 2000, para. 10, available at http://web.lexis-nexis.com/universe.

138. Andrew Zimbalist, "Backtalk; Baseball Makes a Mess in Milwaukee," *New York Times*, December 21, 2003, available at http://web.lexis-nexis.com/universe.

139. "Miller Park," Milwaukeestock.com, March 19, 2007, available at http://cpd.typepad.com/milwaukeestock/2007/03/miller_park.html.

140. Lawrence Wenner, "Playing Dirty: On Reading Media Texts and Studying Sports Fans in Commercialized Settings," in Lawrence W. Hugenberg, Paul M. Haridakis, and Adam C. Earnheardt, *Sports*

Chapter Notes—One

Mania: Essays on Fandom and the Media in the 21st Century (Jefferson, NC: McFarland, 2008), 26.

141. Ibid.

142. Cited in Patrick Hubry, "Love Story; Beer and Sports, So Happy Together," *Washington Post*, July 17, 2003, available at http://web.lexis-nexis.com/universe.

143. Rosensweig, *Retro Ballparks*.

144. Cited in Hubry, "Love Story."

145. As quoted in Dustin Bartholomew, "Razorback Stadium to Sell Beer and Wine in Select Seating Areas," *Fayetteville Flyer*, February 12, 2014, para.5, available at http://www.fayettevilleflyer.com/2014/02/12/razorback-stadium-to-sell-beer-and-wine-in-indoor-club-areas-in-2014/.

146. Ibid.

147. Alain de Botton, *Status Anxiety* (New York: Vintage Books, 2004).

148. Ibid., 65–66.

149. For more on this "divine" theory of power and wealth, see Chris Harman, *A People's History of the World* (New York: Verso, 1999).

150. de Botton, *Status Anxiety*.

151. Ibid., vii.

152. "MLB Fan Cost Index," *Team Marketing*, 2014, available at https://www.teammarketing.com/public/uploadedPDFs/2014+mlb+fci.pdf.

153. Ibid., 2.

154. "NBA Team Marketing Report," *Team Marketing*, November 2014, available at https://www.teammarketing.com/public/uploadedPDFs/2014–15%20nba%20fci.pdf; "NFL Team Marketing Report," *Team Marketing*, September 2014, available at https://www.teammarketing.com/public/uploadedPDFs/2014+NFL+FCI+Final+%282%29.pdf.

155. "10 Wrigley Field Renovations," *NBC Chicago*, n.d., available at http://www.nbcchicago.com/news/local/Wrigley-Renovations-203013231.html.

156. "Captain Morgan Club," Chicago Cubs.com, n.d., available at http://chicago.cubs.mlb.com/chc/ballpark/information/index.jsp?content=captain_morgan_club.

157. Quoted in Carrie Muskat, "Cubs Unveil Renovation Plan for Wrigley Field," MLB.com, January 19, 2003, available at http://m.cubs.mlb.com/news/article/41045120/cubs-unveil-major-renovation-plan-for-wrigley-field, para. 3.

158. Kurt Badenhausen, "MLB Worth $36B as Team Values Hit Record $1.2 Billion Average," Forbes.com, March 25, 2015, available at http://www.forbes.com/mlb-valuations/.

159. As quoted in Neil deMause, "Cubs Can't Sign Free Agents without Wrigley Upgrades, Says Guy Who Signed as Free Agent with Cubs Last Year," Field of Schemes.com, April 26, 2013, available at http://www.fieldofschemes.com/category/mlb/chicago-cubs/page/7/, para. 1.

160. Jack Bouboushian, "Wrigley Field Rootops Battle Jumbotron Plan," Courthouse News Service, January 12, 2015, available at http://www.courthousenews.com/2015/01/12/wrigley-field-rooftops-battle-jumbotron-plan.htm.

161. Neil deMause, "Cubs Add Porta-Potties to Ease Bathroom Crush, Now Neighbors Complain New Sound System Too Damn Loud," Field of Schemes.com, available at http://www.fieldofschemes.com/category/mlb/chicago-cubs/.

162. Blair Sheade, "Wrigley Field Hit with Health Violations," *Chicago Sun Times*, May 21, 2015, available at http://chicago.suntimes.com/baseball/7/71/625809/wrigley-field-hit-health-violations.

163. "Wrigley Field to Keep Serving Up Old Style Beer," TribToday.com, September 8, 2011, available at http://tribune-chronicle.com/page/content.detail/id/146164/Wrigley-Field-to-keepserving-up-Old-Style-Beer-html?isap=1&nav=5034.

164. Ibid., para. 5.

165. Matthew Futterman, "NFL to Charge New York Prices," *Wall Street Journal*, September 17, 2003, available at http://www.wsj.com/articles/SB10001424127887324665604579079424146436620.

166. "Celebrities Spotted at Super Bowl XLVIII," Boston.com, n.d., available at http://www.boston.com/ae/celebrity/2014/02/02/bdc-celebrities-superbowl-gallery/kJeKq3bWaGD2HCmq6tWMPK/pictures.html#slide-17.

167. Thorstein Veblen, *The Theory of the Leisure Class* (Oxford: Oxford University Press, 2007). The original edition by Veblen was published in 1899.

168. Quoted in Nicholas Archer, *Ideological Endzones: NFL Films and the Countersubversive Tradition in American Politics* (PhD diss., University of Massachusetts–Amherst, 2010), 82.

169. Ibid.

170. Frank Luchuk, Blue Jays 1, Expos 0: The Urban Rivalry That Killed Major League Baseball in Montreal (Jefferson, NC: McFarland, 2007).

Chapter Notes—One

171. Andrew Egan, "In Depth: World's Most Expensive Stadiums," Forbes.com, August 6, 2008, available at http://www.forbes.com/2008/08/06/expensive-stadiums-worldwide-forbeslife-cx_ae_0806sports_slide_11.html; Luchuk, *Blue Jays 1, Expos 0*.

172. Butterworth, Baseball and Rhetorics of Purity.

173. Andrew Zimbalist, *May the Best Team Win: Baseball Economics and Public Policy* (Washington, DC: Brookings Institute, 2003), 9.

174. See "Bring MLB Back to MTL," Montreal Baseball Project.com, n.d., available at http://montrealbaseballproject.com/about/.

175. Jonah Keri, *Up, Up and Away* (Canada: Random House, 2014).

176. Quoted in Larry Weisman, "Houston Ponies Up for Sports," *USA Today*, January 27, 2004, 6C, para. 9, available at http://web.lexis-nexis.com/universe.

177. Ibid., para. 12.

178. David Harvey, *A Brief History of Neoliberalism* (Oxford: Oxford University Press, 2007).

179. See Bob Kappstatter, "Carrion Defends Board Firings," [New York] *Daily News*, June 21, 2006, available at http://web.lexis-nexis.com/universe.

180. John Heyman, "Yankees Reach Agreement with Texiera on 8-year, $180M Deal," SI.com, December 23, 2008, available at http://sportsillustrated.cnn.com/2008/baseball/mlb/12/23/texiera; Zirin, *Bad Sports*.

181. See "Martini Bar."

182. Albor Ruiz, "Promises Fade as Budget Cuts Hit Schools Hard," [New York] *Daily News*, March 16, 2008, available at http://web.lexis-nexis.com/universe.

183. Adam Lisberg and Jonathan Lemire, "Mets and Yankees Fans Go Gaga over New Yankee Stadium; Citi Field," New York Daily News.com, April 4, 2009, available at http://articles.nydailynews.com/2009-04-04/sports/17920349_1_jackie-robinson-rotunda-cubsfan-billion-ballpark, paras. 1 and 2.

184. Martin Z. Braun, "Detroit Billionaires Get Arena Help as Bankrupt City Suffers," Bloomberg.com, September 3, 2013, available at http://www.bloomberg.com/news/articles/2013-09-03/detroit-billionaires-get-hockey-arena-as-bankrupt-city-suffers.

185. Ibid.

186. Anna Clark, "Red Wings Gives You Bull," *American Prospect*, August 8, 2013, available at http://prospect.org/article/red-wings-give-you-bull.

187. Braun, "Detroit Billionaires."

188. As quoted in Raad Cawthon, "Detroit Banks on Central Stadium," *Philadelphia Inquirer*, May 29, 2000, available at http://articles.philly.com/2000-05-29/news/25619143_1_gateway-sports-tigers-downtown.

189. As quoted in Braun, "Detroit Billionaires," para. 2.

190. Aaron Wherry, "Motown Tune-Up: Hosting the Super Bowl Is Just One Part of Detroit's Master Plan for Reversing Decades of Decline," *National Post*, January 31, 2006, B9, available at http://web.lexis-nexis.com/universe.

191. As cited in Brent Snavely, "A Super-Suite Deal: Comerica Park Suites to Be Made into a 3500 Square Foot Unit," *Crain's Business Detroit*, January 23, 2006, available at http://www.crainsdetroit.com/article/20060123/SUB/601230881/a-super-suite-deal.

192. Quoted in David Whitfield, "Postcard: Downsizing Detroit," *Time*, March 29, 2010, available at http://0-web.ebscohost.com, para. 7.

193. Quoted in Stephen Yaccino and Michael Cooper, "Cries of Betrayal as Detroit Plans to Cut Pensions," *New York Times*, July 21, 2013, available at http://www.nytimes.com/2013/07/22/us/cries-of-betrayal-as-detroit-plans-to-cut-pensions.html?_r=0.

194. Nathan Bomey, Matt Helms, and Joe Guillen, "Judge Approves Detroit's Exit from Bankruptcy," *USA Today*, November 7, 2014, available at http://www.usatoday.com/story/news/nation/2014/11/07/detroit-bankruptcy-ruling/18640947/.

195. Robert Reich, "Detroit, and the Bankruptcy of America's Social Contract," Reader Supported News.org., January 21, 2013, available at http://readersupportednews.org/opinion2/277-75/18522-detroit-and-the-bankruptcy-of-americas-social-contract.

196. Sidney Fine, Violence in the Model City: The Cavanaugh Administration, Race Relations, and Detroit Race Riot of 1967 (Ann Arbor: University of Michigan Press, 1989); Joseph Howard Kunstler, The Geography of Nowhere: The Rise and Decline of America's Man-Made Landscape (New York: Touchstone, 1993).

Chapter Notes—Two

197. Kunstler, The Geography of Nowhere.
198. Reich, "Detroit."
199. Eisinger, "The Politics of Bread and Circuses."
200. deMause and Cagan, Field of Schemes.
201. As quoted in Bob Nightengale, "Tigers Owner Mike Illitch Driven to Rebuild Detroit," USA Today, April 16, 2012, available at http://www.usatoday.com/sports/baseball/al/tigers/story/2012-04-11/Mike-Illitch-Red-WingsTigers/54227648/1, para. 10.
202. As quoted in Nightengale, "Tigers Owner," para. 12.
203. Louis Aguilar, "$650M Hockey Arena District Moves Forward," Detroit News, 2013, available at http://www.detroitnews.com/article/20130619/BIZ/306190075.
204. Tyler Kepner, "A Former Baseball Cathedral Now Lies Neglected and Decrepit," New York Times, July 10, 2005, available at http://web.lexis-nexis.com/universe.
205. Ibid., para. 24.
206. Lynn Henning, "New Plans for Old Tiger Stadium," Detroit News, February 23, 2015, available at http://www.detroitnews.com/story/opinion/columnists/lynn-henning/2015/02/23/sports-field-honor-tiger-stadium-roots/23864315/.
207. Rosentraub, Major League Losers; Trumpbour, The New Cathedrals.
208. See Bill Shea, "Detroit's $2M Ticket Hangs in the Balance with JLA Talks," Crain's Detroit Business, August 4, 2011, available at http://www.crainsdetroit.com/article/20110814/SUB01/308149993/detroits-2m-ticket-%20hangs-in-the-balance-with-jla-talks#.
209. Brendan Savage, "Report Says Detroit Red Wings Owe Millions to City for Unpaid Cable TV Rights," MLive.com, December 26, 2012, available at http://www.mlive.com/redwings/index.ssf/2012/12/report_says_detroit_red_wings.html.
210. David Muller, "Detroit City Council Narrowly Agrees to New Lease for Joe Louis Arena, Paves Way for New Red Wings Development," MLive.com, March 31, 2014, available at http://www.mlive.com/business/detroit/index.ssf/2014/03/detroit_city_council_narrowly.html.
211. Ibid., para. 11.
212. Both quotes can be found in Muller, "Detroit City Council," para. 5.
213. "Detroit Red Wings," Forbes.com, November 2014, available at http://www.forbes.com/teams/detroit-red-wings/.
214. Michigan Civil Service Commission, "Detroit—Live. Work. Play," n.d., available at https://civilservice.state.mi.us/EICPSEventInfo/EventDisplay.aspx?Event=mgYcwRIPO%2BdrlxccSZ72HQ%3D%3D.

Chapter Two

1. Irving Rein, Philip Kotler, and Ben Shields, The Elusive Fan (New York: McGraw-Hill, 2006), 4.
2. As cited in Brian Sternberg, "The NFL's Biggest Challenge? Keeping Younger Viewers," Variety, September 17, 2014, available at http://variety.com/2014/tv/news/the-nfls-greatest-test-not-ray-rice-but-young-crowds-who-tune-out-games-1201307613/.
3. Ibid., para. 4.
4. See Roger Bennett, "MLS Equals MLB in Popularity with Kids," ESPNFC.com, May 7, 2014, available at http://www.espnfc.com/major-league-soccer/story/1740529/mls-catches-mlb-in-popularity-with-kids-says-espn-poll.
5. As cited and quoted in Tim Marchman, "That ESPN Poll Claiming MLS Is as Popular with Kids as MLB Is Bullshit," Deadspin.com, March 10, 2014, available at http://deadspin.com/that-espn-poll-claiming-mls-is-as-popular-with-kids-as-1539533010.
6. As quoted in Chris Hedges, "The Lonely American," Truthdig.com, June 28, 2015, available at http://www.truthdig.com/report/item/the_lonely_american_20150628.
7. As quoted in Seth Schiesel, "They Got (Video) Game; NBA Finals Can Wait," New York Times, June 21, 2005, available at http://www.nytimes.com/2005/06/21/arts/television/they-got-video-game-nba-finals-can-wait.html.
8. Quoted in Schiesel, "They Got (Video) Game," para. 14.
9. See Fantasy Sports Trade Association, "Industry Demographics," FSTA.org, n.d., available at http://www.fsta.org/?page=demographics.
10. Ibid.
11. Erica Rosenfeld Halverson and Richard Halverson, "Fantasy Baseball: The Case for Competitive Fandom," Games and Culture 3 (2008): 286–308.
12. Luke Howie and Perri Campbell,

Chapter Notes—Two

"The Social and Gender in Fantasy Sports Leagues," in *Playing to Win: Sports, Video Games, and the Culture of Play*, ed. Robert Alan Brookey and Thomas P. Oates, 92–111 (Bloomington: Indiana University Press, 2015).

13. Halverson and Halverson, "Fantasy Baseball."

14. See ibid.; Jim Hu, "Sites See Big Season for Fantasy Sports," *CNet News*, August 8, 2003, available at http://news.cnet.com/2100-1026_3-5061351.html?tag=fd_lede2_hed.

15. Thomas Oates, "New Media and the Repackaging of NFL Fandom," *Sociology of Sport Journal* 26 (2009): 31–49.

16. Todd M. Nesbit and Kerry A. King, "The Impact of Fantasy Sports on Television Viewership," *Journal of Media Economics* 23 (2010): 24–41.

17. See Fantasy Sports Trade Association, "Industry Demographics."

18. Ibid.

19. As cited in Eugene Kim, "Why Draft Kings, a $900 Million Site That Allows Gambling on Fantasy Sports, Is Legal," *Business Insider*, April 6, 2015, available at http://www.businessinsider.com/draft-kings-not-illegal-2015-4.

20. Matt Burke, "Why 'Gambling' at Daily Fantasy Sites DraftKings, FanDuel Is Legal," Metro.com, October 22, 2014, available at http://www.metro.us/news/why-gambling-at-daily-fantasy-sites-draftkings-fanduel-is-legal/zsJnjw-tOAsTVwwwggPI/.

21. Burke, "Why 'Gambling'"; Kim, "Why Draft Kings."

22. Adam Kilgore, "MLB's Deal with DraftKings Should Signal Baseball's Changing Stance on Gambling," *Washington Post*, April 7, 2015, available at http://www.washingtonpost.com/news/sports/wp/2015/04/07/mlbs-deal-with-draftkings-should-signal-baseballs-changing-stance-on-gambling/.

23. Ibid., para. 2.

24. Darren Heitner, "FanDuel and DraftKings Dueling over Team and League Partnerships," Forbes.com, November 14, 2014, available at http://www.forbes.com/sites/darrenheitner/2014/11/14/fanduel-and-draftkings-dueling-over-team-and-league-partnerships/.

25. See Marc Edelman, "Lawyer Who Sued FanDuel Brings Another Gambling Lawsuit Against Winner of DraftDay Contest," Forbes.com, May 24, 2013, available at http://www.forbes.com/sites/marcedelman/2013/05/24/lawyer-who-sued-fanduel-brings-another-gambling-lawsuit-against-winner-of-draftday-contest/.

26. Ibid., para. 10.

27. "ESPN Outside the Lines: Daily Fantasy Sports Special," ESPN, available at https://www.youtube.com/watch?v=xPubMOh_Tw8.

28. Burke, "Why 'Gambling.'"

29. As quoted in ibid., para. 6.

30. Dave Zirin, "The Fantasy That's Ruining Football," *Los Angeles Times*, September 16, 2007, available at http://www.latimes.com/la-op-zirin16sep16-story.html.

31. Oates, "New Media and the Repackaging of NFL Fandom," 32.

32. See Andrea D. Buhrmann, "The Emerging of the Entrepreneurial Self and Its Current Hegemony. Some Basic Reflections on How to Analyze the Formation and Transformation of Modern Forms of Subjectivity," *Forum: Qualitative Social Research* 6, available at http://www.qualitative-research.net/index.php/fqs/article/view/518/1122.

33. Michael Peters, "Education, Enterprise Culture and the Entrepreneurial Self: A Foucauldian Perspective," *Journal of Educational Inquiry* 2 (2001): 58–71.

34. Ibid.

35. See Noam Chomsky, "Education for Whom and for What," *Arizona Connection*, available at https://www.youtube.com/watch?v=8OLJTVnFeo&list=PL46C2186E3EA7D4A5.

36. As quoted in "Margaret Thatcher: A Life in Quotes," *The Guardian*, April 8, 2013, available at http://www.theguardian.com/politics/2013/apr/08/margaret-thatcher-quotes.

37. David Harvey, *A Brief History of Neoliberalism* (Oxford: Oxford University Press, 2007).

38. Oates, "New Media and the Repackaging of NFL Fandom."

39. See Sut Jhally, "Cultural Studies and the Sports-Media Complex," in *The Spectacle of Accumulation: Essays in Culture, Media, & Politics*, ed. Sut Jhally, 129–151 (New York: Peter Lang).

40. As quoted in "Noam Chomsky: Why Americans Know So Much About Sports but So Little About World Affairs," Alternet.com, September 15, 2014, available at http://www.alternet.org/noam-chomsky-why-americans-know-so-much-about-sports-so-little-about-world-affairs.

41. Jim Bouton, *Ball Four: Twentieth Anniversary Edition* (New York: Macmillan, 1990).
42. See David Voigt, American Baseball, vol. 1: From Gentleman's Sport to the Commissioner System (University Park: Pennsylvania State University Press, 1983); Andrew Zimbalist, May the Best Team Win: Baseball Economics and Public Policy (Washington, DC: Brookings Institution, 2003).
43. Ethan Lewis, "A Structure to Last Forever: The Players' League and the Brotherhood War of 1880," Ethanlewis.org., para. 5, 2001, available at http://www.ethanlewis.org/pl/ch1.html.
44. Nick Acocella, "Flood of Free Agency," ESPN Go.com, n.d., available at http://espn.go.com/classic/biography/s/flood_curt.html.
45. As quoted in ibid., para. 22.
46. See David Q. Voigt, American Baseball, vol. 3: From Postwar Expansion to the Electronic Age (University Park: Pennsylvania State University Press, 1983); Zimbalist, May the Best Team Win; and Dave Zirin, A People's History of Sports in the United States (New York: New Press, 2008).
47. See Voigt, American Baseball, vol. 3; Zimbalist, May the Best Team Win; and Zirin, A People's History of Sports in the United States.
48. Michael Schottey, "How Free Agency Changed the NFL Forever," *Bleacher Report*, March 11, 2013, available at http://bleacherreport.com/articles/1561856-how-free-agency-changed-the-nfl-forever.
49. Ibid., para. 11.
50. Ibid.
51. Robert Bradley, "Labor Pains Nothing New to the NBA," The Association for Professional Basketball Research, n.d., available at http://www.apbr.org/labor.html.
52. Ibid.
53. Ibid.
54. Bradley, "Labor Pains"; Matt Petersen, "The Impact of Tom Chambers and Unrestricted Free Agency," NBA.com, July 2, 2014, available at http://www.nba.com/suns/history/impact-tom-chambers-and-unrestricted-free-agency.
55. Bradley, "Labor Pains."
56. A "hard cap" allows for very few exceptions for team owners to spend money on contracts above the capped amount. The NBA, meanwhile, has a "soft cap," so that even though it includes a capped amount, teams are allowed to spend beyond that limit in any number of ways. The most well-known of these exceptions is the "Larry Bird exception," which allows teams to exceed the capped amount in the pursuit of resigning their own players once they hit free agency. For more, see Derek Thompson, "The NBA Lockout: Here's What You Need to Know," *The Atlantic*, June 30, 2011, available at http://www.theatlantic.com/business/archive/2011/06/the-nba-lockout-heres-what-you-need-to-know/241251/.
57. "MLB Team Valuations: Los Angeles Dodgers," Forbes.com, March 2015, available at http://www.forbes.com/teams/los-angeles-dodgers/.
58. As cited in Ike Ejiochi, "How the NFL Makes the Most Money of Any Pro Sport," CNBC.com, September 4, 2014, available at http://www.cnbc.com/id/101884818.
59. This is the only study that I could find on the issue of whether fans are more loyal to their fantasy sports team than their favorite team. See Jeremy Lee, "The Effects of Fantasy Football Participation on Team Identification and NFL Fandom," LSU.edu, May 2011, available at http://etd.lsu.edu/docs/available/etd-04142011-162307/unrestricted/leethesis.pdf.
60. Chris Moyers, "Americans to Bet $2 Billion on 70 Million March Madness Bracket This Year, Says New Research," American Gaming.org., March 12, 2015, available at http://www.americangaming.org/newsroom/press-releases/americans-to-bet-2-billion-on-70-million-march-madness-brackets-this-year.
61. Ibid., para. 2.
62. *Wall Street: Money Never Sleeps*, DVD, directed by Oliver Stone (New York: 20th Century–Fox, 2010).

Chapter Three

1. "Total US Ad Spending to See Largest Increase Since 2004," *EMarketer*, July 2, 2014, available at http://www.emarketer.com/Article/Total-US-Ad-Spending-See-Largest-Increase-Since-2004/1010982.
2. See Entertainment Software Association, "Essential Facts About the Computer and Video Game Industry: 2015 Sales, Demographic, and Usage Data," available at http://www.theesa.com/wp-content/uploads/2015/04/ESA-Essential-Facts-2015.pdf.
3. Ibid.

Chapter Notes—Three

4. Thomas P. Oates and Robert Alan Brookey, "Introduction," in *Playing to Win: Sports, Video Games, and the Culture of Play*, ed. Robert Alan Brookey and Thomas Oates, 1–20 (Bloomington: Indiana University Press, 2015).

5. See Cory Hillman and Michael L. Butterworth, "Keeping It Real: Sports Video Game Advertising and the Fan-Consumer," in *Playing to Win: Sports, Video Games, and the Culture of Play*, ed. Robert Alan Brookey and Thomas Oates, 152–171 (Bloomington: Indiana University Press, 2015).

6. Oates and Brookey, "Introduction," 4.

7. Caitlin Dewey, "The Only Guide to Gamegate You Will Ever Need," *Washington Post*, October 14, 2014, available at http://www.washingtonpost.com/news/the-intersect/wp/2014/10/14/the-only-guide-to-gamergate-you-will-ever-need-to-read/.

8. Milo Yiannopoulous, "Feminist Bullies Tearing the Video Game Industry Apart," Breitbart.com, September 1, 2014, available at http://www.breitbart.com/london/2014/09/01/lying-greedy-promiscuous-feminist-bullies-are-tearing-the-video-game-industry-apart/, para. 1.

9. Ibid., para. 12.

10. The Gamergate backlash extended beyond the cases of Zoe Quinn and Anita Sarkeesian to include several gaming journalists and designers who reported and/or remarked on the harassment these two women received. This included Brianna Wu, who tweeted jokes regarding the Gamergate controversy. Wu co-founded an indie game studio and was driven from her home after receiving a deluge of Twitter threats that included: "I hope you enjoy your last moments alive on this earth. You did nothing worthwhile with your life"; "If you have any kids, they're going to die too. I don't give a @#$%. They'll grow up to be feminists anyway"; and "Your mutilated corpse will be on the front page of Jezebel tomorrow and their isn't jackshit you can do about it." For more, see Dewey, "The Only Guide to Gamergate You Will Ever Need."

11. Oates and Brookey, "Introduction."

12. For example, see Mike Jaccarino, "'Training Simulation': Mass Killers Often Share Obsession with Violent Video Games," FoxNews.com, September 12, 2013, available at http://www.foxnews.com/tech/2013/09/12/training-simulation-mass-killers-often-share-obsession-with-violent-video-games/.

13. Benedict Carey, "Shooting in the Dark," *New York Times*, February 11, 2013, available at http://www.nytimes.com/2013/02/12/science/studying-the-effects-of-playing-violent-video-games.html?_r=0.

14. T.J. Jackson Lears, *Fables of Abundance: A Cultural History of Advertising in America* (New York: Basic Books, 1994).

15. Ibid.

16. Naomi Klein, *No Logo* (New York: Picador, 2000), 6.

17. Lisa Held, "Psychoanalysis Shapes Consumer Culture," American Psychological Association, December 2009, available at http://www.apa.org/monitor/2009/12/consumer.aspx.

18. Darren Rovell, "How Nike Landed Jordan," ESPN.go, February 15, 2013, available at http://espn.go.com/blog/playbook/dollars/post/_/id/2918/how-nike-landed-michael-jordan.

19. Mary G. McDonald and David L. Andrews, "Michael Jordan: Corporate Sport and Postmodern Celebrityhood," in *Sports Stars: The Cultural Politics of Sporting Celebrity*, ed. David L. Andrews and Steven J. Jackson, 20–35 (New York: Routledge, 2001).

20. Ibid.

21. Ibid., 26.

22. Thomas Frank, *What's the Matter with Kansas? How Conservatives Won the Heart of America* (New York: Metropolitan Books, 1994), McDonald and Andrews, "Michael Jordan."

23. As quoted in Dave Zirin, *A People's History of Sports in the United States* (New York: New Press, 2008), 238.

24. Lawrence Wenner, "Brewing Consumption: Sports Dirt, Mythic Masculinity, and the Ethos of Beer Commercials," in *Sport, Beer, and Gender: Promotional Culture and Contemporary Social Life*, eds. Lawrence Wenner and Steven J. Jackson, 121–142 (New York: Peter Lang, 2009).

25. Sut Jhally and Bill Livant, "Watching as Working: The Valorisation of Audience Consciousness," in *The Spectacle of Accumulation: Essays in Culture, Media, & Politics*, ed. Sut Jhally, 45–61 (New York: Peter Lang, 2006).

26. See Matthew P. McAllister, "Super Bowl Advertising as Commercial Celebration," *Communication Review* 3 (1999): 403–428.

Chapter Notes—Three

27. "How the Super Bowl Ate America," *The Week*, February 1, 2015, available at http://theweek.com/articles/536265/how-super-bowl-ate-america.

28. The cost of a 30-second spot for the 2014 Super Bowl averaged $4.5 million, which will probably increase in the future as long as the Super Bowl remains the premier prime-time cultural event that it is currently. As a matter of fact, this figure is nearly double what a similar advertising spot would have cost a decade ago. For more, see ibid.

29. Of course, YouTube and Facebook did not exist when McAllister wrote about the afterlife of Super Bowl advertising, but there is no question that the "best" ads attain viral status on these Web sites. For more, see McAllister, "Super Bowl Advertising as Commercial Celebration."

30. As cited in "How the Super Bowl Ate America."

31. Dave Zirin, "Why I'm Done Defending Women's Sports," Edgeofsports.com, n.d., available at http://www.edgeofsports.com/2015-07-06-1050/index.html., para. 4.

32. Ronald Grover and Tom Lowry, "TV Shows with the Most Product Placement," Bloomberg.com, 2015, para. 2 available at http://www.bloomberg.com/ss/09/04/0423_tv_product_placements/1.htm.

33. Ibid., para. 3.

34. Ibid.

35. *The Office: Season Two*, "Christmas Party," DVD, directed by Charles McDougall (Orlando, FL: Universal Studios, 2006).

36. See Steven Zeitchick, "Steve Jobs 1955–2011; Apple Took Big Bite Out of Product Placement; If You Thought the Logo Was Everywhere on TV and in Films, You Were Right," *Los Angeles Times*, October 8, 2011, available at http://web.lexisnexis.com/universe.

37. Felix Salmon, "Building a Bigger Bubble: What Does the $24 Billion NBA Deal Mean for the Future of TV Sports?," Slate.com, October 7, 2014, available at http://www.slate.com/articles/business/moneybox/2014/10/nba_espn_billion_dollar_deal_when_is_the_tv_sports_bubble_going_to_burst.html.

38. Christina Settimi, "MLB's Most Valuable Television Deals," Forbes.com, March 26, 2014, available at http://www.forbes.com/sites/christinasettimi/2014/03/26/mlbs-most-valuable-television-deals/.

39. As quoted in Christina Settimi, "Baseball's Biggest Cable Deals," Forbes.com, March 21, 2012, available at http://www.forbes.com/sites/christinasettimi/2012/03/21/baseballs-biggest-cable-deals/.

40. Ibid.

41. Salmon, "Building a Bigger Bubble."

42. Jayson Stark, "Stanton Wanted Flexibility for the Marlins," ESPN.com, November 18, 2014, available at http://espn.go.com/mlb/story/_/id/11897600/giancarlo-stanton-325m-miami-marlins-heavily-backloaded.

43. See Salmon, "Building a Bigger Bubble."

44. Dorothy Pomeranz, "Are You Willing to Pay $36 Per Month for ESPN?," Forbes.com, March 25, 2015.

45. These numbers were generated by a study conducted by Michael Nathanson of MoffetNathason Research and are referred to in ibid., para. 6. Of course, under the current subscription model, where customers purchase packages that include a bundle of networks, providers have enough customers to negotiate a lower price with ESPN. If these companies moved to "a la carte" television, this customer base would shrink significantly—not everyone who purchases ESPN through a package actually watches it—and those who still wanted ESPN would have to pay a higher price to offset the lost revenues.

46. Ibid.

47. Ibid., para. 7.

48. Ibid., para. 8.

49. Richard Sandomir, "Here's the Pitch. But First, One from Our Sponsor," *New York Times*, August 18, 2013, available at http://www.nytimes.com/2013/08/19/sports/baseball/radio-broadcasts-balance-baseball-with-advertising.html.

50. Ibid., para. 4.

51. Ibid., para. 6.

52. Ibid., para. 10.

53. Ibid., para. 15.

54. Matthew P. McAllister, The Commercialization of American Culture: New Advertising, Control, and Democracy (Thousand Oaks, CA: Sage, 1996).

55. Mike Littwin, "Jordan Hid Allegiance Under Flag: Cover-up Discloses Nike Won Shoe War," *Baltimore Sun*, August 9, 1992, available at http://articles.baltimoresun.com/1992-08-09/sports/1992222100_1_reebok-nike-jordan-put.

56. Ibid., para. 8.

57. As quoted in Paul White, "The Lengths MLB Goes to Protect Sponsors,"

Chapter Notes—Three

USA Today, October 23, 2013, available at http://www.usatoday.com/story/sports/mlb/2013/10/23/mlbs-protects-its-exclusive-sponsors-in-the-postseason/3174007/, para. 2.

58. Ibid., para. 7.
59. Ibid., para. 8.
60. Ibid., para. 17.
61. Ibid., para. 22.
62. Esther Addley, "Olympics 2012: Branding 'Police' to Protect Sponsors' Exclusive Rights," *The Guardian*, April 13, 2012, available at http://www.theguardian.com/sport/2012/apr/13/olympics-2012-branding-police-sponsors.
63. Dave Zirin, "'Drones, Missiles, and Gunships, Oh My!' Welcome to the 2012 London Olympics," *The Nation*, May 14, 2012, available at http://www.thenation.com/article/drones-missiles-and-gunships-oh-my-welcome-2012-london-olympics/.
64. As quoted in David Segal, "Brand Police Are on the Prowl for Ambush Marketers at London Games," *New York Times*, July 24, 2012, available at http://www.nytimes.com/2012/07/25/sports/olympics/2012-london-games-brand-police-on-prowl-for-nike-and-other-ambush-marketers.html?_r=0, para. 27.
65. Ibid., para. 23.
66. Entertainment Software Association, "Games: In Game Advertising," The Electronic Software Association.com, n.d., available at http://www.theesa.com/wp-content/uploads/2014/11/Games_Advertising-11.4.pdf.
67. Ibid.
68. Ted Trautman, "Excavating the Video Game Industry's Past," *The New Yorker*, April 29, 2014, available at http://www.newyorker.com/business/currency/excavating-the-video-game-industrys-past.
69. Matt Smith, "Searchers Unearth Grave of 'E.T,' the Game Atari Wanted Us to Forget," CNN.com, April 28, 2014, available at http://www.cnn.com/2014/04/27/tech/gaming-gadgets/atari-et-video-game/.
70. Ibid.
71. Trautman, "Excavating the Video Game."
72. Smith, "Searchers Unearth Grave."
73. Trautman, "Excavating the Video Game."
74. Entertainment Software Association, "Games: In-Game Advertising."
75. Ibid., para. 2.
76. With the Playstation 4, for example, gamers who are connected online through the Playstation Network can see which games their "friends" are playing and how often.
77. See Ahmed Ajaz, "Changing the Rules of the Game," *Campaign*, May 15, 1999, available at http://web.lexis-nexis.com/universe; Entertainment Software Association, "Games: In-Game Advertising"; and Matthew Ingram, "Obama Targets Gamers with Ads," *The Globe and Mail*, October 15, 2008, B3, available at http://web.lexis-nexis.com/universe.
78. Entertainment Software Association, "Games: In-Game Advertising."
79. Hillman and Butterworth, "Keeping It Real."
80. "Study Shows In-Game Advertising Maximizes Marketing Dollars in Sports Category," PRNewsWire.com, n.d., available at http://www.prnewswire.com/news-releases/study-shows-in-game-advertising-maximizes-marketing-dollars-in-sports-category-84019197.html.
81. As quoted in ibid., para. 6.
82. As quoted in ibid., para. 2.
83. As cited in ibid., para. 5.
84. Hillman and Butterworth, "Keeping It Real."
85. Lizabeth Cohen, *A Consumer's Republic: The Politics of Mass Consumption in Postwar America* (New York: Alfred A. Knopf, 2003); Greg Dickinson, "Selling Democracy: Consumer Culture and Citizenship in the Wake of September 11," *Southern Communication Journal* 70 (2009): 271–294.
86. Entertainment Software Association, "2015 Sales, Demographic, and Usage Data: Essential Facts About the Computer and Video Game Industry," Entertainment Software Association, available at http://www.theesa.com/wp-content/uploads/2015/04/ESA-Essential-Facts-2015.pdf.
87. "Madden: The $4 Billion Video Game Franchise," CNN Money.com, September 5, 2013, available at http://money.cnn.com/2013/09/05/technology/innovation/madden-25/.
88. Ibid.
89. For more on this partnership, see Thomas Oates, "New Media and the Repackaging of NFL Fandom," *Sociology of Sport Journal* 26 (2009): 31–49.
90. Quoted in Patrick Hruby, "The Full Throttle World of *Madden*," ESPN Page 2, August 6, 2010, http://sports.espn.go.com/

espn/page2/story?page=hruby/100806_madden.

91. "Madden 16 Cover Vote," ESPN Go.com, available at http://espn.go.com/nfl/feature/maddenvote.

92. Rick Marshall, "Coincidence or Curse? Looking Back on Madden's Troubled Cover Athletes," Digital Trends.com, August 23, 2014, available at http://www.digitaltrends.com/gaming/the-madden-curse/.

93. Ibid., para. 2.

94. The video I am referring to here can be found at the end of the article published by Mike Dyce, "Madden 2016: Top 10 Rookies Ratings," July 2015, available at http://fansided.com/2015/07/20/madden-2016-top-10-rookies-ratings/.

95. Hillman and Butterworth, "Keeping It Real."

96. Andy Rosenberg, "In-Game Advertising in Sports Video Games...Why It Works," Andythegiant.com, March 12, 2009, http://andyrosenberg.wordpress.com/2009/03/12/in-game-advertising-in-sports-video-games-why-it-works.

97. At the time I was writing this chapter, Madden 16 had not been released, forcing me to review Madden 15, which was the latest release available for review.

98. Quoted in Larry Stewart, "'Playmakers' Is Sacked by ESPN," *Los Angeles Times*, February 5, 2004, available at http://articles.latimes.com/2004/feb/2005/sports/sp-espn 2005.

99. "Madden: The $4 Billion Video Game Franchise."

100. Meredith M. Bagley and Ian Summers, "Ideology, It's in the Game: Selective Simulation in EA Sports' NCAA Football," in *Playing to Win: Sports, Video Games, and the Culture of Play*, eds. Robert Alan Brookey and Thomas Oates, (Bloomington: University of Indiana Press, 2015): 192.

101. Ibid.

102. As quoted in Bagley and Summers, "Ideology," 210.

103. Ibid., 210.

104. Hillman and Butterworth, "Keeping It Real."

105. I am referring here only to console releases available on either the Playstation, Xbox, or Nintendo. There is a PC text-based simulation game, Out of the Park Baseball, that carries an official MLB license, but because of its format and niche appeal it does not even come close to competing with MLB: The Show in terms of its overall sales.

106. "MLB 15 The Show—New Features and Released Date Revealed," Playstation Blog, January 29, 2015, available at http://blog.eu.playstation.com/2015/01/29/mlb-15-show-new-features-release-date-revealed/.

107. Damian Seeto, "Licensed Gear Is Coming to MLB 15 The Show," Attackofthefanboy.com, March 21, 2015, available at http://attackofthefanboy.com/news/licensed-gear-is-coming-to-mlb-15-the-show/.

108. "Study Shows In-Game Advertising."

109. As quoted in Kyle Newport, "Mike Trout Becomes First MLB Player Since Ken Griffey Jr. to Get Own Nike Cleat," *Bleacher Report*, June 20, 2014, available at http://bleacherreport.com/articles/2104350-mike-trout-becomes-first-mlb-player-since-ken-griffey-jr-to-get-own-nike-cleat.

110. "Retro Michael Jordan and Spike Lee Commercial," YouTube video, :30, posted by SoxFan10, August 15, 2006, available at https://www.youtube.com/watch?v=Abr_LU822rQ.

111. As quoted in Ken Belson, "In Tough Times, Charity Sells for Sponsors," *International Herald Tribune*, July 15, 2009, available at http://web.lexis-nexis.com/universe, para. 12 [emphasis mine].

112. Samantha King, "Pink Ribbons, Inc.: Breast Cancer Activism and the Politics of Philanthropy," *International Journal of Qualitative Studies in Education* 17 (2004): 473–492.

113. Sandy M. Fernandez, "History of the Pink Ribbon: Pretty in Pink," Think Before You Pink.org., available at http://thinkbeforeyoupink.org/before-you-buy/history-of-the-pink-ribbon/.

114. As quoted in *Pink Ribbons, Inc.*, DVD, directed by Lea Pool (National Film Board of Canada, 2011).

115. As quoted in "The Women Behind Pink Ribbons, Inc. Hope to Change the Discourse of Breast Cancer," *Postmedia News*, January 30, 2012, available at http://news.nationalpost.com/arts/the-women-behind-pink-ribbons-inc-hope-to-change-the-discourse-of-breast-cancer, para. 8.

116. "Chemicals in Cosmetics," Breast Cancer Fund.org., available at http://www.breastcancerfund.org/clear-science/environmental-breast-cancer-links/cosmetics/?referrer=https://www.google.com/.

Chapter Notes—Four

117. Pink Ribbons, Inc.
118. Ibid.
119. Smriti Sinha, "The NFL's Pink October Does Not Raise Money for Cancer Research," *Vice Sports*, October 8, 2014, available at https://sports.vice.com/en_us/article/the-nfls-pink-october-does-not-raise-money-for-cancer-research.
120. David Pincus, "The Conflicting Truth About the NFL's Pink Campaign," *SBNation*, October 26, 2012, available at http://www.sbnation.com/2012/10/26/3498376/nfl-pink-flags-breast-cancer-charity.
121. As quoted in Pincus, "Conflicting Truth," para. 6.
122. Sinha, "The NFL's Pink October," para. 9.
123. Ibid.
124. As quoted in ibid., para. 7.
125. There seems, at first glance, to be conflicting evidence regarding whether or not any portion of the NFL's donations actually funds breast cancer research. According to Rick Chandler, "$3.54 of every $100 collected actually goes toward breast cancer research." See Rick Chandler, "The NFL Strongly Opposes Domestic Violence: Now Please Buy This Pink Ray Rice Jersey," *Sports Grid*, September 11, 2014, available at http://www.sportsgrid.com/nfl/the-nfl-strongly-opposes-domestic-violence-now-dont-forget-to-buy-this-pink-ray-rice-jersey-thanks/, para. 2. However, according to ACS spokesperson Tara Peters "the money we receive from [the] NFL has nothing to do with our research program." See Sinha, "The NFL's Pink October," para. 4.
126. Chris Isidore, "P&G Pulls Out of NFL Breast Cancer Campaign," CNN Money.com, September 23, 2014, available at http://money.cnn.com/2014/09/19/news/companies/pg-nfl-breast-cancer/, para. 6.
127. Ibid.
128. As quoted in Chris Bahr, "Pink Problem: MLB's Mother's Day Tribute, Breast Cancer Awareness Plans Become Controversial," *Sporting News*, May 11, 2013, available at http://www.sportingnews.com/mlb/story/2013-05-11/pink-bats-mlb-mothers-day-breast-cancer-louisville-slugger-plouffe-markakis, para. 6.
129. Ibid., para. 8.
130. Matthew P. McAllister, "College Bowl Sponsorship and the Increased Commercialization of Amateur Sports," *Critical Studies in Mass Communication* 15 (1998): 357–381.
131. Matthew P. McAllister, "Hypercommercialism, Televisuality, and the Changing Nature of College Sports Sponsorship," *American Behavioral Scientist* 53 (2010): 18.

Chapter Four

1. Chris Greenberg, "University of Maryland Football Uniforms by Under Armour Create Buzz on Twitter," *New York Times*, September 14, 2011, available at http://web.lexis-nexis.com/universe.
2. Quoted in Mike Tanier, "There's an Exciting Clash on the Field. Oh, That's the Uniform," *New York Times*, September 14, 2011, available at http://web.lexis-nexis.com/universe.
3. Dave Sheinin, "The Changing Colors of Fall Saturdays," *Washington Post*, September 15, 2011, available at http://web.lexis-nexis.com/universe.
4. As quoted in Sheinin, "Changing Colors," paras. 21 and 23.
5. Tanier, "There's an Exciting Clash," para. 7.
6. Gus Turner, "The 20 Most Outrageous Minor League Uniforms," Complex.com, April 11, 2014, available at http://www.complex.com/sports/2014/04/most-outrageous-minor-league-uniforms/., para. 16.
7. Jason McIntyre, "Indiana Pacers Will Wear Hickory Throwback Jerseys," *USA Today Sports*, July 21, 2015, available at http://thebiglead.com/2015/07/21/indiana-pacers-hickory-jerseys-hoosiers/.
8. The phrase "lazy cynicism" is taken from an article written by Matt Ashby and Brendan Carroll, "David Foster Wallace Was Right: Irony Is Ruining Our Culture," Salon.com, April 13, 2014, available at http://www.salon.com/2014/04/13/david_foster_wallace_was_right_irony_is_ruining_our_culture/, para. 1.
9. Ron Bishop, "Stealing the Signs: A Semiotic Analysis of the Changing Nature of Professional Sports Logos," *Social Semiotics* 11 (2001): 23–41.
10. Ibid., 37.
11. G. Michael Green and Roger D. Launius, *Charlie Finley: The Outrageous Story of Baseball's Super Showman* (New York: Walker, 2010).
12. Bishop, "Stealing the Signs"; John Rosengren, Hammerin' Hank, George Almighty, and the Say Hey Kid: The Year

Chapter Notes—Four

That Changed Baseball Forever (Naperville, IL: Sourcebooks, 2008).

13. During the 1960s as the revolutionary energy of the decade became more visible in popular culture, conservative groups believed that sports, understood to be the defender of traditional values, should be kept "pure" from these influences. For more, see David W. Zang, *Sports Wars: Athletes in the Age of Aquarius* (Fayetteville: University of Alabama Press, 2001).

14. As quoted in Rosengren, *Hammerin' Hank*, 31.

15. C.K. Lendt, *Kiss and Sell: The Making of a Supergroup* (New York: Watson-Guptill, 1997).

16. "Spiked on Top: Brooklyn Dodgers Caps Are a Hot Headgear Trend," *New York Times*, July 3, 1989, available at http://web.lexis-nexis.com/universe.

17. As quoted in "Celebrating Baseball: Hats Off to the Game," *New York Times*, July 3, 1989, available at http://web.lexis-nexis.com/universe, para. 14.

18. Quoted in Robert Strauss, "P-Diddy's Jersey Connection; for the Hippest of the Hip-Hop, Vintage Uniforms Just like New," *Washington Post*, February 9, 2003, available at http://web.lexis-nexis.com/universe.

19. Ibid.

20. Matthew Grimm, "Baseball Pursues Field of Marketing Dreams; Major League Uses Nostalgia to Lure Family of the '90s Back to the Park," *Adweek*, September 10, 1990, available at http://web.lexis-nexis.com/universe.

21. As quoted in Jim McLennan, "Baseball's Greatest Scandals, #10: Steinbrenner vs. Winfield," *SB Nation: AZ Snake Pit*, April 18, 2011, available at http://www.azsnakepit.com/2011/4/18/2095444/baseballs-greatest-scandals-steinbrenner-winfield.

22. For more on the rhetoric of purity as it is often mobilized in discussions of baseball, see Michael L. Butterworth, *Baseball and Rhetorics of Purity* (Tuscaloosa: University of Alabama Press, 2010).

23. "Field of Dream Quotes," Internet Movie Database, available at http://www.imdb.com/title/tt0097351/quotes.

24. Grimm, "Baseball Pursues Field of Marketing Dreams."

25. Ibid.

26. Ibid., para. 23.

27. Charles Fruehling Springwood, *Cooperstown to Dyersville: A Geography of Baseball Nostalgia* (Boulder, CO: Westview Press, 1996), 2.

28. Alexander Cartwright has been credited with creating the first set of rules for baseball while the first "organized" baseball game took place June 19, 1846, in Hoboken, New Jersey, located across the river from Manhattan. The Doubleday creation myth was the product of sporting goods magnate Albert Spalding, who believed Doubleday's status as a war veteran, as well as the pastoral quality of Cooperstown, both were the perfect symbols to solidify baseball's status as the American game. According to Dave Zirin, "the myth was powerful enough and repeated enough that Cooperstown is now the site of the baseball hall of fame. There is no evidence that Doubleday ever set foot in Cooperstown." In fact, the surviving personal letters from Doubleday make no mention of baseball nor does his 1893 obituary printed in *The New York Times*. For more, see Dave Zirin, *A People's History of Sports in the United States* (New York: New Press, 2008).

29. Springwood, *Cooperstown to Dyersville*.

30. Ibid., 15.

31. Grimm, "Baseball Pursues Field of Marketing Dreams," para. 15.

32. Charles Johnson, "Comiskey Park Revisits 1917; Uniforms, Popcorn Price Straight Out of History," *USA Today*, July 12, 1990, available at http://web.lexis-nexis.com/universe.

33. Ibid., para. 10.

34. Ibid., para. 14.

35. Ibid.

36. See Zang, *Sports Wars*.

37. Barry M. Bloom, "Robinson's Legacy Celebrated at Shea," MLB.com, April 15, 2008, available at http://m.mlb.com/news/article/2531842/.

38. As quoted in Jerry Brankowski, "White Sox Set Aside May to Remember Negro Leagues," *USA Today*, May 1, 1992, available at http://web.lexis-nexis.com/universe.

39. There are many different theories regarding why fewer African Americans are participating in organized baseball. One is the growing wealth gap between white and African American households, which stood at $84,00 in 1984 and $236,500 in 2009. Consequently, it is theorized, most African American families cannot afford the escalating ticket prices or finance the increasing cost of youth sports leagues dominated by for-profit camps, showcases, and travel leagues. Others note the deteri-

Chapter Notes—Four

oration of baseball fields and parks in inner cities. Perhaps the most prominent theory is that the NFL and the NBA have become more popular among African American fans due to the surplus of black players in both sports. According to *Sporting News* journalist Michael Gentry, this contributes to the perception that some sports (football, basketball) are "black" sports while baseball is increasingly seen as "white," even in spite of the growing number of Latin-born players. For more, see Michael Gentry, Black Cloud (2015). *Sporting News: Baseball Yearbook 2015*, 16–23.

40. Andy Bernstein, "NHL Thaws Out Retro Jerseys, Hope to Boost Category to $250M," *Sports Business Daily,* July 7, 2003, available at http://www.sportsbusinessdaily.com/Journal/Issues/2003/07/20030707; David Steinhart, "Jersey Colour Is Money Green: Pro Sports Teams Find Revenue in Alternate Uniforms," *National Post,* December 6, 2003, available at http://web.lexis-nexis.com/universe.

41. As quoted in Steinhart, "Jersey Colour," paras. 13–14.

42. The phrase "memories for sale" is taken from Greg Dickinson, "Memories for Sale: Nostalgia and the Construction of Identity in Old Pasadena," *Quarterly Journal of Speech* 83 (1997): 1–27.

43. Adam Dietz, "The Ugliest Uniforms in Sports History," Bleacher Report, June 24, 2011, available at http://bleacherreport.com/articles/747718-the-ugliest-uniforms-in-sports-history/page/4; Randy Pennell, "Networking Inspires Retro Jersey Craze," Associated Press, June 19, available at http://www.enquirer.com/editions/2003/06/19tem0619retrojerseys.html.

44. Quoted in Rene A. Guzman, "Old-School Basketball Jerseys Bounce Back with a Slammin' Retro Style," *San Antonio Express,* May 16, 2003, available at http://www.seattlepi.com/lifestyle/article/Old-school-basketball-jerseys-bounce-back-with-a-1114924.php.

45. As quoted in "Rims and Rhymes: NBA's New Icons: Players with Street Cred, Style," *Chicago Tribune,* February 18, 2005, available at http://articles.chicagotribune.com/2005–0218/news/0502190026_1_mitchell-ness-hip-hop-jerseys.

46. Kembrew McLeod, "Authenticity within Hip-Hop and Other Cultures Threatened with Assimilation," *Journal of Communication* 49 (1999): 134–150.

47. "1999 Time Magazine: Lauryn Hill Hip-Hop Nation," Prostores.com, available at http://store03.prostores.com/servlet/dccollectibles/the-21710/1999-Time-Magazine-cln-Lauryn/Detail.

48. McLeod, "Authenticity Within Hip-Hop."

49. James Bernard, "Why the World Is After Vanilla Ice," *New York Times,* February 3, 1991, available at http://www.nytimes.com/1991/02/03/arts/why-the-world-is-after-vanilla-ice.html?pagewanted=1, para. 8.

50. McLeod, "Authenticity Within Hip-Hop."

51. As quoted in Jeff Chang, "Rapping the Vote with Chuck D," *Mother Jones,* September/October 2004, available at http://www.motherjones.com/media/2004/09/chuck-d.

52. As quoted in Annette John-Hall, "Hip-Hop Haberdasher Center City's Mitchell & Ness—Once a Sleepy Outpost for Replica Sports Apparel—Is Now a Hot Name in Urban Fashion," *Philadelphia Inquirer,* December 12, 2002, available at http://web.lexis-nexis.com/universe, para. 10.

53. Ibid., para. 13.

54. As quoted in William Hageman, "Rockin' the Jerseys: Some Were Kickin' It Old-School Before Old-School Was Cool," *Chicago Tribune,* March 16, 2003, available at http://articles.chicagotribune.com/2003–03-16/features/0303160468_1_peter-capolino-hip.

55. "Retro Jerseys All the Rage," SI.com, available at http://printthis.clickability.com/pt/cpt?expire=&url11ID=5358759&action=cpt&partner, para. 16.

56. Eric Fisher, "NBA: Hot or Not? Merchandise Sales Up; TV Ratings Are Down," *Washington Times,* May 5, 2004, available at http://web.lexis-nexis.com/universe.

57. Michael Heistand, "Sports Gear So Out of Style, It's in Style," *USA Today,* August 18, 2002, available at http://www.usatoday.com/sports/2002-08-19-retrofocus_x.htm.

58. Ibid., para. 5.

59. As quoted in Eric Fisher, "Old Jerseys Have Become the 'Now' Thing for Many Fans," *Washington Times,* May 12, 2002, available at http://web.lexis-nexis.com/universe, para. 14.

60. Larry Eischel, "NHL Hope Retro Look Will Bring Black Fans," *Philadelphia Inquirer,* August 5, 2003, available at http://web.lexis-nexis.com/universe.

Chapter Notes—Four

61. Bernstein, "NHL Thaws Out Retro Jerseys," para. 4.
62. Guzman, "Old-School Basketball Jerseys."
63. Heistand, "Sports Gear So Out of Style."
64. As quoted in John-Hall, "Hip-Hop Haberdasher," para. 7.
65. As quoted in Heistand, "Sports Gear So Out of Style," para. 16.
66. As quoted in "Retro Jerseys All the Rage," para. 9.
67. As quoted in Heistand, "Sports Gear So Out of Style," para. 31.
68. Christy Wampole, "How to Live Without Irony," November 17, 2012, available at http://opinionator.blogs.nytimes.com/2012/11/17/how-to-live-without-irony/, para. 2.
69. Sheinin, "Changing Colors."
70. As quoted in Michael Kruse, "How Does Oregon Football Keep Winning?," *Grantland,* August 30, 2011, available at http://www.grantland.com/story/_/id/6909937/how-does-oregon-football-keep-winning.
71. Ibid., para. 8.
72. Mike Tanier, "There's an Exciting Clash."
73. As quoted in Kruse, "How Does Oregon Football Keep Winning?," para. 27.
74. As quoted in Dave Sheinin, "College Football Uniforms Are Getting More Outrageous, Thanks to Nike, Under Armour," *Washington Post,* September 14, 2011, para. 8., available at http://www.washingtonpost.com/sports/college-football-uniforms-are-getting-more-outrageous.
75. Jesse Max Price, "Players Poll: Oregon Uniforms Voted NCAA's Best," *Oregon Ducks Football Examiner,* August 11, 2011, available at http://www.examiner.com/oregonducksfootball-in-portland/players-poll-oregon-uniforms-voted-ncaa-s-best.
76. As quoted in ibid., para. 2.
77. As quoted in Adam Fusfeld, "Florida Gators Change Uniforms in Order to Help Fans Buy More Stuff," *Business Insider Sports Page,* October 29, 2010, available at http://articles.businessinsider.com/2010-10-29/sports/30021877_1_uniforms-nike-pro-combat-gators.
78. Sheinin, "Changing Colors," para. 3.
79. Michael McCarthy, "Nike Schools Will Be Outfitted for Tradition," *USA Today,* September 1, 2010, available at http://web.lexis-nexis.com/universe.
80. Sheinin, "College Football Uniforms Are Getting More Outrageous."
81. Ibid.
82. Zito Madu, "Here Are 13 New College Football Uniforms for 2015. Are They Lit or Not?," SBNation.com, August 7, 2015, available at http://www.sbnation.com/college-football/2015/8/17/9153219/new-ncaa-football-uniforms-2015.
83. Julia T. Wood, *Gendered Lives: Communication, Gender, & Culture,* 11th ed. (Stamford CT: Cengage Learning, 2015), 232.
84. See Thomas H. Davenport and John C. Beck, *The Attention Economy: Understanding the New Currency of Business* (Accenture: United States, 2001).
85. Lindsay Foltin, "Johnny Baseball? Manziel Picked by Padres in 28th Round of MLB Draft," *Fox Sports Ohio,* June 7, 2014, available at http://msn.foxsports.com/ohio/story/johnny-baseball-manziel-selected-in-28th-round-of-mlb-draft-060714.
86. Ibid.
87. Ken Gee, "Johnny Manziel (Kind of) Joins the Padres," *Maxim,* June 9, 2014, available at http://www.maxim.com/sports/johnny-manziel-drafted-by-the-san-diego-padres, para. 3.
88. Mark Townsend, "Johnny Everything—Padres Draft Johnny Manziel in 28th Round," Yahoo! Sports, June 7, 2014, available at http://sports.yahoo.com/blogs/big-league-stew/johnny-everything-%E2%80%94-padres-draft-johnny-manziel-in-28th-round-211258872.html, para. 1,3,4.
89. "Padres Minor Leaguer Tweets a Johnny Manziel Jersey," *Lobshots,* June 11, 2014, available at http://www.lobshots.com/2014/06/11/padres-minor-leaguer-tweets-a-johnny-manziel-jersey.
90. Michael C. Jones, "Johnny Manziel MLB Draft: Padres GM Defends Decision Late-Round Selection," *Sports Out West,* June 10, 2014, available at http://www.sportsoutwest.com/2014/06/10/johnny-manziel-mlb-draft-padres-gm-defends-selection, para. 8.
91. Jeff Sanders, "Johnny Baseball? Padres Draft Manziel," *UT San Diego,* June 7, 2014, available at http://www.utsandiego.com/news/2014/Jun/07/padres-draft-johnny-manziel-cleveland-browns-qb, para. 13.
92. As quoted in Chris Hedges, *Empire of Illusion: The End of Literacy and the Triumph of Spectacle* (New York: Nation Books, 2009), 22–23.

93. Daniel J. Lair, Katie Sullivan, and George Cheney, "Marketization and the Recasting of the Professional Self," *Management Communication Quarterly* 18 (2005): 307–343.
94. Kenneth Burke, *A Rhetoric of Motives* (New York: Prentice-Hall, 1950), 55.

Chapter Five

1. I am borrowing the phrase "consumer's republic" from the title and thesis of Lizabeth Cohen's book *A Consumer's Republic: The Politics of Mass Consumption in Postwar America* (New York: Vintage Books, 2003).
2. See David Harvey, *A Brief History of Neoliberalism* (Oxford: Oxford University Press, 2007).
3. "The Core Principles of the League of Fans," League of Fans (n.d.), para. 2, available at http://leagueoffans.org/cor.
4. "Ralph Nadar Launches Campaign to Make the NCAA Live Up to Its Stated Purpose," League of Fans (n.d.), available at http://leagueoffans.org/2011/11/22/ralph-nadar-launches-campaign-to-make-the-NCAA-live-up-to-its-stated-purpose.
5. Ken Reed, "It's Time to Establish a National Sports Commission," League of Fans, October 26, 2011, available at http://leagueoffans.org/pdf/Manifesto9.pdf.
6. "What's Going On with Youth Sports?," PHITAmerica.org., May 19, 2015, available at http://www.phitamerica.org/News_Archive/What_s_Going_On.htm.
7. Daniel Kaplan, "NFL Sets Stadium Wi-Fi/Cell Standards," *Sports Business Daily*, October 21, 2013, available at http://www.sportsbusinessdaily.com/Journal/Issues/2013/10/21/Leagues-and-Governing-Bodies/NFL-WiFi.aspx.
8. Ibid., para. 5.
9. As quoted in ibid., para. 4.
10. As quoted in Edward C. Baig, "NFL Goal: Better Wi-Fi in Stadiums," *USA Today*, November 19, 2014, para. 11, available at http://www.usatoday.com/story/tech/columnist/baig/2014/11/19/nfl-hopes-to-boost-wifi-in-stadiums-via-extreme-networks/19285451/.
11. Kaplan, "NFL Sets Stadium Wi-Fi/Cell Standards."
12. Ibid., para. 10.
13. Aaron Gordon, "The Stupid Sports Stadium Clause That's Screwing You Over," *Vice Sports*, April 7, 2015, available at https://sports.vice.com/en_us/article/the-stupid-sports-stadium-clause-thats-screwing-you-over.
14. Ibid.
15. Ibid.
16. As quoted in Kaplan, "NFL Sets Stadium Wi-Fi/Cell Standards," para. 15.
17. Bill Shaikin, "Few New Details in Dodgers' Sale in Court Documents," *Los Angeles Times*, April 6, 2012, available at http://articles.latimes.com/2012/apr/06/sports/la-sp-0407dodgers-sale-20120407.
18. See Robert Reich, Supercapitalism: The Transformation of Business, Democracy, and Everyday Life (New York: Vintage Books, 2007).
19. Karl Marx, *The Communist Manifesto* (United States: Empire Books, 1848/2011).
20. Matthew P. McAllister, "Hypercommercialism, Televisuality, and the Changing Nature of Sports Sponsorship," *American Behavior Scientist* 53 (2010): 1489.
21. Dave Zirin, Bad Sports: How Owners Are Ruining the Games We Love (New York: Scribner, 2010).
22. Ibid.
23. Nick Trujillo and Bob Krizek, "Emotionality in the Stands: Expressing Self Through Baseball," *Journal of Sports and Social Issues* 18 (1994): 1994.
24. The phrase "compensatory fulfillment" is taken from Sut Jhally, "Cultural Studies and the Sports Media Complex," in *Media, Sports, and Society*, ed. Lawrence Wenner (Newbury Park, CA: Sage, 1989), 71. The phrase itself refers to how sports provide emotional compensation for the often physically exhausting and dull experience of having to go to work.
25. McAllister, "Hypercommercialism, Televisuality, and the Changing Nature of College Sports Sponsorship."
26. Harvey, A Brief History of Neoliberalism.
27. Cork Gaines, "Milwaukee Is in Danger of Losing the Bucks, and It Could Be Worth $1 Billion to the Other NBA Owners," *Business Insider*, July 8, 2015, available at http://www.businessinsider.com/milwaukee-bucks-could-move-with-out-arena-deal-2015–7.
28. Ibid., para. 10.
29. A.J. Bayatpour, "Gov. Walker Signs Milwaukee Bucks Arena Funding Bill: 'This is Much More than an Arena," Fox 6 Now. com, August 12, 2015, available at http://fox6now.com/2015/08/12/governor-scott-

walker-to-sign-milwaukee-bucks-arena-funding-bill-at-state-fair-park/.

30. Valeria Strauss, "Gov. Scott Walker Savages Wisconsin Public Education in New Budget," *Washington Post,* July 13, 2015, available at http://www.washingtonpost.com/blogs/answer-sheet/wp/2015/07/13/gov-scott-walker-savages-wisconsin-public-education-in-new-budget/.

31. Noel Tomas Radomski, director at the University of Wisconsin–Madison Center for the Advancement of Postsecondary Education, as quoted in Danielle Douglas-Gabriel, "Scott Walker's Real Record on Higher Education in Wisconsin," *Washington Post,* August 13, 2015, available at http://www.washingtonpost.com/news/wonkblog/wp/2015/08/13/scott-walkers-real-record-on-higher-education-in-wisconsin/, para. 10.

32. As cited in Thomas Barrabi, "Milwaukee Bucks New Arena Secures $250M in Public Funding Despite Questions About Benefits," *International Business Times,* August 6, 2015, available at http://www.ibtimes.com/milwaukee-bucks-new-arena-secures-250m-public-funding-despite-questions-about-2042212.

33. As quoted in ibid., para. 3.

34. Dennis Coates and Brad R. Humphreys, "Do Economists Reach a Conclusion on Subsidies for Sports Franchises, Stadiums, or Mega-Events?," North American Association of Sports Economists, August 2008, available at http://college.holycross.edu/RePEc/spe/Coates Humphreys_LitReview.pdf.

35. Harvey, A Brief History of Neoliberalism.

36. Grant Jarvie, "Sport, Social Change, and the Public Intellectual," *International Review for the Sociology of Sport* 42 (2007): 411.

37. Josh Boyd, "Selling Home: Corporate Stadium Names and the Destruction of Commemoration," *Journal of Applied Communication Research* 28 (2000): 330–346.

Bibliography

Abercrombie, Nicholas, and Brian Longhurst. *Audiences.* London: Sage, 1998.
Andrews, David. "Disneyization, Debord, and the Integrated NBA Spectacle." *Social Semiotics* 16 (2006): 89–102.
Archer, Nicholas R. "Ideological Endzones: NFL Films and the Countersubversive Tradition in American Politics." Unpublished Dissertation, University of Massachusetts—Amherst, 2010.
Aristotle. *The Politics.* Edited by Steven Everson. Cambridge: Cambridge University Press, 2003.
Babcock, William, and Virginia Whitehouse. "Celebrity as a Postmodern Phenomenon, Ethical Crisis for Democracy, and Media Nightmare." *Journal of Mass Media Ethics* 20 (2005): 176–191.
Bagdikian, Ben. *The New Media Monopoly.* 2nd ed. Boston: Beacon Press, 2004.
Barber, Benjamin. *Consumed: How Markets Corrupt Children, Infantilize Adults, and Swallow Citizens Whole.* New York: W.W. Norton, 2007.
____. "Jihad vs. Mcworld." *The Atlantic,* March 1992. Accessed April 1, 2012. http://www.theatlantic.com/magazine/archive/1992/03/jihad-vs-mcworld/3882/.
Baudrillard, Jean. *Simulacra and Simulation.* Translated by Shelia Faria Glaser. Ann Arbor: University of Michigan Press, 1995.
Beauregard, Robert. *When America Became Suburban.* Minneapolis: University of Minnesota Press, 2006.
Best, Steven, and Douglas Kellner. *The Postmodern Adventure: Science, Technology, and Culture Studies at the Third Millennium.* New York: Guilford Press, 2001.
Bishop, Ron. "Stealing the Signs: A Semiotic Analysis of the Changing Nature of Professional Sports Logos." *Social Semiotics* 11 (2001): 23–41.
Black, Edwin. *Rhetorical Criticism: A Study in Method.* New York: Macmillan, 1965.
____. "The Second Persona." In *Contemporary Rhetorical Theory: A Reader,* edited by John L. Lucaites, Celeste M. Condit, and Sally Caudill, 331–340. New York: Guilford Press, 1998.
Blakely, Edward J., and Mary Gail Snyder. *Fortress America: Gated Communities in the United States.* Washington, D.C.: Brookings Institute, 1999.
Boyd, Josh. "Selling Home: Corporate Stadium Names and the Destruction of Commemoration." *Journal of Applied Communication Research* 28 (2000): 330–346.
Braun Levine, Suzanne. "A New Consumer's Bill of Rights." In *Consuming Desires: Consumption, Culture, and the Pursuit of Happiness,* edited by Roger Rosenblatt, 97- 110. Washington, D.C.: Island Press, 1999.
Breckenridge, Saylor R., and Pat Rubio Goldsmith. "Spectacle, Distance, and Threat: Attendance and Integration of Major League Baseball, 1930–1961." *Sociology of Sport Journal* 26 (2009): 296–319.

Bibliography

Bryman, Allan. *The Disneyization of Society.* London: Sage, 2004.
Burd, Gene. "Mediated Sports, Mayors, and the Marketed Metropolis." In *Sporting Dystopias: The Making and Meanings of Urban Sports Culture,* edited by Ralph C. Wilcox, David L. Andrews, Robert Pitter, and Richard L. Irwin, 35–63. Albany: SUNY Press, 2003.
Burke, Kenneth. *A Rhetoric of Motives.* New York: Prentice Hall, 1950.
Butterworth, Michael L. *Baseball and Rhetorics of Purity.* Tuscaloosa: University of Alabama Press, 2010.
_____. "The Politics of the Pitch: Claiming and Contesting Democracy Through the Iraqi National Soccer Team." *Communication and Critical/Cultural Studies* 4 (2007): 184–203.
_____. "Purifying the Body Politic: Steroids, Rafael Palmeiro, and the Rhetorical Cleansing of Major League Baseball." *Western Journal of Communication* 72 (2008): 145–161.
_____. "Ritual in the 'Church of Baseball': Suppressing the Discourse of Democracy After 9/11." *Communication and Critical/Cultural Studies* 4 (2005): 107–129.
Butterworth, Michael L., and Stormi Moskal. "Football, Flags, and 'Fun': The Bell Helicopter Armed Forces Bowl and the Rhetorical Production of Militarism." *Communication, Culture, and Critique* 2 (2009): 411–433.
Chomsky, Noam. *Deterring Democracy.* New York: Hill and Wang, 1992.
Clarke, Gregory. *Rhetorical Landscapes: Variations on a Theme from Kenneth Burke.* Columbia: University of South Carolina Press, 2004.
Clavio, Galen, Patrick M. Kraft, and Paul M. Pedersen. "Communicating with Consumers Through Video Games: An Analysis of Brand Development Within the Video Game Segment of the Sports Industry." *International Journal of Sports Marketing and Sponsorship* 10 (2009): 143–156.
Coates, Dennis, and Brad Humphreys. "Can New Stadiums Revitalize Urban Neighborhoods?" *Significance* 8 (2011): 65–69.
Cohen, Lizabeth. *A Consumer's Republic: The Politics of Mass Consumption in Postwar America.* New York: Alfred A. Knopf, 2003.
Combs, James. *The Reagan Range: The Nostalgic Myth in American Politics.* Bowling Green, OH: Bowling Green State University, 1993.
Connolly, William E. *Capitalism and Christianity American Style.* Durham, NC: Duke University Press, 2008.
Crawford, Garry. *Consuming Sport: Fans, Sport, and Culture.* London: Routledge, 2004.
Crowley, Sharon. *Toward a Civil Discourse: Rhetoric and Fundamentalism.* Pittsburgh, PA: University of Pittsburgh Press, 2006.
Dahlberg, Lincoln. "The Habermasian Public Sphere: Taking Difference Seriously?" *Theory and Society* 34 (2005): 111–136.
DaSilva, Fabil, and Jim Fraught. "Nostalgia: A Sphere and Process in Contemporary Ideology." *Qualitative Sociology* 5 (1982): 47–61.
Davis, Nikolas W., and Margaret Carlisle Duncan. "Reinforcing Masculine Privilege Through Fantasy Sport League Participation." *Journal of Sport and Social Issues* 30 (2006): 244–264.
Debord, Guy. *The Society of the Spectacle.* Translated by Donald Nicholson-Smith. New York: Zone Books, 1994.
de Botton, Alan. *Status Anxiety.* New York: Vintage Books, 2005.
Delaney, Kevin J., and Rick Eckstein. *Public Dollars, Private Stadiums: The Battle Over Building Sports Stadiums.* New Brunswick, NJ: Rutgers University Press, 2003.
deMasue, Neil, and Joana Cagan. *Field of Schemes: How the Great Stadium Swindle*

Bibliography

Turns Public Money Into Private Profit. Lincoln: University of Nebraska Press, 2008.

Dickinson, Greg. "Memories for Sale: Nostalgia and the Construction of Identity in Old Pasadena." *Quarterly Journal of Speech* 83 (1997): 1–27.

———. "Selling Democracy: Consumer Culture and Citizenship in the Wake of September 11." *Southern Communication Journal* 70 (2005): 271–284.

Duncan, James, and Nancy Duncan, "The Aesthetization of the Politics of Landscape Preservation." *Annals of the Association of American Geographers* 91 (2001): 387–409.

Eisinger, Peter. "The Politics of Bread and Circuses." *Urban Affairs Review* 35 (2000): 316–333.

Eitzen, D. Stanley. "Classism in Sport: The Powerless Bear the Burden." *Journal of Sport and Social Issues* 20 (1996): 95–105.

Engels, Jeremy. "Demophilia: A Discursive Counter to Demophobia in the Early Republic." *Quarterly Journal of Speech* 97 (2011): 131–154.

Ewen, Stuart. *PR! A Social History of Spin.* New York: Basic Books, 1996.

Fainstein, Susan S., and Robert J. Stokes. "Spaces for Play: The Impacts of Entertainment Development on New York City." *Economic Development Quarterly* 12 (1998): 150–165.

Fine, Sidney. *Violence in the Model City: The Cavanaugh Administration, Race Relations, and Detroit Race Riot of 1967.* Ann Arbor: University of Michigan Press, 1989.

Fishman, Robert. *Bourgeois Utopias: The Rise and Fall of Suburbia.* New York: Basic Books, 1987.

Foley, Douglas E. "The Great American Football Ritual: Reproducing Race, Class, and Gender Inequality." *Sociology of Sport Journal* 7 (1990): 111–135.

Fort, Rodney. "Direct Democracy and the Stadium Mess." In *Sports, Jobs, and Taxes*, edited by Roger Noll and Andrew Zimbalist, 146–177. Washington, D.C.: Brookings Institution, 1997.

Foucault, Michel. *The History of Sexuality: An Introduction,* vol. 1. New York: Vintage Books, 1990.

Frank, Thomas. *The Conquest of Cool.* Chicago: University of Chicago Press, 1997.

———. *What's the Matter with Kansas? How Conservatives Won the Heart of America.* New York: Metropolitan Books, 1994.

Gabler, Neil. *Life: The Movie: How Entertainment Conquered Reality.* New York: Vintage Books, 1998.

Grano, Dan. "Ritual Disorder and the Contractual Morality of Sport: A Case Study in Race, Class, and Agreement." *Rhetoric and Public Affairs* 10 (2007): 445–473.

Gratton, Chris, and Harry Solberg. *The Economics of Sports Broadcasting.* New York: Routledge, 2007.

Green, G. Michael, and Roger D. Launius. *Charlie Finley: The Outrageous Story of Baseball's Super Showman.* New York: Walker, 2010.

Griffin, Rachel Alicia, and Bernadette Marie Calafell. "Black Masculinity and (In)Visible Whiteness in the NBA." In *Critical Rhetorics of Race*, edited by Michael L. Lacy and Kent Ono, 117–136. New York: New York University Press, 2011.

Guttmann, Alan. *A Whole New Ballgame: An Interpretation of American Sports.* Chapel Hill: University of North Carolina Press, 1988.

Habermas, Jurgen. *The Structural Transformation of the Public Sphere: An Inquiry into a Category of Bourgeois Society.* Translated by Thomas Burger and Frederick Lawrence. Cambridge: MIT Press, 1989/1999.

Hall Jamieson, Kathleen. *Eloquence in the Electronic Age: The Transformation of Political Speechmaking.* New York: Oxford University Press, 1990.

Bibliography

Halverson, Erica Rosenfield, and Richard Halverson. "Fantasy Baseball: The Case for Competitive Fandom." *Games and Culture* 3 (2008): 286–308.

Hariman, Robert, and John L. Lucaites. *No Caption Needed: Iconic Photographs, Public Culture, And Liberal Democracy*. Chicago: University of Chicago Press, 2007.

Harrington, Andrew Gordon. "The House That Cultural Capital Built: The Saga of the New Yankee Stadium." *NINE: A Journal of Baseball History and Culture* 19 (2011): 77–92.

Harvey, David. *A Brief History of Neoliberalism*. Oxford: Oxford University Press, 2007.

Haskel, Molly. "Movies and the Selling of Desire." In *Consuming Desires: Consumption, Culture, and the Pursuit of Happiness*, edited by Roger Rosenblatt, 123–136. Washington, D.C.: Island Press, 1999.

Hauser, Gregory A. *Vernacular Voices: The Rhetoric of Publics and Public Sphere*. Columbia: University of South Carolina Press, 1999.

Hedges, Chris. *Empire of Illusions: The End of Literacy and the Triumph of Spectacle*. New York: Nation Books, 2009.

Herman, Edward S., and Noam Chomsky. *Manufacturing Consent: The Political Economy of the Mass Media*. 2nd ed. New York: Pantheon Books, 2002.

Highsmith, Andrew R. "Demolition Means Progress: Urban Renewal, Local Politics, and State-Sanctioned Ghetto Formation in Flint, Michigan." *Journal of Urban History* 35 (2009): 348–368.

Hill, John Paul. "Commissioner A.B. 'Happy' Chandler and the Integration of Major League Baseball: A Reassessment." *NINE: A Journal of Baseball History and Culture* 19 (2010): 28–51.

Hoberman, John M. *Sport and Political Ideology*. Austin: University of Texas Press, 1984.

Hohendahl Peter U. "Critical Theory, Public Sphere, and Culture: Jurgen Habermas and His Critics." *New German Critique* 16 (1979): 89–119.

Hughes, Richard. *Myths America Lives By*. Urbana, IL: University of Chicago Press, 2003.

Ivie, Robert L. *Democracy and America's War on Terror*. Tuscaloosa: University of Alabama Press, 2005.

Jarvie, Grant. "Sport, Social Change, and the Public Intellectual." *International Review for The Sociology of Sport* 42 (2007): 411–424.

Jhally, Sut. "Advertising as Religion: The Dialectic of Technology and Magic." In *The Spectacle of Accumulation: Essays in Culture, Media, & Politics*, edited by Sut Jhally, 85–97. New York: Peter Lang, 2006.

———. "Cultural Studies and the Sports-Media Complex." In *The Spectacle of Accumulation: Essays in Culture, Media, & Politics*, edited by Sut Jhally, 129–151. New York: Peter Lang, 2006.

———. "The Political Economy of Culture." In *The Spectacle of Accumulation: Essays in Culture, Media, & Politics*, edited by Sut Jhally, 45–61. New York: Peter Lang, 2006.

———. "Sports and Cultural Politics: The Attraction of Modern Spectator Sports." In *The Spectacle of Accumulation: Essays in Culture, Media, & Politics*, edited by Sut Jhally, 153–160. New York: Peter Lang, 2006.

Jhally, Sut, and Bill Livant. "Watching as Working: The Valorisation of Audience Consciousness." In *The Spectacle of Accumulation: Essays in Culture, Media, & Politics*, edited by Sut Jhally, 25–43. New York: Peter Lang, 2006.

Karpinnen, Kari, Hallvard Moe, and Jakob Svensson. "Habermas, Mouffe, and Political Communication." *Javnost* 15 (2008): 5–21.

Katz, Cindy. "Power, Space, and Terror: Social Reproduction and the Public Environ-

Bibliography

ment." In *The Politics of Public Space,* edited by Seth Low and Neil Smith, 105–122. New York: Picador, 2000.

Kellner, Douglas. "Sports, Media Culture, and Race—Some Reflections on Michael Jordan." *Sociology of Sport Journal* 13 (1996): 458–467.

King, Samantha. "Pink Ribbons Inc.: Breast Cancer Activism and the Politics of Philanthropy." *International Journal of Qualitative Studies in Education* 17 (2004): 473–492.

Klein, Naomi. *No Logo.* New York: Picador, 2000.

Kraft, Rachel, and Barry Brummett. "Why Sports and Games Matter: Performative Rhetorics in Popular Culture." In *Sporting Rhetoric: Performance, Games, & Politics,* edited by Barry Brummett, 9–25. New York: Peter Lang, 2009.

Kunstler, Joseph H. *The Geography of Nowhere: The Rise and Decline of America's Man-Made Landscape.* New York: Touchstone, 1993.

Lasch, Christopher. *The Culture of Narcissism: American Life in an Age of Diminishing Expectations.* New York: W.W. Norton, 1979.

———. *The Revolt of the Elites and the Betrayal of Democracy.* New York: W.W. Norton, 1995.

Lavine, Amy, and Norman Oder. "Urban Redevelopment Policy, Judicial Deference to Unaccountable Agencies, and Reality in Brooklyn's Atlantic Yards Project." *Urban Lawyer* 42 (2010): 287–373.

Lee, Ronald, and Shawn T. Wahl. "Justifying Surveillance and Control: An Analysis of Media Framing of Pedophiles and the Internet." *Texas Speech Communication Journal* 32 (2007): 495–508.

Lefebvre, Henri. *The Production of Space.* Translated by Donald Nicholson-Smith. Oxford: Blackwell, 1994.

Lippmann, Walter. *Public Opinion.* New York: Free Press, 1922/1965.

Luchuk, Frank. *Blue Jays 1, Expos 0: The Urban Rivalry That Killed Major League Baseball in Montreal.* Jefferson, NC: McFarland, 2007.

Macek, Steve. *Urban Nightmares: The Media, the Right, and the Moral Panic Over the City.* Minneapolis: University of Minnesota Press, 2006.

Marcuse, Herbert. *One Dimension Man.* Boston: Beacon Press, 1964.

Marx, Karl. *Capital,* vol. 1. Translated by Ben Fowkes. New York: Penguin, 1990.

———. *The Communist Manifesto.* Translated by Samuel Moore. New York: Washington Square Press, 1906.

McAdon, Brad. "Reconsidering the Intention or Purpose of Aristotle's *Rhetoric.*" *Rhetoric Review* 23 (2004): 216–234.

McAllister, Matthew P. "College Bowl Sponsorship and the Increased Commercialization of Amateur Sports." *Critical Studies in Mass Communication* 15 (1998): 357–381.

———. *The Commercialization of American Culture: New Advertising, Control, and Democracy.* Thousand Oaks, CA: Sage, 1996.

———. "Hypercommercialism, Televisuality, and the Changing Nature of College Bowl Sponsorship." *American Behavioral Scientist* 53 (2008): 1476–1491.

———. "Super Bowl Advertising as Commercial Celebration." *Communication Review* 3 (2001): 403–428.

McChesney, Robert. "Media Made Sport: A History of Sports Coverage in the United States." In *Media, Sport, and Society,* edited by Lawrence Wenner, 49–67. Newbury Park, CA: Sage, 1989.

McKerrow, Raymie. "Critical Rhetoric: Theory and Praxis." *Communication Monographs* 56 (1989): 91–111.

McLeod, Kembrew. "Authenticity Within Hip-Hop and Other Cultures Threatened with Assimilation." *Journal of Communication* 49 (1999): 134–150.

Bibliography

McMurria, John. "Desperate Citizens and Good Samaritans: Neoliberalism and Makeover Reality TV." *Television New Media* 9 (2008): 305–332.

Miller, Jackson B. "'Indians,' 'Braves,' and 'Redskins': A Performative Struggle for Control of an Image." *Quarterly Journal of Speech* 85 (1999): 188–20.

Mitchell, Don. "The Annihilation of Space by Law: The Roots and Implications of Anti-Homeless Laws in the United States." *Antipode* 29 (1997): 303–335.

_____. "The End of Public Space? People's Park, Definitions of the Public, and Democracy." *Annals of the Association of American Geographers* 85 (1995): 108–133.

_____. "The SUV Model of Citizenship: Floating Bubbles, Buffer Zones, and the Rise of the Purely 'Atomic' Individual." *Political Geography* 24 (2005): 77–100.

Mouffe, Chantal. *The Democratic Paradox*. London: Verso, 2000.

Nesbit, Todd M., and Kerry A. King. "The Impact of Fantasy Sports on Television Viewership." *Journal of Media Economics* 23 (2010): 24–41.

Oates, Thomas. "New Media and the Repackaging of NFL Fandom." *Sociology of Sport Journal* 26 (2009): 31–49.

O'Leary, Cecilia Elizabeth. *To Die For: The Paradox of American Patriotism*. Princeton, NJ: Princeton University Press, 1999.

Pinskey, Drew P., and S. Mark Young. *The Mirror Effect: How Celebrity Narcissism Is Seducing America*. New York: HarperCollins, 2009.

Plato. *The Republic of Plato*, vol. 1. 3rd ed. Translated by Benjamin Jowett. London: Oxford University Press, 1927.

Postman, Neil. *Amusing Ourselves to Death: Public Discourse in the Age of Show Business*. 20th anniversary ed. New York: Penguin, 2005.

Quirk, James, and Rodney Fort. *Hardball: The Abuse of Power in Pro Team Sports*. Princeton, NJ: Princeton University Press, 1999.

Real, Michael R. "The Super Bowl: Mythic Spectacle." In *Mass-Mediated Culture*, edited by Michael R. Real, 91–117. Englewood Cliffs, NJ: Prentice Hall, 1977.

Reich, Robert. *Aftershock: The Next Economy and America's Future*. New York: Alfred A. Knopf, 2010.

_____. *Supercapitalism: The Transformation of Business, Democracy, and Everyday Life*. New York: Random House, 2008.

Rein, Irving, Philip Kotler, and Ben Shields. *The Elusive Fan*. New York: McGraw-Hill, 2006.

Reisch, George. "Is Radiohead the New Pink Floyd of the 21st Century." In *Radiohead and Philosophy*, edited by Brandon W. Forbes and George A. Reisch. Chicago: Open Court, 2009.

Rhoden, William. *40 Million Dollar Slaves: The Rise, Fall, and Redemption of the Black Athlete*. New York: Random House, 2006.

Ritzer, George. *Enchanting a Disenchanted World*. 2nd ed. Thousand Oaks, CA: Pine Forge Press, 2005.

Ritzer, George, and Todd Stillman. "The Postmodern Ballpark as Leisure Setting: Enchantment and Simulated De-McDonaldization." *Leisure Sciences* 23 (2001): 99–113.

Rosengren, John. *Hammerin' Hank, George Almighty, and the Say Hey Kid: The Year That Changed Baseball Forever*. Naperville, IL: Sourcebooks, 2008.

Rosensweig, Daniel. *Retro Ballparks: Instant History, Baseball, and the New American City*. Knoxville: University of Tennessee Press, 2005.

Rosentraub, Mark. *Major League Losers: The Real Cost of Sports and Who's Paying for Them*. New York: Basic Books, 1999.

_____. *Major League Winners: Using Sports and Cultural Centers as Tools for Economic Development*. Boca Raton, FL: CRC Press, 2010.

Bibliography

Rushkoff, Douglas. *Media Virus: Hidden Agendas in Popular Culture.* 2nd ed. New York: Ballantine Books, 1996.
Sage, George H. *Power and Ideology in American Sport.* 2nd ed. Champaign, IL: Human Kinetics, 1998.
Santo, Charles. "Beyond the Economic Catalyst Debate: Can Public Consumption Benefits Justify a Municipal Stadium Investment." *Journal of Urban Affairs* 29 (2007): 455–479.
Scherer, Jay, and Michael P. Sam. "Public Consultation and Stadium Developments: Coercion and Polarization of Debate." *Sociology of Sport Journal* 25 (2008): 443–461.
Schor, Juliet. "What's Wrong with Consumer Society? Competitive Spending and the 'New' Consumerism." In *Consuming Desires: Consumption, Culture, and the Pursuit of Happiness,* edited by Roger Rosenblatt, 37–50: Washington, D.C.: Island Press, 1999.
Sites, William. *Remaking New York: Primitive Globalization and the Politics of Urban Community.* Minneapolis: University of Minnesota Press, 2003.
Sperb, Jason. "Islands of Detroit: Affect, Nostalgia, and Whiteness." *Culture, Theory, and Critique* 49 (2008): 183–201.
Springwood, Charles Freuhling. *Cooperstown to Dyersville: A Geography of Baseball Nostalgia.* Boulder, CO: Westview Press, 1996.
Spirou, Costas, and Larry Bennett. *It's Hardly Sporting: Stadiums, Neighborhoods, and the New Chicago.* Dekalb: Northern Illinois University Press, 2003.
Stahl, Roger. *Militainment, Inc.: War, Media, and Popular Culture.* New York: Routledge, 2010.
Sze, Julie. "Sports and Environmental Justice: 'Games' of Race, Nostalgia, Power in Neoliberal New York City." *Journal of Sport and Social Issues* 33 (2009): 111–129.
Thomas, G. Scott. *The United States of Suburbia: How the Suburbs Took Control of America and What They Plan to Do with It.* Amherst, NY: Prometheus Books, 1998.
Thompson, Heather Ann. *Whose Detroit? Politics, Race, and Race in a Modern American City.* Ithaca, NY: Cornell University Press, 2001.
Trujillo, Nick. "Hegemonic Masculinity on the Mound: Media Representations of Nolan Ryan and American Sports Culture." *Critical Studies in Mass Communication* 8 (1991): 290–308.
Trujillo, Nick, and Bob Krizek. "Emotionality in the Stands and in the Field: Expressing Self Through Baseball." *Journal of Sport and Social Issues* 18 (1994): 303–325.
Trumpbour, Robert. *The New Cathedrals: Politics and Media in the History of Stadium Construction.* Syracuse, NY: Syracuse University Press, 2007.
Twenge, Jean M. *Generation Me: Why Today's Young Americans Are More Confident, Assertive, Entitled—And More Miserable than Ever Before.* New York: Free Press, 2006.
Von Burg, Ron. "Yearning for a Past That Never Was: Baseball, Steroids, and the Anxiety of the American Dream." *Critical Studies in Media Communication* 26 (2009): 351–371.
Wander, Philip. "The Third Persona: An Ideological Turn in Rhetorical Theory." In *Contemporary Rhetorical Theory: A Reader,* edited by John L. Lucaites, Celeste M. Condit, and Sally Caudill, 357–379. New York: Guilford Press, 1998.
Wenner, Lawrence. "The Dream Team, Communicative Dirt, and Marketing Synergy." In *Critical Readings: Sport, Culture, and the Media,* edited by David Rowe, 70–83. London: Open University Press, 2004.
_____. "Media, Sports, and Society: The Research Agenda." In *Media, Sports, and Society,* edited by Lawrence Wenner, 13–48. Newbury Park, CA: Sage, 1989.

Bibliography

____. "Playing Dirty: On Reading Media Texts and Studying Sports Fans in Commercialized Contexts." In *Sports Mania: Essays on Fandom and Media in the 21st Century*, ed. Lawrence W. Hugenberg, Paul M. Haridakis, and Adam C. Earnheardt, 13–22. Jefferson, NC: McFarland, 2008.

White, Curtis. *The Barbaric Heart: Faith, Money, and the Crisis of Nature*. Sausalito, CA: PoliPoint Press, 2009.

Zagacki, Kenneth S., and Dan Grano. "Radio Sports Talk and the Fantasies of Sport." *Critical Studies in Media Communicatio*, 22 (2005): 45–63.

Zimbalist Andrew. *May the Best Team Win: Baseball Economics and Public Policy*. Washington, D.C.: Brookings Institution, 2003.

____. *Unpaid Professionals: Commercialism and Conflict in Big-Time College Sports*. Princeton, NJ: Princeton University Press, 1999.

Zinn, Howard. *A People's History of the United States*. 20th anniversary ed. New York: Harper Perennial Modern Classics, 2010.

Zirin, Dave. *Bad Sports: How Owners Are Ruining the Game We Love*. New York: Scribner, 2010.

____. *A People's History of Sports in the United States*. New York: New Press, 2008.

____. *Welcome to the Terrordome: The Pain, Promise, and Politics of Sport*. New York: Haymarket Books, 2007.

Zukin, Sharon. *Landscapes of Power: From Detroit to Disney World*. Berkeley: University of California Press, 1991.

Index

Aaron, Hank 29
Adams, Bud 64
Adorno, Theodor 51
advertising 92, 108; formulas 95–102; in sports 104–105
Alamodome 36
alcohol sponsorships 52–55
American Airlines Arena 39
American Association 54
American Basketball Association (ABA) 87
American dream 7, 135
American exceptionalism 7
American Idol 102
American League 24
Anaheim Angels 15
Anaheim Mighty Ducks 15
Anderson, Elijah 33
Angels in the Outfield 134
antitrust exemption 85
The Apprentice 102
Astrodome 64
Atari 93, 109
Atlanta Braves 44
AT&T Stadium 20
"Attention economy" 143, 146

The Bad News Bears 135
Baker Bowl 27
Baltimore Colts 25, 87
Ball Four 83
Bank of America Stadium 61
Bernays, Edward 97
Bernie the Brewer 52–53
The Biggest Loser 102
Bird, Larry 141
Blackmun, Harry 85
Bloomberg, Michael 65
Boise State University 144
Boston Braves 40
Boston Red Sox 30, 106
Bouchard, Lucien 64

branding 9, 11, 14, 15; personal 143–144
Brochu, Claude 64
Brookey, Robert Alan 93
Brooklyn Dodgers 29–30, 130
Brooklyn Nets 15, 77
Brotherhood of Professional Baseball Players 84
Brown v. The Board of Education 30
Bryant, Paul "Bear" 144
Buffalo Bills 47–48
Burke, Kenneth 147–148
Busch Stadium 31
Butkus, Dick 54

Cagan, Joana 24, 41
Camden Yards *see* Oriole Park at Camden Yards
Candlestick Park 10
capitalism *see* neoliberalism
cause-related marketing 121–123
CBS 73
Central Market Gateway Project 24
Chicago American Giants 135
Chicago Bulls 77, 98, 129
Chicago Cubs 53, 57–59, 79
Chicago White Sox 32, 59, 132–135
Chomsky, Noam 82
Citizens United v. Federal Election Commission 12, 153, 158
Cincinnati Bengals 27, 152
Cincinnati Reds 28, 131, 132
Cleveland, Ohio 31; new stadium construction 23; poverty and census data 27
Cleveland Browns 23, 25, 27
Cleveland Browns Stadium 23
Cleveland Cavaliers 23–26, 32, 71
Cleveland Indians 23–26
Cleveland Municipal Stadium 23, 25–26, 40
"Code of the Street" 33
Cold War 7
Colorado Rockies 42

Index

color barrier 29, 135–136
Comerica Park 66, 69
Comiskey Park 32, 155
communism 7
conspicuous consumption 7
consumer culture 6–8, 11, 14–16, 71
"Consumer Republic" 7, 149
Cooperstown, New York 132
Coors Field 42
"corporate welfare" 41
Costas, Bob 5
Costner, Kevin 61
County Stadium 40, 52–53
Crisis of overproduction 7, 12
Cromartie, Warren 63
Cuban, Mark 14, 79–80

Dallas Cowboys 20–21
Dallas Mavericks 77, 79
de Botton, Alain 56
Denver Broncos 61, 100
DeMause, Neil 24, 41, 152
democracy 6–7, 16, 82, 149; as metaphor for sports 11
Detroit 1; bankruptcy 65–68; economic development 65–66, 71; race riots 31
Detroit Lions 32, 66, 69, 129
Detroit Pistons 32, 69
Detroit Red Wings 65–66, 69–70
Detroit Renaissance Board 68
Detroit Tigers 1–2, 66, 69, 106
Dodger Stadium 5–6
Donald W. Reynolds Razorback Stadium 55
Doubleday, Abner 133
DraftKings 77–78
"The Dream Team" 105–106

Edward Jones Dome 152
Eisenhower, Dwight D. 31
Emmert, Mark 10
Engler John 66
entrepreneurial self 79–81
Epstein, Theo 79–80
ESPN 21, 72–73, 75, 111, 113, 116, 143; subscription costs 103–104
E.T. the Extra Terrestrial (video game) 108–109
Extreme Home Makeover 102

Fan Cost Index 57
FanDuel 77, 78
Fantasy sports 74–78, 88; effects on fandom 81–83
Fantasy Sports Trade Association 74–75
federal tax-exempt bonds 23
Federal Works Commission 23
Fenway Park 30, 106, 145

Field of Dreams 131–134
Finley, Charlie 16, 86, 129
First Amendment 12
First Energy Stadium *see* Cleveland Browns Stadium
Flood, Curt 84–85
Florida Everblades 128
Florida Panthers 38
Forbes Field 29
Ford, William Clay, Jr. 66
Ford Field 66
Foster, Rube 29
Fox (media conglomerate) 73, 77
Fox Sports 72, 104
Fox Theatre 68
franchise tag 87
Frankfurt School 51
free agency 83, 86, 87; history of 84–85
free trade agreements 8
Fresno Grizzlies 128
Freud, Sigmund 97

"Gamergate" 94–95
gated communities 49–51
Giamatti, A. Bartlett 131
Gibson, Kirk 5
Gilbert, Dan 71
Great Depression 7, 12
Green, Pumpsie 30
Green Bay Packers 154–155
Greenspan, Alan 61
Griffey, Ken, Jr. 119
Griffith Stadium 30
Gund Arena 23–25

Haley, Charlotte 122
Hamilton, Josh 44
Harvey, David 13, 81, 156
hip hop 136–141
Holiday Bowl 9
Holt, Peter 36
Hoosiers 128
Houston Oilers 64
Hubert H. Humphrey Metrodome 63
Hunter, Catfish 85
Hunter, Torii 106

Ilitch, Mike 66–70
income inequality 13
incremental affinity 110–111
Indianapolis Colts 25–27, 64
Indiana Pacers 128
International Monetary Fund (IMF) 12–13
International Olympic Committee (IOC) 62
Interstate Highway Act 31
Invesco Field at Mile High Stadium 61

192

Index

Jack Murphy Stadium 32
Jackson, Reggie 131
Jacksonville Jaguars 21
Jacobs Field 23–25, 44
Jarry Park 62
Jay-Z 14–15
Jethroe, Sam 30
Jhally, Sut 8
Jennings, Peter 78
"Jerry Vision" 21
Jobs, Steve 14
Joe Louis Arena 65, 69; lease agreement 70
Jones, Jerry 20
Jordan, Michael: endorsement of Nike 97–98, 120; Olympic sponsorship controversy 105–106

Kauffman Stadium 45
Keynes, John Maynard 12
Kingdome 42
Kiss (band) 130
Knight, Phil 142–143
Kuhn, Bowie 84

Lake Front Park 28
League of Fans (LF) 149
Leary, Denis 61
Lee, Spike 61, 120, 130
licensed merchandise 15, 128, 144–148; nostalgia movement 131–135
Little Big League 134
Los Angeles Dodgers 5–6, 86, 88, 104; bankruptcy, 153
Los Angeles Lakers 140
Louisiana State University (LSU) 10
Lowell Spinners 128
Luck, Oliver 64

Mackey v. NFL 86
Madden, John 54
Madden NFL Football (video game) 110, 112, 113; "Madden curse" 113–114; ratings system 117–118
Major League Baseball (MLB), 10, 22, 24, 35, 46, 51, 56–58, 62, 69, 73, 77, 129, 131–132, 135, 140; free agency 85–86, 104; sponsorships 120–123; 129, 131–132, 135, 140
Major League Baseball Players' Association 85
Major League Soccer (MLS) 22, 73
Mantle, Mickey 54, 130
Manziel, Johnny 146–147
March Madness 9, 90
Marlins Park 19
"Maryland Pride" uniforms 127
Mays, Willie 29–30

McAllister, Matthew P. 9, 154
M.C. Hammer 138
Media 8, 15–16; blackout policies 101; expansion of sports coverage 8, 72; sports television rights deals 88–90, 103
meritocracy 55–56
Messersmith, Andy 86
MetLife Stadium 60–61
Metropolitan Sports Facilities Commission 63
Miami Arena 37–39
Miami Dolphins 19, 46
Miami Heat 37–39, 44
Miami Marlins 19–20, 103
Michaels, Al 21
Michigan & Trumbull Group 69
Michigan Economic Development Corporation 65
millennials 11, 73
Miller, Jeffrey 48
Miller Brewing Company 52
Miller Lite 54
Miller Park 52–53
Milwaukee Braves 1, 40
Milwaukee Brewers 52–53
Milwaukee Bucks 156
Minneapolis Lakers 140
Minnesota Twins 62–63
Minnifield, Frank 87
Mississippi State University 144
Mitchell & Ness 131, 137–141
MLB.com. 52
MLB: The Show (video game) 112, 118–119
MLB TV 89
Modell, Art 25–26, 64
Monster Park 10
Montreal Expos 62–64, 86
mythology 29

Nadar, Ralph 150
Narrowcasting 100
National Basketball Association (NBA) 15, 22, 35, 36, 46, 73, 77, 103–104, 122, 136, 140, 156–157; free agency 84; merger 87
National Basketball League (NBL) 87
National Collegiate Athletic Association (NCAA) 9, 73, 122, 150; bowl games 10; commercialization 10, 15; student-athlete definition 10
National Football League (NFL) 9, 26, 35, 36, 37, 46, 47, 48, 51, 54, 64, 66, 73, 104, 116, 118, 136, 140; free agency 84, 86; "NFL Pink" campaign 122–125; wi-fi policy 150–152, 155
National Hockey League (NHL) 22, 35, 46, 73, 77, 84, 122, 136, 140, 150–152, 155
National League 19, 28, 54
The National Post 21

193

Index

National Sports Commission 150–151
Nationals Park 23
NBC 73
NCAA Football (video game) 117
Negro Leagues 29, 30, 135–136
neoliberalism 13, 16, 41, 56, 64–65, 69, 153, 156, 159; definition 13; impact on citizenship 90
New Orleans Pelicans 9
New Yankee Stadium 51, 65
New York Knicks 77
New York Stock Exchange 12
New York Yankees 16, 65, 83, 104
NFL Network 73
Nietzsche, Friedrich 50
Nike 96–98, 105, 111, 118, 120, 141–144
Norris, Bruce 69
nostalgia 131–136

Oakland Athletics 5, 16, 85–86, 129
Oakland Raiders 36
Oates, Thomas 79, 93
Obama, Barack 90, 110
The Office 102
Ohio State University 10, 144
Okrent, Dan 75
Old Style Brewing Company 59
Old Tiger Stadium Conservancy 69
Olympia Development Company 68
Olympia Entertainment 70
Olympic Stadium 62–64
Olympics Games 9, 23, 62, 107
On the Genealogy of Morals 50
O'Neill, Buck 30
Oregon State University 144
Oriole Park at Camden Yards 32, 34–35, 44, 64, 135
Orlando Magic 77
Orr, Kevyn 66
Outkast 136
Owens, R.C. 86

Paige, Satchel 29
Philadelphia Flyers 131
Philadelphia Phillies 84, 131
pink marketing 122–125
Pink Ribbons, Inc. 122
Playmakers 116
Political action committees (PAC's) 12
Polo Grounds 27
Pontiac Silverdome 69
Prince, Chris 78
Progressive Field *see* Jacobs Field
Protestantism 27
"purification policies" 28, 46, 53

Quicken Loans Arena *see* Gund Arena
Quinn, Zoe 94

Ratner, Bruce 15
Reagan, Ronald 12, 13
Reich, Robert 67
Reinsdorf, Jerry 32
reserve clause 84–85
retro jerseys *see* throwback jerseys
Rice, Ray 125
Ricketts, Tom 58–59
Rickey, Branch 30
Riggins, John 79
Riley, Pat 38
Riverfront Stadium 32
Robinson, Jackie 29–30, 135
Rock and Roll Hall of Fame 23
Rookie of the Year 134
Rose, Pete 131
Rose Bowl 40
Rosensweig, Daniel 46
Rotisserie baseball 75
Rozelle Rule 87
Ryan, Nolan 44, 133, 141

Sabbathia, C.C. 65
St. Louis Cardinals 85
San Antonio Spurs 36, 37
San Diego Padres 146, 155
San Francisco 49ers 87
The Sandlot 134
Sarkeesian, Anita 94
Seattle Mariners 1, 42
Seattle Seahaws 100
Selig, Bud 10, 62–63, 68, 135
Shea Stadium 32
Silver, Adam 15
"sin tax" 24–25
Smoothie King Center 9
Snell, Matt 54
Snyder, Dan 61, 79
Snyder, Rick 65, 66
social media 14, 100–101, 145–147
social status 7, 14, 56, 57, 61
Soldier Field 40
Southeastern Conference (SEC) 55
Soviet Union 7
Spalding, Albert 28
Spider Man (film) 2, 10
sponsorship 2, 149–159; event control 105–108
"Sports Dirt" 53
sports gambling 28, 89–90
Sports Illustrated 26
sports stadiums 1, 15, 20, 22, 28, 31, 40–41, 45; economic impact 22, 42–43; Fan Code of Conduct 50; funding 40–45; multipurpose stadiums 31–33, 46; retro stadiums 19, 32–34; state of the art clause 151–152
Stanton, Giancarlo 103

194

Index

Star Wars (film) 128, 130
"statuscape" 60
Stautner, Eddie 54
Steinbrenner, George 16, 131
Steiner, Charlie 104
Stern, David 73–74
Stranded at the Corner 69
Strat-O-Matic 74
Suburbanization 7, 33–34, 49–50; effect on sports 31–32
Sun Belt 31
Sun Life Stadium 46
Super Bowl 9, 53, 60–61, 66, 79; advertising and consumerism 100–101
Supreme Court 12
Survivor 102

Tampa Bay Lightning 128
Tennessee Titans 64
Texas Rangers 44
Texas Stadium 20
Texeira, Mark 65
Thatcher, Margaret 81
3Com Park at Candlestick Point 10
Three Rivers Stadium 32
throwback jerseys 134–137, 140–141
Tiger Stadium 1, 2, 69
Toledo Mud Hens 128
Torches of Freedom campaign 97
Trapasso, A.J. 21
trickle down economics 12
Trost, Leon 51
Trout, Mike 119–120
Turner Field 44

Unlawful Internet Gambling Enforcement Act 76–78
University of Alabama 144
University of Arkansas 55
University of Connecticut 9
University of Maryland 127

University of Miami (FL) 127, 144
University of Michigan 10
University of Notre Dame 10
University of Oregon 127–128; sponsorship deal with Nike 141–145
upward mobility 14; *see also* social status
U.S. Cellular Field 9

Vanilla Ice 138
vicarious management 79
Vincent, Fay 24

Walker, Scott 157–158
Wall Street 67; bailout 156
Wall Street (film) 79
Wall Street: Money Never Sleeps (film) 91
Walt Disney 15
Ward, John Montgomery 84
Washington Nationals 63
Washington Redskins 61, 77, 79
Watkins Glen International 73
Wembley Stadium 63
Wenner, Lawrence 53
White, Michael 26
white flight 31; *see also* suburbanization
Williams, Marvin 30
Winfield, Dave 16, 131, 141
Women's National Basketball Association (WNBA) 122
Wood, Kerry 58
World Series 5, 19, 58, 79
World War I 29
World War II 7, 34
Wrigley Field 53; renovation of 57–59

Yankee Stadium 29–30, 51
Yawkey, Tom 30
"yuppization" 59

Zimbalist, Andrew 63
Zirin, Dave 27, 51, 79, 101, 154

www.ingramcontent.com/pod-product-compliance
Ingram Content Group UK Ltd.
Pitfield, Milton Keynes, MK11 3LW, UK
UKHW042009140426
5217IPUK00015B/1076